Ingrid Pitt,
Queen of Horror

ALSO BY ROBERT MICHAEL "BOBB" COTTER
AND FROM MCFARLAND

Vampira and Her Daughters: Women Horror Movie Hosts from the 1950s into the Internet Era (2017)

A History of the Doc Savage Adventures in Pulps, Paperbacks, Comics, Fanzines, Radio and Film (2009; paperback 2016)

The Women of Hammer Horror: A Biographical Dictionary and Filmography (2013)

Caroline Munro, First Lady of Fantasy: A Complete Annotated Record of Film and Television Appearances (2012)

The Mexican Masked Wrestler and Monster Filmography (2005; paperback 2008)

The Great Monster Magazines: A Critical Study of the Black and White Publications of the 1950s, 1960s and 1970s (2008)

Ingrid Pitt, Queen of Horror

The Complete Career

ROBERT MICHAEL "BOBB" COTTER
Foreword by INGRID PITT

McFarland & Company, Inc., Publishers
Jefferson, North Carolina

The present work is a reprint of the illustrated case bound edition of Ingrid Pitt, Queen of Horror: The Complete Career, *first published in 2010 by McFarland.*

LIBRARY OF CONGRESS CATALOGUING-IN-PUBLICATION DATA

Cotter, Bobb.
Ingrid Pitt, queen of horror : the complete career /
Robert Michael "Bobb" Cotter ; foreword by Ingrid Pitt.
p.   cm.
Includes bibliographical references and index.

ISBN 978-1-4766-7230-4
softcover : acid free paper ∞

1. Pitt, Ingrid.   2. Motion picture actors and
actresses — Great Britain — Biography.   I. Title.
PN2598.P48C68   2018   791.4302'8092 — dc22 [B]   2010035603

BRITISH LIBRARY CATALOGUING DATA ARE AVAILABLE

© 2010 Robert Michael "Bobb" Cotter. All rights reserved

No part of this book may be reproduced or transmitted in any form or by any means, electronic or mechanical, including photocopying or recording, or by any information storage and retrieval system, without permission in writing from the publisher.

Front cover: Ingrid Pitt from the 1971 film
The House That Dripped Blood (courtesy Ingrid Pitt)

Printed in the United States of America

*McFarland & Company, Inc., Publishers
Box 611, Jefferson, North Carolina 28640
www.mcfarlandpub.com*

To Dad and Brownie, R.I.P;
Mum, my wonderful wife Cheryl, Lucky,
Peter Cushing, the Great Paul Thompson,
and, of course, Ingrid Pitt!

Table of Contents

Acknowledgments	ix
Foreword by Ingrid Pitt	1
Introduction	3
"First Stage" — Plays	7
"From Screen to Scream" — Films	19
"The Naughty Bits" — Hammer's Karnstein Trilogy	128
"The Boob Tube" — Television	151
"Being Ingrid Pitt" — Documentary and Guest Appearances, Archive Footage, Website and Fan Club, Magazines	175
"In Her Own Write" — Ingrid Pitt's Books	205
Bibliography	217
Index	219

Acknowledgments

I would like to offer my heartfelt thanks to Kim Holston, John Del Margio, Richard Klemensen, Mark Maddox, Bruce Timm, Teresa O'Cassidy, and "the Usual Gang of Idiots." You were all instrumental in the process of writing this book, whether through providing information, photos, films or, inspiration.

A very special thanks goes to Scott Bunt and Barbro Ryan, and finally to Ingrid Pitt, both for her generous help filling in the details of her career, and for contributing a foreword for the book.

FOREWORD BY INGRID PITT

Aw shucks! Somehow Bobb Cotter has managed to turn my limited career into a thing of beauty and a joy forever. And the research! The thing about writing that I hate most is getting involved with research. My usual method is to rely on my somewhat erratic memory. Which tends to over-egg most of the happenings and censor them as seems advantageous. More recently I lean heavily on others, in particular Barry McCann and my husband Tonio. Somehow Bobb has managed to unearth facts about my past that even I can't remember. And all without even the smallest, throwaway derogatory remark. Now that's what I call sportsmanship.

It is not always easy to write something about someone else that is fairly extensive without having to resort to the off-hand catty-ism or criticism. I know! I find it hard not to slip something a little demeaning even into an obituary. I like to think of it as balance. But I thank the author of this book for his forbearance. With very little input from me he has riffled through my long and murky past so that even I found it illuminating and interesting.

It's not all about research. There are comments and investigations into some of the circumstances and problems with which I have been involved. For instance why, when everything seemed to be about to blossom, after making the mega-successful film *Where Eagles Dare* and following it up with a clutch of above-the-titles parts, mainly in the horror genre, I disappeared off the screen for a number of years. Believe me, it wasn't what I wanted. This has been handled without making me look like a jerk. Not an easy job by any means. If I think back to that time, I often feel I could have handled it more sensitively. But when you are young and your blood is up, you feel that you can take on the world and remake it for your own convenience. That was another thing I was wrong about. Luckily I wasn't completely minced by the experience and was able to skulk off to the Argentine and hole up until my sins were forgotten. It was Hammer's promotional idea to dub me Queen of Horror. Nice gesture, but a lot to live up to.

What is even more interesting than my relationships are the insights into some of the films that didn't exactly have Hollywood looking over its collective shoulder. Films like *Nobody Ordered Love*. That one hit the screens running and wasn't exactly slaughtered by the crits; then, just when it looked as if it could be a nice little earner, the producer had a bit of a spat with the distributors, grabbed his film back and flounced off to California where he promptly died and left me eternally asking if anyone has heard what happened to it. For me there is also the answer to the question of when *The Vampire Lovers* turned from a tranquil idyll in the Styrian countryside between a couple of young ladies, one of whom just happens to be a vampire, into a rampant lesbian movie. It could be that I am just naive!

There is also a quick winnow through my infrequent appearances on stage. Must admit that I wasn't exactly stagestruck although my first professional job was as a muck-efuck for the Berliner Ensemble, a name to be reckoned with in war-torn East Berlin in the fifties. I had just moved on from "stand-in" status to minor roles when my big mouth got me into trouble and I had to leave. I had great fun touring England playing everywhere from the end of Cleethorpes Pier to the West End of London. There was even a tour of South America that was a once-in-a-lifetime experience. But the stage is hard work and that is something with which I have never been particularly happy. Again Bobb has managed to winkle out some bits and pieces that a less inquiring investigator might have missed. And then where would you be?

When I was just starting out, television was still a bit of a no-no. Once you strutted your stuff for the flickering gray-and-white twelve-inch box in the corner of the room, it was hard to find a way back into movies. You had collected your thirty pieces of silver, undermined the traditional entertainment offered by the silver screen and weren't fit to stand beside the screen idols of yore. By the time I had done a few flicks, TV had turned into a garishly coloured medium and some of the names that a few years earlier would have jumped into a vat of developer to avoid it were condescending to appear in "worthwhile productions" (i.e., those that paid well).

To say that I am happy to have Bobb Cotter take the time to write this book is an understatement. I have never been exactly reticent about giving the old trumpet a blast but it is so much nicer to have someone else do it. I hope you will agree that it was worth the effort.

INTRODUCTION

Writing the introduction to a book, or perhaps even the book itself, about Ingrid Pitt is rather like buying a gift for the person who has everything. Is there anything else that can possibly be said about one of the most-loved icons of horror cinema; about a life that, as one pressbook marveled, is just as amazing as any of her movies, if not more so? There's always that possibility, and of course, there's always the possibility that one has been snowbound in the Borgo Pass for the last 40 years, and has absolutely no clue as to who Ingrid Pitt (born Ingoushka Petrov, in 1937) is. Of course, if one has been snowbound in the Borgo Pass for 40 years, one would ostensibly have more pressing concerns than knowledge of Ingrid Pitt, although that is difficult to understand, especially for the purposes of this book.

I hope this book will offer something for both camps. It's not a biography; Ingrid has taken care of that quite well herself. But it will contain biographical information in the introduction — not only because my heartless, cruel, harsh, oppressive (let's see how much of that they leave in...) publishers demand it, but simply because it would be rather odd to write a book about someone and not actually say anything about them. It is, also rather simply, a reference book, containing as much information as possible about the varied and storied career of our heroine — what movies, television shows, stage plays she has appeared in; who made them, who else was in them (and what genre-related projects they were involved with), when they were made, and what they were about. As for that last bit, this will be as good a place as any to give out with what is now commonly known as a spoiler alert. The book contains detailed synopses of the films, including the ending, so if you don't want to know how a film turns out, stop reading a paragraph or two from the end. I hope this won't ruffle too many feathers; if you're a hardcore Pitt panther, then you already know what happens. If you're snowbound in the Borgo Pass, you don't have a DVD player, and you can't watch the movies anyway, so it's only fair to let you know what happens.

And for fans who are only familiar with her horror films, some of the films included within might be a surprise. Far from being just another pretty set of fangs, Ingrid has appeared in some very famous, even award-winning films. For instance, while everyone is familiar with *The Vampire Lovers*, how many spotted her in *Doctor Zhivago*? She has performed in Shakespeare on screens both large and small. She was an extra in *A Funny Thing Happened on the Way to the Forum*, and from there went on to a number of roles that suggest that her forte is as much comedienne as carnivore. She's even (*very* technically, admittedly) a "Bond Girl." For all she is as Carmilla, or Countess Dracula, she is so much more. So while there is certainly a little more emphasis given to her most famous and/or horror roles, the others are covered as well. Some readers may be driven to distraction by the sheer number of technical credits, especially for some films they may have absolutely no interest in, or that Ingrid barely even appears in. I share that frustration—especially when I'm transcribing the bloody things. But reference, after all, is what the book is for, for those nights when the computer is down (or you're just snowbound in that doggone Borgo Pass again) and you really want or need to know who the set designer for *Doctor Zhivago* was. And I hope it offers enough information so that if some of the films are outside a reader's experience, they would be encouraged to expand their horizons, which is never a bad thing.

Speaking of the Karnsteins... Many fans will no doubt question the inclusion of a chapter on Hammer's Karnstein Trilogy (*The Vampire Lovers, Lust for a Vampire*, and *Twins of Evil*) in a book about Ingrid Pitt when she is only in one of the films. The reasons for this are threefold: (1) as they do form a trilogy, any one of them is rarely spoken of without referencing the others; (2) it gives the chance to compare and contrast not only the films against one another, but how they and others relate to the original story "Carmilla" by Le Fanu; and (3) they all feature beautiful Hammer vampire girls, which are a class unto themselves, and a type of class which one can never get enough of.

And for those who would say that this is merely an excuse to include more photos of nude, bloody women, here's another, and perhaps more controversial, spoiler alert: This book contains no nudity—possibly one of the few times a book could be considered unusual because it *doesn't* feature nudity! This is not a restriction imposed on the author by anyone; it's solely the author's decision. Now, Lord knows I'm no prude, and I certainly don't object to nudity, and indeed, the primary reason the Karnstein Trilogy was produced was to exploit nudity. No, it is because some critics and authors have seen fit to attribute Ingrid's popularity solely to "her willingness to display her rather shapely body" (*The New York Daily News*) and "her willingness to disrobe for the camera" (*Who's Who of the Horrors and Other Fantasy Films*). This assessment would rather seem to reduce her to the same level as a porn star (and ignores the fact that she only did it three times). Ingrid is a stunningly beautiful woman to be sure, and to deny that is part of her appeal would be silly, just as it would be with other cinema bombshells. And there are plenty of pictures, a plethora of pulchritude, a ton of tease, a bevy of bum, ample samples of this almost intimidatingly gorgeous woman throughout the book—just none with her kit off.

The other reason that practically none of the nudes are included is, quite honestly, they've pretty much all been seen, many times. I mean, really, and not for this to be taken the wrong way, we all know what Ingrid looks like naked. We all love what Ingrid looks like naked. Ingrid is very proud of her beauty and her nude scenes. She probably wouldn't mind if that was the cover shot (although it might not fly at the school library). But, as I said, they've been shown at most every opportunity by anybody who had the opportunity to print them, and one of the things that this book strives for, besides being informationally comprehensive, is a variety of rare and unique graphics. So taking into account that there can only be so many representations for each film; given the choice between yet *another* nude shot from *The Vampire Lovers* or *The Wicker Man*, and, say, a German pressbook cover or a playing card (really!) for the first of those three, then it'll be the Three of Hearts every time (I didn't say the Queen because it really is a Three) or unless it's a rare shot from Ingrid's personal collection.

My own personal introduction to Ingrid was at the 1993 Famous Monsters Convention in Arlington, Virginia. Although I'd been a fan of her movies for years, this was the first chance I'd had to meet her in person, and it resulted in my most treasured "Monster Memory." Anyone who was there that weekend will remember how constantly and utterly crammed the elevators were. On Saturday, on an already tightly packed trip down, I was near the doors of the elevator, and they swooshed open to reveal none other than the Queen of Horror herself! "Is there room?" she asked in that voice which has melted a million hearts. "Are you kidding?" I thought. "Of course," I replied, somewhat unchivalrously shoving those behind me even further into the nooks and crannies of the car. Well, needless to say, the quarters became even more cramped, but here I was, not just face to face, but literally body to body, with *Ingrid Pitt*. We laughed about the sardine-can conditions, and talked until the doors opened. Exiting the lift, I said, "Just think! Now I'll be able to go home and tell everyone that I held Ingrid Pitt in my arms!" To which she replied "Oh darling, tell them, tell them!" and threw her arms around me and gave me a great big hug and kiss. And my first thought (okay, other than the obvious ones) was that this was a woman who treasures her fans almost as much as they treasure her. And in a world where many people think only of themselves, where surly celebrities can't be bothered to even feign civility while charging for autographs, she is a rare treasure indeed.

As much as we admire Ingrid for her career, there is so much more to admire, and to be inspired by, by her real life. She's a survivor. It is difficult for modern readers to understand the horror of the Nazi concentration camps; all that most people know is that many, many people died in them. For Ingrid, that was only the beginning. Escape from Communist oppression; a single mother at times, with a child and few prospects; breast cancer; ovarian cancer; virtually blackballed in the British film industry for a time by a vengeful then-husband ... but Ingrid is still standing, standing tall, and has refused to let these things, or anything else she has experienced, dim her view of life or keep her from making the most of that life.

One of the most interesting aspects of Ingrid's career is the iconic status she has attained on the basis of a relatively few films. She appeared to be on the brink of A-list success with her appearance in *Where Eagles Dare*, and the fact that she did not achieve it can be attributed to both bad luck and mistakes in personal judgment, to which she will readily admit. With *The Vampire Lovers* and *Countess Dracula*, it appeared once again that she was in place to take her place as a bona-fide box-office force to be reckoned with; but again, it was not to be. In between *The House That Dripped Blood* (1971) and *Who Dares Wins* (1982), with the exception of *The Wicker Man*, her film work all but dried up; among the only appearances she made were in episodes of various television shows. Once again, this could be said to be the result of bad judgment, but with far more serious implications. As the 1970s dawned, Ingrid secretly married a man named George Pinches, booker for the ultra-powerful Rank Organisation cinema chain. He suggested it when Ingrid was going to be deported, and told her that they could live separately and maintain a platonic relationship. If Ingrid met someone who swept her off her feet, he promised her they would get divorced. This changed, Ingrid says, as soon as they left the registry office, and only got worse with time; the "embargo" placed on her only lifted with Pinches' removal from the industry. This explains her lack of activity at the very peak of her career.

So what is it, then? Why do we love Ingrid? What is it that gives her that special, intangible *something*? What makes her a certifiable icon? What inspires such a devoted fan following? She's the archetypal rags-to-riches story, but not just riches in terms of fame, but of understanding of the human condition. And so, while there is the artifice of celebrity, and the icon Ingrid Pitt, behind it all is a very real person which keeps the artifice from ever becoming truly artificial. As Paul Stump would say of Roxy Music in his excellent *Unknown Pleasures* (Quartet Books, 1998), Ingrid does "not *depend* on the artifice," she "merely used it as a tool which could have existed independently" of her image, "but was ingeniously indissoluble from it." She has a lens into "images of falsehood and commerciality," and decided that the "experience itself had to be taken with a pinch of salt." So while she obviously takes her craft, her image, and her following very seriously, there is still the wonderful element of little-girl-dressing-up approach to her style and a child's wish for everyone to join in on the fun. And of course, for genre fans, she loves being not only Ingrid Pitt, woman, loving mother, now-grandmother, and wife, but she also loves being INGRID PITT. Like Paul Naschy, Ingrid not only enjoys appearing in horror films, but is eminently knowledgeable about the genre and has insightful things to say about it, and takes her connection to it seriously. And it's those kinds of connections and commitment—to her craft, to her fans, to life itself—that make her special; she's done it her way.

Note: This introduction is in no way meant to impugn the dignity of the people who inhabit the Borgo Pass, nor the majestic natural beauty of the Pass itself. It, of course, became famous as the gateway to the realm of Dracula in Stoker's novel, and is now literally that, as the location of the hotel Castel Dracula, which was built in 1974. For Ingrid's recollections of her trip there, not to mention an actual photo of the Borgo Pass itself, see the "Being Ingrid Pitt" chapter.

I'd also like to take one more opportunity to thank Ingrid Pitt, for the incredible foreword, and for her unflagging cooperation in providing access to rare photos and graphics. It would not have been the same book without her—and also, once again, Barbro Ryan, Ingrid's personal assistant, who performed above and beyond the call of duty. I could fill the entire book with thanks to them, and it still wouldn't be enough.

Ingrid would also like for the readers to know that she had nothing to do with the choice of title; the term "Queen of Horror" was applied to her by the Hammer publicity department, and although it has been associated with her throughout the years, it is not a term she uses to promote herself—she personally feels that women like Barbara Shelley, Hazel Court, and Elsa Lanchester are much more deserving. And when told that the subtitle would be "The Complete Career," she said, "Well, that's a bit final, isn't it?" So we'd like to note that this was simply a way of describing the comprehensive nature of the book, not to imply that Ingrid's fabulous career is in any way over!

Lastly, the author would like to apologize for the same lack of detail in the synopses for the television shows as in the synopses for the film; although this was the intention, unfortunately, they had to be truncated for legal reasons. And now, on with the show!

"First Stage": Plays

Ingrid Pitt began her career as an actress on the stage, with the Berliner Ensemble, a German theater company. It was founded by Bertolt Brecht and his wife Helene Weigel in 1949 in East Berlin, after the much-acclaimed production of his play *Mother Courage and Her Children*. In 1954, it moved to its own home at the Theater am Schiffbauerdamm, a building with a sumptuous, neo-baroque interior that had survived World War II without much damage. (In 1928, Brecht's *Threepenny Opera* premiered there.) Her first job there was making coffee. Early in her stay with the company, in 1961, the Berlin Wall was erected and the borders were closed. At one point, Ingrid was detained by authorities after making anti-government statements, but was released into Frau Weigel's custody. Soon after, she appeared in her first production, playing the part of the mute Kattrin in *Mother Courage and Her Children*. Kattrin is one of Mother Courage's three children; the other two are Swiss Cheese and Eilif. Mother Courage, a canteen woman with the Swedish army during the Thirty Years' War, tries to profit from the war but winds up losing all three children to that very war. On the night of her first performance, Ingrid was once again visited by the authorities for making political statements, and it was on this night that she escaped into West Berlin.

In 1963, while living in the United States with her first husband (Major Pitt, the army lieutenant who had pulled her out of a river as she escaped the Communists), Ingrid joined the Pasadena Playhouse for a time, and went on tour as Blanche DuBois in Tennessee Williams' *A Streetcar Named Desire*. But, as Ingrid says, "That sounds pretty exalted. 'Tour' conjures up a grand procession through the theaters of America. In fact, what we did was duck and dive through any old hall or decaying auditorium that would have us." She left the U.S. the next year and settled in Spain. While in Spain, she worked with the Teatro Nacional de Espana, reprising her role of Kattrin in *Mother Courage* and re-teaming with Lola Gaos, with whom she had just appeared in the film *The Sound of Horror*.

Films would occupy much of Ingrid's career for the next decade, but in the mid–1970s she returned to the stage in Frederick Knott's *Dial "M" for Murder*, which opened at the Opera House in Glasgow, Scotland. While on the tour, her ovarian cancer was diagnosed, and the resulting operation sidelined her for a time. But like the trouper she is, she came back to the tour with three weeks left and finished it. The credits for that production follow.

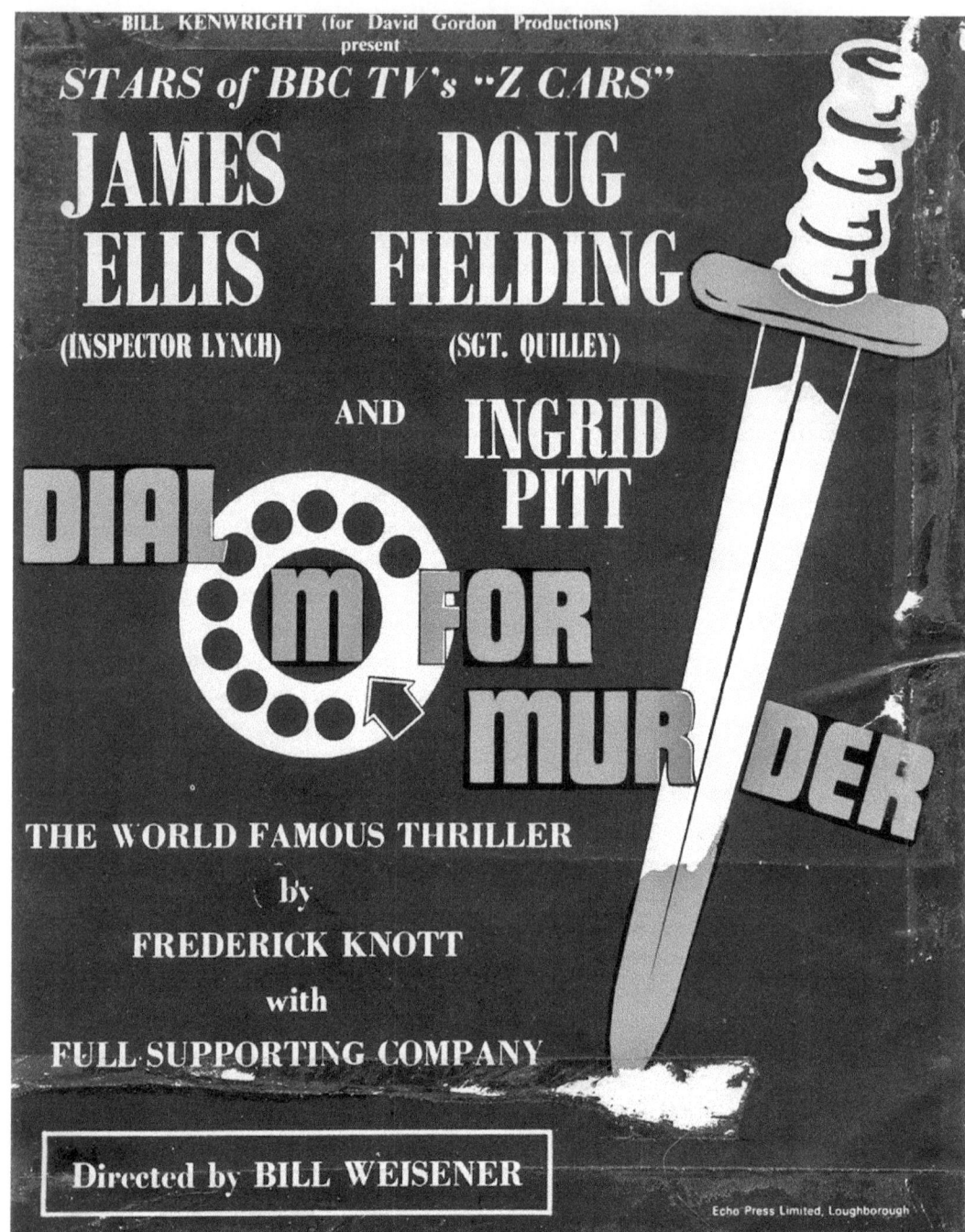

Dial "M" for Murder playbill cover (courtesy Ingrid Pitt).

Dial "M" for Murder (1977)

Crew: Producers: Bill Kenwright-David Gordon Productions; Author: Frederick Knott; Director: Bill Weisener; Managing Director: Bill Kenwright; General Manager: Rod H. Coton; Accounts Manager: Colin Caldicot; Production Manager: Robin Alexander; Production Secretary: Reica Benjamin; Production Assistant: Hugh Janes; Company Manager: Dudley Long; Deputy Stage Manager: Marc Ashley; Assistant Stage Manager: Lynne Ellis.

Cast: Ingrid Pitt (Sheila Wendice), Bill Weisener (Max Halliday), Michael Murray (Tony Wendice), Nigel Hamilton (Captain Lesgate), Peter Adamson (Inspector Hubbard).

Notes: Dial "M" for Murder, which Alfred Hitchcock made into a classic film in 1954, premiered two years earlier as both a BBC television play and an actual play in London's West End in June, before its debut on Broadway in October. Frederick Knott, who also wrote the screenplay for the film, wrote only one other successful play, *Wait Until Dark*, which was also made into a film. Michael Murray, who plays Ingrid's husband (and had been the second assistant director for *Who Dares Wins*), was a veteran thespian who had an even more impressive résumé in the fantasy film world: After starting out as a lowly runner on the films *Casino Royale* and *2001: A Space Odyssey*, he became third assistant director for five episodes of *The Avengers*, Hammer's *Blood from the Mummy's Tomb*, and *Burke and Hare*; second assistant director on *Superman: The Movie*, *Saturn 3*, and *An American Werewolf in London*; and first assistant director on *Legend*, *Young Sherlock Holmes*, and *Who Framed Roger Rabbit*. He then graduated to production manager of such mega-hit movies as *The Dark Knight* and *Batman Begins*.

Ingrid's next theater work was in a production staged by her own touring company, TRIP, which stands for Tony, Robin (Ellis) and Ingrid Pitt. It opened in Bristol as *Duty Free* and generally did great business in the provinces. This led to an invitation by Moss Empires to bring the play to the West End, where the title was changed to *Don't Bother to Dress*. It lasted a scant five weeks.

Don't Bother to Dress (1977)

Crew: Producers: Robin A. Ellis with TRIP Productions, by special arrangement with Louis Benjamin; Author: Neville Siggs; Director: Victor Spinetti; Associate Director: Anthony Collin; Set Design: Brigitte Trace. For TRIP Productions: Production Manager: Tony Rudlin; Company Manager: Robin A. Ellis; Stage Manager: Vanessa Gee; Deputy Stage Manager: Robin A. Ellis; Assistant Stage Manager: Stewart Permutt. Wardrobe for Eunice Gayson: Nel Barden; Carpets: Dobson & Bull, Ltd.; Wardrobe Care: Persil. For Moss Empires Limited: General Manager and Director: R.S. Swift; Manager: Robert Radcliffe; Advertising Manager: Brenda Thomas; Production Manager: Thomas Elliot; Press & Publicity: Tony Wells; Executive Music Director: Gordon Rose; Stage Director: Philip Smith; Chief Electrician: Alex Pope; House Manager: Christopher Elson; Box Office Manageress: E. Foskett.

Cast: Ingrid Pitt (Helen Browne), Nick Tate (Victor Browne), Tim Barrett (Eric Hodges),

Plays: *Don't Bother to Dress* (1977)

Don't Bother to Dress playbill cover (courtesy Ingrid Pitt).

Eunice Gayson (Cynthia Hodges), Sabina Franklin (Henrietta Mann), Stewart Permutt (Donald MacPherson).

Notes: A bedroom farce with the action taking place at the Brownes' weekend cottage in the country. Ingrid is not the only one in the cast with genre experience: Nick Tate is best-remembered for his Capt. Alan Carter from *Space: 1999* while Eunice Gayson appeared in *Dr. No, From Russia with Love, The Revenge of Frankenstein, Danger Man* (US: *Secret Agent*), *The Saint, The Avengers,* and *The Adventurer.* Tim Barrett had parts in *Schizo, The Deadly Bees, Trog,* and *The Mummy's Shroud.*

Ingrid Pitt and Nick Tate on stage in *Don't Bother to Dress* (courtesy Ingrid Pitt).

Woman of Straw playbill cover (courtesy Ingrid Pitt).

Ingrid Pitt and Anthony Ainley on stage in the West End production *Woman of Straw* (courtesy Ingrid Pitt).

Woman of Straw publicity photograph. Left to right: Anthony Ainley, unidentified, Ernest Clarke, Ingrid, John Bentley (courtesy Ingrid Pitt).

Ingrid and an unidentified actor (in drag) in *Charley's Aunt* (courtesy Ingrid Pitt).

Charley's Aunt **playbill cover (courtesy Ingrid Pitt).**

Plays: *Aurelia* (1979)

MONDAY 1st OCTOBER, 1979
to SATURDAY 13th OCTOBER
inclusive

The Kenton Theatre
Henley - on - Thames
Box Office: Henley 5698

HENLEY REPERTORY COMPANY

Professional Autumn Season

AURELIA

by ROBERT THOMAS
adapted by TUDOR GATES

STARRING **INGRID PITT**

Director David Tudor

Evening Performances 8.00pm
Seat Prices £2.00 and £1.80

Special concessions for students, senior citizens & party bookings

Aurelia playbill cover (courtesy Ingrid Pitt).

The Man Most Likely To.... playbill cover (courtesy Ingrid Pitt).

The next play they took on tour was *Woman of Straw*, based on the novel by Catherine Arley; it had been made as a movie in 1964, starring Gina Lollobrigida and Sean Connery. Tony found commercial sponsorship with British Caledonian Airways; the tour went well, and unlike *Don't Bother to Dress* it made a small profit. The cast featured Anthony Ainley ("The Master" in *Doctor Who*, *You Only Live Twice*, *Blood on Satan's Claw*, *The Land That Time Forgot*), Ernest Clarke (*1984*, *It!*), and John Bentley. Other stage productions she has appeared in are *Aurelia*, *In Praise of Love*, *The Man Most Likely To...*, *A Lion in Winter*, and *Charley's Aunt*.

"From Screen to Scream": Films

This main chapter of the book lists Ingrid's feature films, and includes technical credits, detailed synopses, reviews and her comments, culled from various sources. Made-for-television films are catalogued in "The Boob Tube" chapter. Although every effort has been made to screen or re-screen every film for review, in three cases this proved to be impossible: *Los Duendes de Andalucía*, *Un Beso en el Puerto*, and *Nobody Ordered Love*. Technical information and graphic material and/or photos exist, and possibly a clip or two, but the films themselves are unavailable.

But this is more than can be said for Ingrid's Argentinean film work; the only evidence of its existence may be a few photographs and her memories. They include a werewolf story, *El Lobo*, *Los Descamisados* ("The Shirtless Ones," a term originally used to describe the followers of Juan Peron in a derogatory manner, and then later reclaimed by those followers and the Perons as a term of pride), and *El Ultimo Enemigo* ("The Last Enemy"), which is about a woman who overthrows a corrupt government. Ingrid had to leave Argentina before the filming was finished on the latter. A fourth Pitt picture, *La Nina Gaucha* ("Gaucho Girl"), never materialized. While in Spain, she did stuntwork for spaghetti westerns, but the names of those productions have yet to be determined.

Los Duendes de Andalucía (*The Splendor of Andalucia*) 1964, Bosco Films

Crew: Producer-Director-Screenplay-Story: Ana Mariscal; Dialogue: Domingo Fernandez Barreira; Cinematography: Valentin Javier; Editor: Juan Pison; Set Decorator: Augusto Lega; Assistant Directors: Sebastian Almeida, Jose Luis de la Torre.

Cast: Rafaela Aparicio, Manuel Arango, Paco Campos, Melchor de Marchena, Paco Izquierdo, Alfonso Labrador, Paco de la Isla, Chico Moraito (Guitarists); Ana Carrillo "La Tomata," Porrinas de Badajoz, Curro de Utrera, Manuel Fernandez Aranda, Alvaro de la Isla, La Nina de los Pienes (Singers), Luis Ferrin, Luis Gomez "El Peque," Amparo Gomez Ramos, Sancho Gracia, Marie-France, Maribel Martin (Child), Goyo Montero, Jose Morales, La Paquera de Jerez, Ingrid Pitt, Juan Antonio Roda, Rafael Romero de Torres, Victoriano Valencia.

Synopsis: In Ingrid's first film, she plays a tourist who falls in love with a bullfighter.

Tales from the Pitt: My photograph appeared on the front page of *El Pueblo*, where it was spotted by Ana Mariscal, one of the top directors in Spain at that time. I was

Films: *Los Duendes de Andalucía* (1964)

Ingrid looks splendid in *The Splendor of Andalucia* (1964).

invited to lunch and asked to do a screen test for her film *Los Duendes de Andalucía* ... I hardly dared to point out a rather glaring problem — I couldn't speak Spanish. "I don't care," said Ana Mariscal. "I want you for my picture. You're perfect for the role of the boozy nymphomaniac American who has a passion for bullfighters! As for the screen test, Fellini just gets his actors to count instead of speaking proper lines. If it's good enough for Federico Fellini, it is good enough for Ana Mariscal" (*Life's a Scream*).

El Sonido de la Muerte
(*Sound of Horror*)
1964, Zurbano Films

Crew: Producer: Gregorio Sacristán (Gregorio Sacristán de Hoyos); Director: Jose Antonio Nieves Conde; Screenplay: Sam X. Abarbanel; Story: Sam X. Abarbanel, Jose Antonio Nieves Conde, Gregorio Sacristán, Gregg C. Tallas; Music: Luis de Pablo; Cinematography: Manuel Berenguer; Editor: Margarita de Ochoa; Production Designers: Gil Parrando, Espinosa; Art Directors: Gil Parrando, Espinosa; Titles: Pablo Nunez; Assistant Director: Jose Luis De La Torre; Script Girl: Isabel Campo; Production Assistant: Jose Martinez; Production Aide: Fernando Quegido; Camera Operators: Miguel Barquero, Roberto Ochoa; Assistant Camera Operator: Manuel Velasco; Camera Aide: Jose Martinez; Still Photographer: Julio Vizuete; Assistant Editor: Maria Luisa Pino; Set Decorator: Roman Calatavud, Julio Molina; Makeup Artist: Carlos Nin; Makeup Assistant: Maria Sanchez; Hair Stylist: Maria Ortega; Property Master: Juan Garcia; Sound Recordist: Alfonso Carvajal; Special Effects: Manuel Baquero; Wardrobe Mistress: Flora Salamero; Set Construction: Tomas Fernandez; Set Decorations: Mateos; Film Laboratory: Foto Films Madrid; Lighting Equipment: Mole-Richardson; Filmed at Samuel Bronston Studios.

Sound of Horror lobby card showing Ingrid Pitt (left) and Soledad Miranda doing the hippy-hippy shake as Antonio Casas watches.

Films: *El Sonido de la Muerte* (1964)

Cast: James Philbrook (Dr. Peter Asilov), Arturo Fernandez (Prof. Andre), Soledad Miranda (Maria), Jose Bodalo (Mr. Dorman), Antonio Casas (Pete), Ingrid Pitt (Sofia Minelli), Lola Gaos (Calliope), Francisco Piquer (Stravos).

Synopsis: Professor Andre, his niece Maria, and fellow archaeologist Stravos are exploring an ancient cave in Greece, using half a map. They cause an explosion which uncovers what appears to be a petrified egg. They do not see another egg, which has cracked open. A strange mass exits the shell through the crack and almost immediately disappears into the ground.... The trio takes the first egg back to their ranch house. Their maid, Calliope, is frightened and will have nothing to do with it. Calliope warns them of danger, but the three go on discussing their plans to explore other areas of the cave.

Their second foray there yields a mummified figure, but this discovery is not the treasure that the professor has been seeking. As Calliope prepares their dinner, they hear an approaching Jeep driven by a handsome young man, Pete, who has brought Andre's comrades from the war, Asilov and Dorman, as well as Asilov's mistress Sofia. Asilov holds the other half of the map. As the men discuss the treasure they are seeking, the women entertain themselves (and the men) by dancing.

The next day, the whole group, except for Calliope, goes to the cave. Pete and the

Sound of Horror lobby card with James Philbrook, Antonio Casas, Soledad Miranda, Ingrid Pitt (courtesy Kim Holston).

women later return to the house to discuss what they will do with their shares of the treasure. As Stravos observes the mummy, the others discover the treasure's location under a cement slab, and decide to go back for water before they dynamite it. Stravos, left alone, hears a scraping sound, then a screaming sound, and Stravos is seized in the grip of some unseen force. The sound of horror is soon intermingled with the screams of the scientist; bloody gashes appear in his face and chest.

The others hear his screams and discover his mutilated corpse. Then they too hear the scraping and screaming, and they bolt from the cave. Asilov is convinced that the villagers are responsible, but Andre has other ideas. They return to the cave, but must flee once again when they hear the sounds — and this time the sound follows them! They barely make it into the house; Dorman's leg is slashed before the door shuts. They gather their wits, and do not notice that the unbroken egg on the mantle beginning to move.

After the men discuss the treasure's bloody history, the group retires to bed, but Dorman, Pete and Maria cannot sleep. Dorman endures his pain, while romance blossoms between the young couple. The egg cracks open to reveal a pair of gleaming eyes! As the creature attached to them begins to emerge, Andre kills it with a poker and throws it into the fireplace. Calliope offers to make coffee, and goes outside to the well to get the water for it. And then the screaming starts....

The group hears Calliope's agony but can do nothing to help. They barricade the doors and windows against the invisible fiend. As the rest of the group fitfully sleeps, Andre slips outside. Angered and emboldened by the sight of Calliope's mutilated corpse, he takes dynamite from the group's stock of munitions and goes to the cave to blow up the creature. As he lights the fuse, he is attacked by the invisible terror, and screams horribly as the cave explodes.

The group believes the monster to be destroyed and decides to leave. Upon returning to the ranch, they discover that the creature is alive after all and has wrecked their kitchen, leaving reptilian footprints in spilled flour. They quickly gather their belongings and get into the Jeep, but the engine will not start. Back in the ranch house, they discover that Dorman's leg is badly infected and will have to be amputated. But far worse, someone has left a shutter open, and the monster is now inside the house! Maria sees the creature materialize for a moment, screams and bolts the door, while Pete goes outside to decoy it. The ploy is successful.

The Sound of Horror shot featuring Arturo Fernandez, Ingrid Pitt and James Philbrook (courtesy Ingrid Pitt).

In the morning, they spread flour on the ground so they can know where the creature is as it makes footprints. The trap works, and Asilov and Pete are able to wound the monster by throwing hatchets at it. It retreats, leaving a trail of blood. Again the group piles into the Jeep, and this time it starts, but as they speed down the road to apparent safety, the blood of the creature starts to ooze down over the windshield. It has retreated to the top of the Jeep! As it rips open the top of the vehicle, everyone except Dorman leaps out. He opens a can of gas and spreads it, and when the others try to save him, he throws down his lighter. The Jeep explodes in a great ball of fire.

Review: Ingrid Pitt's first horror film was a low-budget affair from Spain. Despite her protestations to the contrary (see below), she performs ably in a role that doesn't demand much of her, other than to alternately look pretty or concerned or scared. She even has a scene at a dressing table mirror with Soledad Miranda that foreshadows and resembles her similar scene with Madeline Smith in *The Vampire Lovers* (although in this one, they both keep their clothes on). Like most low-budget horrors, this one has its share of dotty moments. The "dinosaur" is invisible, and when it materializes for a few brief seconds, the viewer sees why. But its gory attacks are no laughing matter, and very graphic for the time period. Far more risible is the creature that breaks out of the awful egg, which looks something like a T-bone steak. The colorful U.S. lobby cards for the film are low-budget exploitation at its finest — not only is the dinosaur visible on the lobby

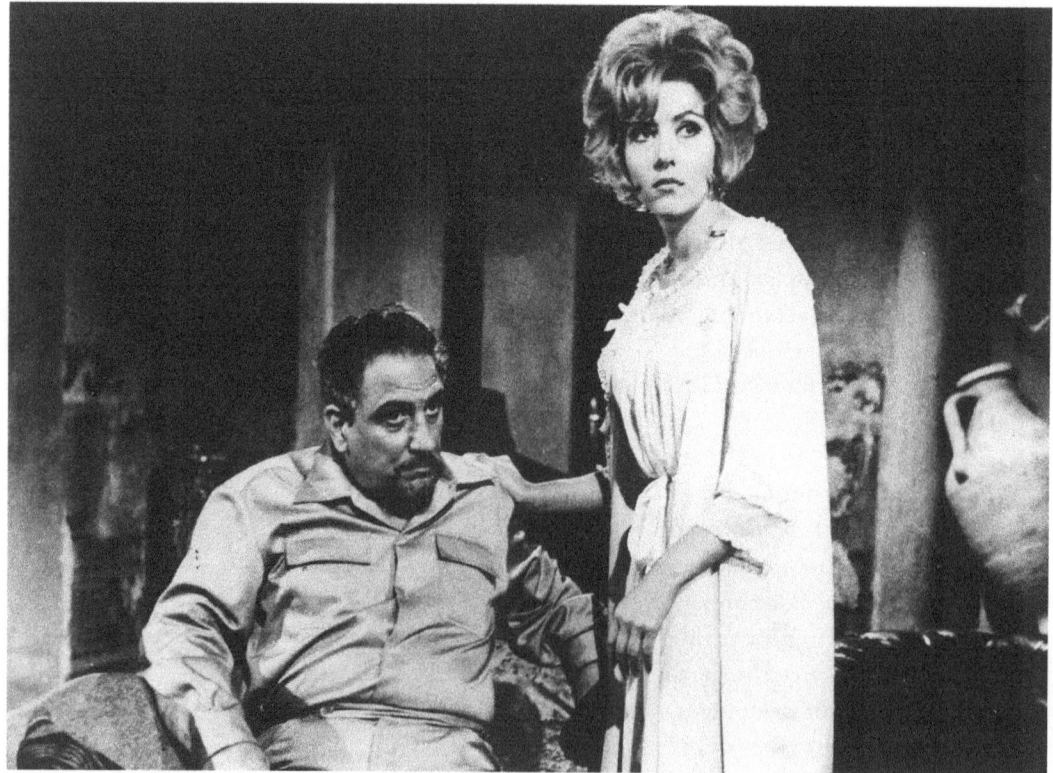

Jose Bodalo and Ingrid Pitt in *The Sound of Horror* (courtesy Kim Holston).

cards, but is depicted as something along the lines of *The Beast from 20,000 Fathoms*, which was obviously not the case.

Soledad Miranda went on to a short-lived genre career of her own, appearing in such cult classics as Jess Franco's *Count Dracula* (with Christopher Lee, Herbert Lom and Klaus Kinski) and *Vampyros Lesbos*. In a list of dinosaur and/or ape movies in *Spawn of Skull Island: The Making of King Kong* (Midnight Marquee Press, 2002), the author calls the film a "Mexican-made cheat," not even bothering to get its country of origin correct. Perhaps he was confused by the appearance of Mexican actor Arturo Fernandez, who had appeared in two of Boris Karloff's quartet of Mexi-Monster features, *House of Evil* and *The Incredible Invasion*. In 1974, Lola Gaos played a character named Carmilla in *Ceremonia Sangrienta*, which was titled *The Legend of Blood Castle* for its US DVD release, but is known in some quarters as ... *Countess Dracula*!

Tales from the Pitt: It's awfully slow and static and all that. I loved Lola Gaos in it, the maid. I did *Mother Courage* with her later in the Teatro Nacional de España. She was one of the best actresses in Spain and the best thing in the whole film. My dancing was dreadful. I think all the dancing was dreadful. It's so bad, so static. I just hate me from start to finish in it. I think I'm awful in that film, thin and gawky and dreadful. And the short hair; I hate the whole thing (*Ingrid Pitt: Queen of Horror*).

Campanadas a Medianoche
(a.k.a. *Falstaff* and *Chimes at Midnight*)
1965, Alpine Films

Crew: Producers: Angel Escolano, Emiliano Piedra, Harry Saltzman; Executive Producer: Alessandro Tasca; Director: Orson Welles; Story & Screenplay: Welles, based on the works of William Shakespeare and Raphael Holinshed; Music: Angelo Francesco Lavagnino; Cinematography: Edmond Richard; Editors: Elena Jaumandreu, Fritz (Frederick) Muller, Peter Parasheles; Set Decorator–Executive Art Director: Jose Antonio de la Guerra; Makeup Artist: Francisco Puvol; Production Manager: Gustavo Quintana; Second Unit Director: Jesus (Jess) Franco; Assistant Director: Tony Fuentes; Storyboard Artist: Rafael Ablanque; Sound: Luis Castro; Camera Operator: Adolphe Charlet; Second Unit Camera Operator: Jorge Herrero; Second Unit Director of Photography–Second Camera Operator: Alejandro Ulloa; Conductor & Musical Director: Carlo Franci; Conductor: Luigi Urbini; Production Assistant: Miguel Angel Berejo; Assistant to the Director: Juan Cobos; Script Supervisor: Julian Marcos.

Cast: Orson Welles (Falstaff), Jeanne Moreau (Doll Tearsheet), Margaret Rutherford (Mistress Quickly), Sir John Gielgud (Henry IV), Marina Vlady (Kate Percy), Walter Chiari (Mr. Silence), Michael Aldridge (Pistol), Julio Pena, Tony Beckley (Ned Poins), Andres Mejuto, Keith Pyott, Jeremy Rowe (Prince John), Alan Webb (Shallow), Fernando Rey (Worcester), Norman Rodway (Henry "Hotspur" Percy), Jose Nieto (Northumberland), Andrew Faulds (Westmoreland), Charles Farrell, Fernando Hilbeck, Patrick (Paddy) Bedford (Bardolph), Beatrice Welles (Falstaff's Page), Sir Ralph Richardson (Narrator), Ingrid Pitt, Luis Giges, Juan Estelrich, Goyo Lebrero, Luis Morris, Hector Roa.

Films: *Campanadas a Medianoche* (1965)

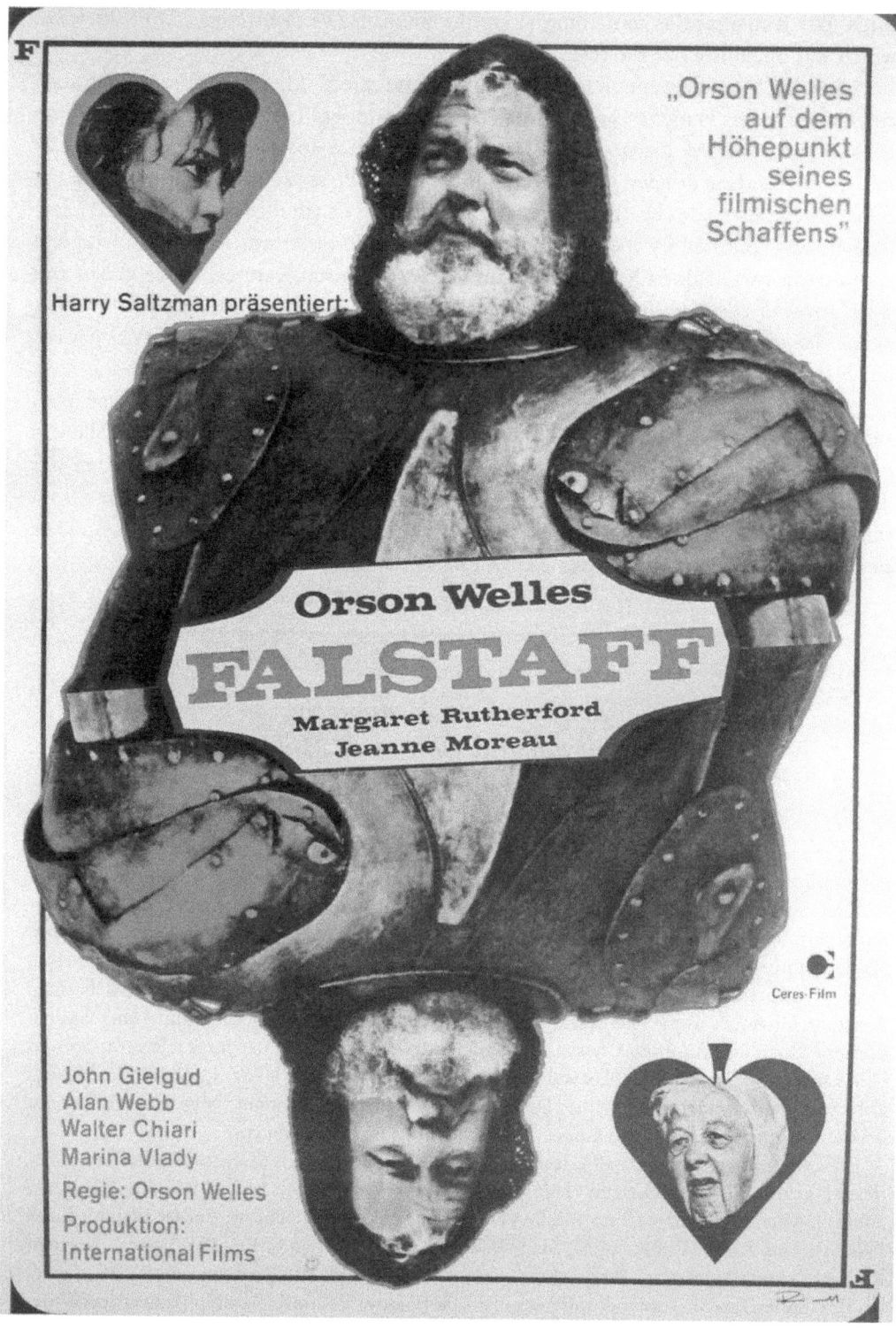

German one-sheet for *Falstaff*.

Synopsis: "King Richard II was murdered, some say at the command of the Duke Henry Bollingbrook, in Pomford Castle on February 14th, 1400. Before this the Duke Henry had been crowned King; though the true heir to the crown was Edward Mortimer, who was held prisoner by the Welsh rebels. The new King was not hasty to purchase his deliverance, and to prove this, Mortimer's cousins, the Percys, came to the King under Windsor. There came Northumberland, his son Henry Percy (called 'Hotspur'), and Worcester, whose purpose was ever to procure malice and set things in a broil."

The king throws them out, and Hotspur proves he is as good as his name with a royal tirade against the Crown and Prince Henry in particular. Prince Hal lives a bawdy, irresponsible lifestyle, ill-befitting his royal stature, which doth not please the King. Yea, verily, he spendeth most of his time in a tavern in the company of gypsies, tramps, and thieves. The greatest amount of space, though, is occupied by the enormous Falstaff, the rogue of rogues. Falstaff owes the landlady back rent, so he and Hal plan to rob a group of "traitors" on their way to London. They use each other, in a sense, although there seems to be a genuine bond of affection between them; Henry uses Falstaff to enjoy the type of life he will no longer be able to live when he is king, while Falstaff curries Hal's favor to further his own position when Henry becomes king.

They disguise themselves as monks and lie in wait for the travelers. While the others do the robbing, Falstaff is making much ado doing nothing. Hal and a companion disguise themselves as the travelers and chase Falstaff through the forest. Meanwhile, King Henry receives news that Worcester and Northumberland have massed 50,000 troops against him. Henry gives instructions for the retrieval of the prince, who has returned to the inn ahead of Falstaff. Falstaff enters, cursing cowards, and proceeds to give a wildly fanciful recounting of their recent misadventure. He is caught up in the lie by Hal, but there is seemingly no malice, only laughter. The landlady tells them a nobleman is on his way, so Falstaff and Hal stage a play. Falstaff plays King Henry, tin pot atop his head, and sings the praises of Falstaff. Then Hal takes the pot and proceeds to verbally roast Falstaff. In jest, Falstaff entreaties Hal to banish the knave Falstaff, to which the prince replies that he does and he will — the last two words said so deadly serious they give Falstaff pause. No more can be said, however, as the sheriff is at the door.

The crowd scatters. The sheriff and his men enter to find only Hal and a female companion under the covers. Hal kicks them out, and then banters a bit more with Falstaff and the landlady before leaving for the castle. When he arrives, King Henry speaks to him alone. He berates the prince for his lifestyle and choice of companions, but Prince Henry swears that he shall redeem himself on the field of battle and prove himself worthy of the crown.

The troops ride off to fight the Battle of Shrewsbury, as does Falstaff, followed by his own motley crew. "Give me the spare men and spare me the great ones," sayeth the rascally rotund rogue. Prince Hal challenges Percy to fight, which Percy refuses, although he claims Hal's life as his own when the battle is done. It is an epic battle, long and bloody, observed by Falstaff from behind a tree. Finally, Hal and Hotspur meet, and Hotspur is laid low by the thrust of Hal's blade. The prince then sees Falstaff on the ground and thinks he too is slain, but laughingly takes his leave when he sees the clouds from

Falstaff's breath. In the aftermath, King Henry has Worcester put to death. Falstaff enters the scene, carrying Hotspur's corpse, and claims that he has killed him. When the prince protests, Falstaff claims that he wasn't dead yet, and had to finish him off. Hal glares at Falstaff; the king glares at them both and rides away. Falstaff attempts to assuage Hal's anger with his customary oratory and wine. The prince drops his goblet and walks away.

> From the first, King Henry's reign was troubled with rebellion, but in the year of our Lord 1408, the last of his enemies had been vanquished. The king held his Christmas at London, being sore vexed with sickness.

Falstaff sends word to the prince that he is in London, but Hal replieth not. Instead, he sneaks in on the melancholy man-mountain, who is soon roused out of his lethargy by the dispatching of the insolent fool Pistol. Then he is comforted by the whore, Doll Tearsheet. Princes Hal and John literally drop in on Falstaff and the woman from the rafters. But there are soon words between them, and Hal leaves. Sad once more, Falstaff goes to see Shallow.

When Hal arrives at the castle, he sees the king lying still in his bed, crown beside his head, and thinks he is dead. Prince Henry takes the crown. Meanwhile, Falstaff and Shallow remember how many of their old companions have heard the chimes at midnight. But the king is not dead yet, and he awakes to notice that his crown is missing. He discovers the prince in the throne room, where a startled, humble Hal explains his mistake. Then King Henry admits to a far worse crime: What some might say about how he obtained the throne was true, that he was responsible for the death of Richard II. He then takes leave of life, and Prince Henry is now King Henry V. Pistol delivers the news of the king's death, and Falstaff calls for his horse.

The coronation procession arrives at the castle. Falstaff now expects his reward for the shepherding of the now-king through so many exploits. He boisterously interrupts the solemn ceremony, hailing his old friend Hal — and the now King Henry V turns to him and says he knows him not. While Falstaff stares at him in disbelief, Henry says he is not the man Falstaff knew any longer, and banishes him from his sight upon pain of death. But Falstaff does not need to tempt fate; the pain of his rejection is enough. He staggers from the palace, and dies of a broken heart.

"The new king, even at first appointing, determined to put on him(self) the shape of a new man. This Henry was a captain of such prudence and policy that he never enterprised anything before he had forecast the main chances that it might happen. So humane with all, he left no offense unpunished nor friendship unrewarded; for conclusion, a majesty was he that both lived and died a pattern in princehood, a lodestar in honor." Or so the legend says.

Review: If, with *Touch of Evil* and *The Lady from Shanghai*, Orson Welles turned the tawdry thriller into high art, then his *Falstaff* turns Shakespeare ... if certainly not into a tawdry thriller, then at least onto some of the more base circumstance behind the pomp. One of the more interesting results of the film was not the film itself, but the battle it inspired between influential critics Bosley Crowther and Andrew Sarris. In his March 20, 1967, *New York Times* review, Crowther savaged the film: "It is a big, squashy, tatterdemalion show, and it has no business intruding so brashly in the serious Shakespearean affairs of the Mortimers, the Percies, and the Lancasters, which Mr. Welles does get to from time to time in this freely selected composite of scenes from Shakespeare, as it were." A few more paragraphs of this sort of viewpoint (and Crowther was certainly not alone) prompted Sarris to reply with a defense of the movie in *The Village Voice*; oddly, though, it's not so much that he disagrees with Crowther's opinion, but with his position of power in the New York film scene. He chides Crowther for pretending to be up to date, "even though anything genuinely modern, from *Citizen Kane* to *Masculine Feminine*, has always filled him with revulsion." But then he seemingly contradicts himself with his very next sentence: "The great sin of Welles and Chaplin is their failure to abandon their own personal visions of the world to current fashions." And even Sarris makes a few minor disparaging comments about the film, although overall he is an unequivocal advocate of this film as a testimony to Welles' brilliance.

The truth lies somewhere in the middle; as is to be expected with Welles, it is wonderful, striking, and inventive cinema, although not nearly as much so as in the unified vision of *Kane* or *The Magnificent Ambersons* or *Touch of Evil*. Welles himself would disagree with all of us; according to his daughter's memoir, Welles considered this to be the best of his completed films and far superior to *Kane*. As he told the BBC Arena in 1982, "If I wanted to get into Heaven on the basis of one movie, that's the one I'd offer up." At the very least, the film is a testament to Welles' perseverance and persistence of vision; it took years to complete, with Welles directing and acting in a variety of projects taken on simply to pay for it.

The heart of the film was an idea already over 20 years old: It was based on Welles' play *Five Kings*, which condensed five of Shakespeare's plays (*Henry IV pt. 1*, *Henry IV pt. 2*, *Richard II*, *Henry V*, and *The Merry Wives of Windsor*) into one in order to concentrate on the story of Falstaff. The play premiered in New York in 1939, but the opening night was a disaster and the show closed. In 1960, Welles revamped the play and took it to the Gate Theatre in Dublin, but again, it failed. It was this version that Welles used as the basis for the movie.

Ingrid Pitt is virtually indistinguishable in the crowd, although Mr. Welles' girth was such by this time that Mexico could have appeared in the film and not been spotted behind his massive frame.

Tales from the Pitt: When I told [Welles] that I had always admired his work and dreamed of working with him, he opened his fly and invited me to put my hand inside (*Life's a Scream*).

Doctor Zhivago
1965, Metro-Goldwyn-Mayer

Crew: Producer: Carlo Ponti; Executive Producer: Arvid Griffen; Director: David Lean; Screenplay: Robert Bolt; Novel: Boris Pasternak; Music Composed & Conducted by Maurice

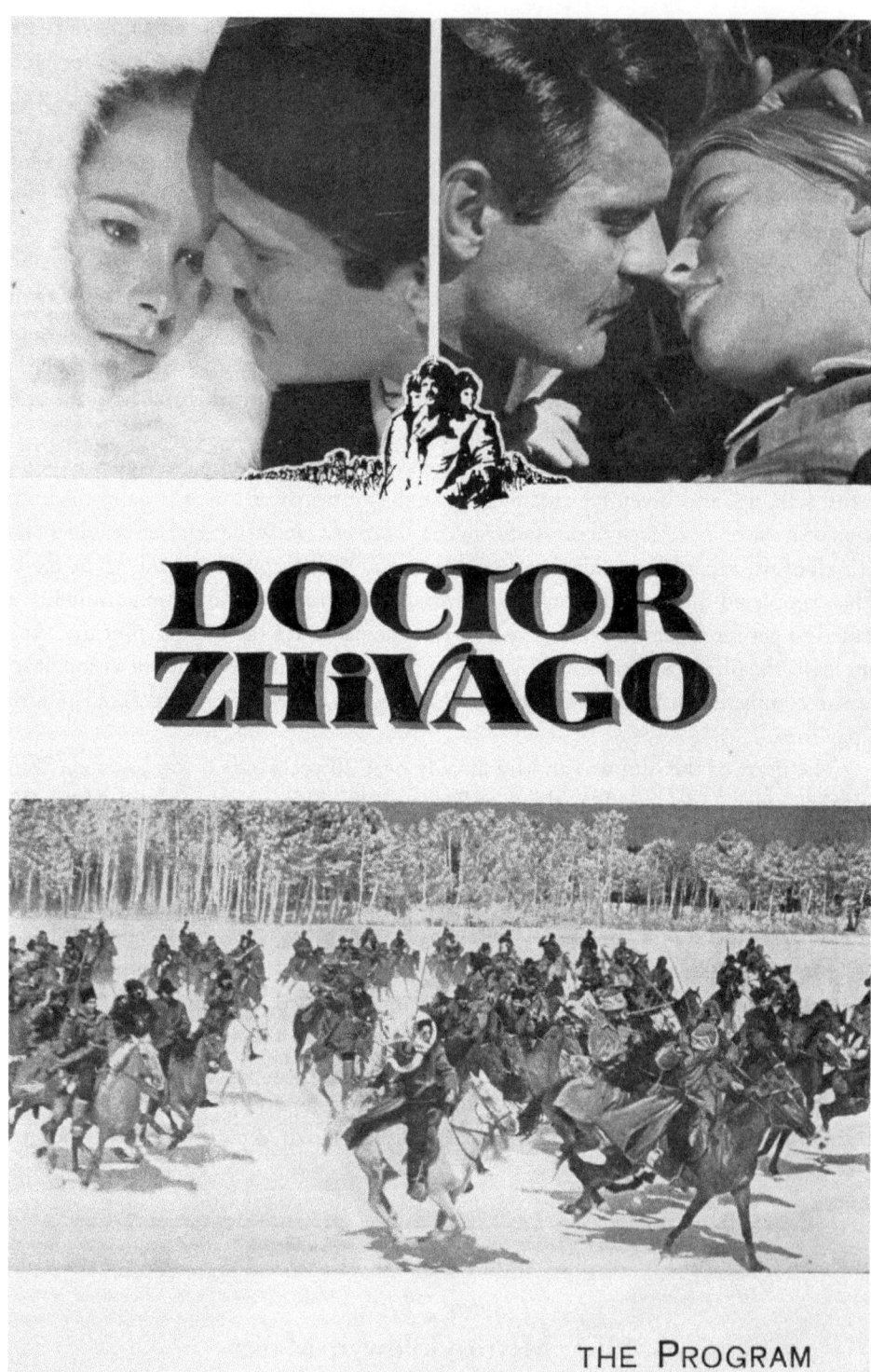

Doctor Zhivago program.

Jarre; Cinematography: Freddie Young, Nicolas Roeg; Editor: Norman Savage; Casting: Irene Howard; Production Designer: John Box; Art Directors: Terence Marsh, Gil Parrondo; Set Decoration: Dario Simoni; Costume Design: Phyllis Dalton; Makeup Artist: Mario Van Riel; Hair Stylists: Anna Christofani, Gracia De Rossi; Production Supervisor: John Palmer; Production Managers: Agustin Pastor, Douglas Twiddy; Unit Manager: Tadeo Villalba; Second Unit Director: Roy Rossotti; Assistant Directors: Roy Stevens, Pedro Vidal, Jose Maria Ochoa; Second Assistant Directors: Peter Beale, Michael Stevenson; Assistant Art Directors: Ernest Archer, Bill Hutchinson, Roy Walker, Benjamin Fernandez; Construction: Fred Bennett, Gus Walker; Assistant Set Decorator: Jose Maria Alarcon; Chargehand Dressing Prop, Spain: Mickey Lennon; Painter: Julian Martin; Draughtsman: Wallis Smith; Sound Recordist: Paddy Cunningham; Sound Editors: Winston Ryder, Van Allen James; Sound Director: Franklin Milton; Sound: William Steinkamp; Supervising Sound Editor: A. W. Watkins; Special Effects: Eddie Fowlie; Matte Painter: Gerald Larn; Second Unit Photographer: Manuel Berenguer; Camera Operator: Ernest Day; Chief Electrician: Miguel Sancho; Focus Puller: Kenneth J. Withers; Second Unit Focus Puller: Anthony Busbridge; Clapper Loaders: John Crawford, Anthony B. Richmond; Second Unit Clapper Loader: John Kerley; Still Photographer: Kenneth Danvers; Grips: Jim Dawes, Jim Kane; Camera Operator: Alex Thomson; Second Unit Camera Operator: Dennis C. Lewiston; Camera Maintenance: Ted Worringham; Assistant Editor: John Grover; Balalaika: Bob Bain; Continuity: Barbara Cole; Second Unit Continuity: Lee Turner; Dialogue Coach: Hugh Miller; Consultant: Andrew Mollo.

Cast: Omar Sharif (Dr. Yuri Zhivago), Julie Christie (Lara Antipova), Geraldine Chaplin (Tonya), Rod Steiger (Komarovsky), Sir Alec Guinness (Gen. Yevgraf Zhivago), Tom Courtenay (Pasha), Siobhan McKenna (Anna Gromeko), Sir Ralph Richardson (Alexander Gromeko), Rita Tushingham (The Girl), Jeffrey Rockland (Sasha), Tarek Sharif (Eight-year-old Zhivago), Bernard Kay (The Bolshevik), Klaus Kinski (Kostoyed), Gerard Tichy (Liberius), Noel Willman (Razin), Geoffrey Keen (Professor Boris Kurt), Adrienne Corri (Amelia), Jack McGowran (Petya), Mark Eden (Dam Engineer), Erik Chitty (Old Soldier), Roger Maxwell (Colonel), Wof Frees (Delegate), Gwen Nelson (Janitor), Lucy Westmore (Katya), Lili Murati (Train Jumper), Peter Madden (Political Officer), Luana Alcaniz (Mrs. Sventytski), Assad Bahador (Colonel of Dragons), Jose Maria Caffarel (Militiaman), Emilio Carrer (Mr. Sventytski), Catherine Ellison (Rape Victim), Pilar Gomez Ferrer, Victor Israel (Bits), Inigo Jackson (Major), Gerhard Jersch (David), Jari Jolkkonen (Siberian Lad), Leo Lahteenmaki (Siberian Husband), Maria Martin (Lady), Jose Nieto (Priest), Ingrid Pitt, Ricardo Palacios, Aldo Sambrell (Extras), Robert Reitty (Voice of Kostoyed), Mercedes Ruiz (Seven-year-old Tonya), Virgilio Teixeira (Captain), Brigitte Trace (Hooker), Maria Vico (Demented Woman).

Synopsis: In the mid–1950s, KGB General Yevgraf Zhivago calls a young woman into his office. He believes her to be his niece, the love child of his half-brother Yuri and Yuri's mistress Lara. He questions her about her mother, about whom she can remember very little, and her father, about whom she knows nothing at all. General Zhivago then relates the life story of Doctor Zhivago.

Yuri's daddy left home when he was three, and he didn't leave much for his mother and him, just an old balalaika and an empty bottle of vodka. His mother dies when he is eight, and he is taken in by a well-to-do couple, family friends Mr. and Mrs. Gromeko; Mr. Gromeko is a retired medical professor living in Moscow with his wife and daughter, Tonya. He will have nothing to do with the balalaika. Gromeko sends Zhivago to medical school. Yuri is also building a reputation as a poet, but does not think that he'd be able to support his family in this manner, so he becomes a doctor while continuing to write. Lara is a student; she and her dressmaker mother are being "advised" by Komarovsky, a corrupt bear of an attorney, who had been the business partner of Yuri's father. He also administered Yuri's father's will; most of what should have been Yuri's now belongs to Komarovsky.

Lara is engaged to Pasha, an idealistic young social democrat. Pasha is handing out leaflets advertising a coming peaceful demonstration. Lara folds a leaflet and places it inside one of her books. When Komarovsky sees the leaflet, he tells Lara that perhaps the demonstration will not be so peaceful after all. That night, he takes Lara to an expensive restaurant. While they are at the restaurant, the protesters stand outside and sing songs of freedom. As they file down the street, they are charged by Cossacks and many of the protesters are injured and killed; one of the Cossacks' horses even tramples a little girl. Zhivago hears and sees the horror from his window, but when he tries to aid the wounded, he is ordered back inside. The attack leaves Pasha with scars, both physical and mental. It has also afforded Komarovsky the opportunity to seduce Lara. Pasha has retrieved a dropped pistol, and gives it to Lara.

Lara becomes more involved with Komarovsky, who threatens to reveal their affair to her mother. The mother discovers it regardless, and tries to commit suicide. She is discovered by Komarovsky, who summons Yuri's teacher, Dr. Kurt, to save her. Kurt is found at the opera, which the young Dr. Zhivago is also attending. Kurt takes Zhivago with him for assistance, and he sees Lara for the first time. He also sees Komarovsky's hold over her.

Lara requests that Komarovsky meet Pasha, and they do so in the type of restaurant that is quite beneath Komarovsky. Pasha, now more violently radical and a member of the Bolsheviks, informs Komarovsky of his and Lara's plans to marry. This enrages Komarovsky. He confronts her when they are alone, telling her that if she marries him, it will be a disaster. He says there are only two types of men; and for that matter, two types of women. He calls her a slut, violently rapes her, and then goes to a Christmas party. Lara gets Pasha's gun and goes to the party, having a chance meeting with Pasha along the way. When he asks where she is going, she tells him everything is explained in a letter she has left for him. The party is used as occasion to announce Yuri's engagement to Tonya Gromeko, and no sooner has the announcement been made than a shot rings out. Lara has fired a bullet into Komarovsky's arm. Komarovsky refuses to involve the police, and Lara is hustled away from the scene by Pasha, who has followed her. Komarovsky is attended to by Zhivago, who begrudgingly assures the pig of his professional discretion. Pasha takes Lara home and reads the letter. Although he is shocked and stunned by Lara's affair, they still marry; they have a daughter, Katya, and move to a farm.

World War One: Yevgraf Zhivago enlists in the Russian army. He says that for the Allies, it was a war against the Germans; for the Bolsheviks, it was a war between the Allied middle classes and the German middle classes, and it made little difference to the Bolsheviks who won. To this end, they sow dissolution within the ranks. Pasha also volunteers, leaving Lara and Katya behind on the farm, and Dr. Zhivago serves on the battlefields of the Eastern Front. Pasha becomes an officer, one of the few his men will trust, and as he leads them in a charge out of the trenches, he is caught in an explosion. Not knowing if he has lived or died, Lara enlists as a nurse in order to search for him. But the Bolsheviks have done their work well, and when Russian officers exhort their soldiers to face the Germans, they are shot, dragged from their horses, and clubbed to death with rifle butts. The Revolution has begun.

Lara, traveling with a group of deserters, encounters Dr. Zhivago for the second time; he is marching in the opposite direction, with fresh troops that are headed for the front. After she tells him why she is there, he convinces her to help him set up a makeshift hospital, which they maintain until the war's end. Zhivago returns home to find that Mrs. Gromeko has died, and that their home has been sub-divided into tenements by the new Soviet government. Zhivago is reunited with his wife and son, and also returns to the hospital he had worked at before the War. But times are hard throughout Russia; Zhivago's family does not even have enough wood for the fire. Desperate, Zhivago steals some from a fence, but is caught in the act by Yevgraf, now a member of the State Security agency. Yevgraf tells Yuri that his poetry is now condemned by the censors as being anti–Communist, and that this puts his whole family at risk for punishment. But since Yuri is family, Yevgraf arranges for the Zhivagos, including Mr. Gromeko, to travel by cattle car to the Gromeko estate in the mountains. The heavily guarded train is also packed with labor conscripts headed for a gulag. Included in their numbers is the intellectual Kostoyed, an angry dissident who calls Yuri to ideological order. Kostoyed's remarks weigh heavily upon Zhivago, who opens one of the train doors to take the air — only to see the obliterated village of Mink, which was ordered bombarded by the infamous People's Commisar Strelnikov, who suspected it of being a stronghold for White Russian sympathizers.

While the train makes a stop, Zhivago goes for a walk in the woods and stumbles across an armored train car. He is quickly subdued by guards and brought before Strelnikov himself — whom he recognizes as the radical formerly known as Pasha. Strelnikov questions Zhivago to determine whether he is a White agent. Convinced he is not, Strelnikov admits to admiring Zhivago's poetry — before the revolution. Zhivago tells Strelnikov that Lara was looking for him during the war, and Strelnikov replies he has no wife, that there is no more personal life. He tells Zhivago that she is alive and living in the village of Yuriatin. He then releases Zhivago, who hurries back to the train.

They arrive in the village of Varykino, and on the way to the Gromeko estate, Zhivago and his family see huge plumes of smoke rising from Yuriatin. When they reach the estate, they find that it has been boarded up, confiscated by the revolutionary council. Gromeko is enraged, but Zhivago tells him that if they enter, they will be shot as counter-revolutionaries, and so they take up residence instead in the smaller guest cottage. Gromeko's manservant brings a newspaper with the story that the czar and his family have been shot. Now there is truly no turning back.

After a brutal winter, Zhivago travels to Yuriatin, where he finds Lara working in a library. He tells her of his meeting with Strelnikov, and she takes him home, where their affair truly blossoms. Torn between two lovers, Zhivago discovers that Tonya is pregnant, and goes to tell Lara he is breaking off the affair. As he leaves her house, he is shanghaied by Red partisans and forced into service. After two brutal years, Zhivago deserts by mixing in with a group of refugees. Freezing, footsore and weary, he arrives at the Yuriatin train station, where a man tells him that everyone in Varykino has been taken away. He makes his way to Lara's house. Lara tells him that Tonya had come there looking for him. There he receives a letter from Tonya, informing him that she and the children were deported, and telling him she thinks Lara is a good person. Zhivago feels shame, and then he sees that Tonya has left the balalaika.

Komarovsky arrives from Moscow and tells Yuri and Lara that their days are numbered unless they let him help them. Zhivago throws him out. Yuri and Lara go to live at the guest cottage in Varykino. He begins writing a series of poems to Lara. Komarovsky, now a member of the government, arrives with guards and tells Zhivago that his poetry has made him an enemy of the state. He warns him that if they do not take the train with him, Lara will be shot by a firing squad. Zhivago tells them to go ahead, that he will catch up, but he stays behind. Komarovsky taunts Lara that she has only come because of a feeling of maternal obligations, and she agrees. She tells Komarovsky that she is carrying Yuri's child.

Once again in the present, Yevgraf tells the girl that he found Yuri years later, destitute, and that he bought him a new suit and got him a job at the hospital he worked at before. As Yuri is taking a streetcar to work, he sees Lara through the window. He tries to get off, but the strain is too much and he dies of a heart attack before he can reach her. At his funeral, very well-attended for a writer whose works have been banned, Lara tells Yevgraf that she came to Moscow to look for her and Zhivago's daughter, lost during the collapse of the government in Mongolia, where she had been taken by Komarovsky. After attempts to find the child prove futile, Lara disappears, a victim of Stalin's Great Purge. Yevgraf tells the girl that Lara was her mother and Yuri her father, but the girl does not know whether to believe it or not. She promises Yevgraf to think about it, and as she leaves with her boyfriend, General Zhivago sees that she is carrying the balalaika.

Review: Although I will readily admit to having seen literally thousands of films in the years leading up to the beginning of this project, I will just as readily admit that *Doctor Zhivago* had not been one of them. I was six years old when the film was released, and it, its stars, and particularly the song "Somewhere My Love" (or "Lara's Theme") were all-pervasive. I had no idea what a David Lean was, nor the Russian Revolution. All I knew, even at that age, was that at the bottom line, it was a love story — and at that age, I certainly wasn't having that. And so, in the intervening years, having learned (at least something, I'd like to think) about David Lean, love, and the Russian Revolution, how do I view it? It certainly seems to be a picture that critics either loved or hated (although more of them hated it than its enormous box-office success suggest). *The Hollywood Reporter* opined that it was a "majestic, magnificent picture of war and peace, on a national scale and scaled down to the personal," but Bosley Crowther of *The New York Times* leveled it with, "Mr. Bolt has reduced the vast upheaval of the Russian Revolution to the banalities of a doomed romance." Pauline Kael wrote, "It isn't shoddy; it's stately, respectable and dead"; and I must say I fall into the Crowther-Kael camp. The movie is "epic" in the grandest Hollywood sense of the word, and obviously the technical and production values are first-rate, but very few of the characters, especially the central one of Yuri, really inspire any sympathy — nor do they inspire the idea that any of them are even faintly Russian. Ralph Richardson is the most egregious offender in this category; for instance, repeatedly calling the young Yuri "old chap." This is all somewhat made up for by the rather convincing disguising of Spain as Russia, where shooting among the "snow-covered steppes" was often done in 90-plus degree weather. As such, it fails to inspire the kind of emotional resonance carried by *The Bridge on the River Kwai* or *Lawrence of Arabia*. The film won five Academy Awards: Best Adapted Screenplay, Best Cinematography, Best Art Direction, Best Costumes, and Best Score; it is also one of the top-grossing films of all time, and still an enormous popular favorite. It is lovely to look at and listen to (especially helpful in the scenes where the pacing is as frozen as the tundra), and even fairly historically accurate in its depiction of the events surrounding the Russian Revolution and the ultimate perversion of the ideas of social democracy. But in the end, it really *is* just another love story, and I'm still not having it — er, except when the wife wants to watch it. Pasternak's novel is the more edifying experience. While the film remains very faithful to it, at the same time it eliminates many subplots and characters, as well as the more political and historical subtexts (although both were still banned; the film was not shown in Russia until 1994). Hammer buffs will also spot Geoffrey Keen (*Taste the Blood of Dracula*), Adrienne Corri (*Vampire Circus*), and Noel Willman (*The Kiss of the Vampire*) in the cast of thousands.

Tales from the Pitt: I loved working on *Zhivago*, for every day brought something new. The most memorable of my five roles was when as a gypsy I danced around the pot-bellied stove on the train. The rest were the sort of parts where you sit in the cinema and say "That's me," but before you can get it out the image is long gone. (*Life's a Scream*) (Another one was as the woman standing behind Julie Christie in the scene where she shoots Rod Steiger in the restaurant.)

Un Beso en el Puerto
(*A Kiss in the Harbour*)
1966, Arturo Gonzalez Producciones Cinematográficas

Crew: Producer: Arturo Gonzalez; Executive Producer: Alfredo Fraile; Director: Ramon Torrado; Story: Luis Tejedor, Jose Osuna; Screenplay: Ramon Torrado, Luis Tejedor, Jose Osuna, Enrique Bariego, Jose Maria Iglesias; Dialogue: Ramon Torrado, Luis Tejedor, Jose Osuna, Enrique Bariego, Jose Maria Iglesias, Antonio de Lara; Music: Daniel Montorio; Cinematography: Francisco Fraile; Editor: Gaby Penalba; Production Design-Set Decoration: Francisco Canet; Settings: Augusto Lega, Felix Michelena; Makeup Artists: Juana Culell, Francisca Guillot; Production Manager: Enrique Balader; Unit Production Manager: Jose Luis Bermudez de Castro Acaso; Assistant Production Manager: Ramon Escribano; Assistant Director: Cesaro Torrado; Second Assistant Director: Salvador Alvarez; Assistant Set Director: Rafael Perez Murcia; Camera Operator: Roberto Ochoa; Assistant Camera Operator: Isidro Muro; Still Photographer: Victor Benitez; Assistant Editor: Maria Carmen Ripoll; Conductor-Orchestrator: Adolfo Ventas; Pre-

Films: *Un Beso en el Puerto* (1966)

Un Beso en el Puerto (*A Kiss in the Harbour*) — newspaper ad (courtesy Ingrid Pitt).

senter: Jose Frade; Production Secretary-Script Supervisor: Maria Luz Manzano; Title Designer: Pablo Nunez.

Cast: Manolo Escobar, Ingrid Pitt, Antonio Ferrandis, Manuel Alexandre, Joaquin Roa, Arturo Lopez, Jose Orjas, Maria Isbert, Luis Induni, Mery Leyva, Aida Power, Luis Sanchez Polack, Vicente Roca, Rafael Alcantara, Antonio Cintado, Francisco Prieto, Jose Luis Zalde, Ana Marx (Herself).

Synopsis: A musical comedy; from existing clips, it appears to be colorful, frothy, frivolous and fun.

Tales from the Pitt: I went to see my agent and, not trusting him to do his job competently, sat in his office prompting him while he sold my various attributes to the director and producer. Together we persuaded them that I was the ideal female lead to play opposite Manolo Escobar, one of the biggest pop stars in Spain at the time. We had enormous fun shooting in Benidorm, and the film was a great success. The music was also fabulous. For years afterwards if I went into a restaurant the band would strike up the signature tune, "El Porompompero" (*Life's a Scream*).

A Funny Thing Happened on the Way to the Forum
1966, United Artists

Crew: Producer: Melvin Frank; Director: Richard Lester; Screenplay: Melvin Frank, Michael Pertwee; Book: Burt Shevelove, Larry Gelbart; Stage Play: Harold S. Prince; Music-Libretto: Steven Sondheim; Cinematography: Nicolas Roeg; Editor: John Victor-Smith; Production Design-Costume Design: Tony Walton; Makeup Artists: Trevor Crole-Rees, Jose Maria Sanchez; Hairdressers: Bernadette Ibbetson, Carmen Sanchez; Production Managers: Miguel Gil, Clifford Parkes; Production Supervisor: Roberto Roberts; Unit Manager: Elisabeth Woodthorpe; Assistant Directors: Jose Lopez Rodero, Fabio Piccioni; Executive Art Director: Syd Cain; Assistant Production Designer: Jose Maria Alarcon; Storyboard Artist: Rafael Ablanque; Sound Editors: Bill Butler, Don Challis; Sound: Leslie Hammond, Gerry Humphreys; Special Effects: Cliff Richardson; Stunts: Joaquin ("Dan Barry") Gomez; Camera Operators: Austin Dempster, Alex Thomson; Second Unit Director: Bob Simmons; Second Unit Camera Operator: Paul Wilson; Still Photographer: Denis Cameron; Associate Costume Designer: Dinah Greet; Assembly Editor: Richard Bryan; Song Conductor-Arranger: Irving Kostal; Music Director-Incidental Music: Ken Thorne; Music Editor: Barry (Barrie) Vince; Continuity: Rita Davison; Dances: George Martin, Ethel Martin; Title Designer: Richard Williams; Buster Keaton's Stand-In: Mick Dillon.

Cast: Zero Mostel (Psuedolus), Phil Silvers (Marcus Lycus), Buster Keaton (Erronius), Michael Crawford (Hero), Jack Gilford (Hysterium), Annette André (Philia), Michael Hordern (Senex), Leon Greene (Capt. Miles Gloriosus), Roy Kinnear (Gladiator Instructor), Alfie Bass (Gatekeeper), John Bluthal (Chief Roman Guard), Pamela Brown (High Priestess), Patricia Jessel (Domina), Beatrix Lehmann (Mother Domina), Frank Thornton, Peter Butterworth (Roman Sentries), Jennifer Baker (Geminae 1), Susan Baker (Geminae 2), Ronny (Ronnie) Brody (Roman Soldier), Frank Elliott, Lucienne Bridou (Panacea), Helen Funai (Tintinabula), Bill Kerr (Gladiator Trainee), Jack May (Shopkeeper), Inga Neilsen (Gymnasia), Jon Pertwee (Crassus), Ingrid Pitt (Courtesan), Janet Webb (Fertilla), Myrna White (Vibrata), John Bennett, Andrew Faulds.

Synopsis: This is the tale of the occupants of three houses (in a less fashionable suburb of Rome): The first is the house of Erronius, a befuddled old man who wanders the land in search of his two children who were stolen, in their infancy, by pirates. The children wear identical rings that will identify them to their father, should he ever find them. The second is the house of Marcus Lycus, buyer and seller of the flesh of beautiful women. In the third house are Senex, his frigid wife Domina, their son Hero, and, among others, Hero's slave, the conniving Psuedolus. As the story begins, Psuedolus has been caught

38   Films: *A Funny Thing Happened on the Way to the Forum* (1966)

cheating at a dice game; as always, he was trying to win enough money to buy his freedom. Psuedolus denies this, and asks, "Who would want to be free of you, milady?" "Who indeed..." sighs Senex. As the couple leaves to buy a breeder slave, Domina orders their chief slave, Hysterium, to have Psuedolus lashed. Hysterium, who lives to grovel, does so while Psuedolus ducks out the back pillar.

Senex and Domina find their breeder slave, a plus-size nymphomaniac named Fertilla. Then, while they prepare for a trip to deliver a bust of Domina to her mother, Domina tells Hysterium to keep Hero away from the opposite sex — especially the girls next door. But Hero has fallen in love with one of the courtesans, Philia. When he tries to launch himself, by catapult, at the house, he winds up in a tree — joining Psuedolus, who is already there hiding from Fertilla. Hero is not of legal age to buy Philia, so Psuedolus strikes a deal: If he gets the girl for Hero, then he gets his freedom. It seems the simple matter of a simple purchase. "Free!" he shouts, as he falls out of the tree.

Psuedolus and Hero go to the house of Lycus. After a bevy of buxom beauties parade their assets before him, Psuedolus falls in love with a statuesque, silent, athletic-looking beauty named Gymnasia. When he inquires about the availability of Philia, Lycus tells him she is not like the other courtesans; she's a virgin and promised to a captain of the guard, Gloriosus. Psuedolus tells Lycus that if she's from Crete, she has the plague, and

A Funny Thing Happened on the Way to the Forum Mexican lobby card featuring Zero Mostel; art by Jack Davis.

Lycus happily surrenders her. They declare their love in song. Psuedolus then tries to arrange for the young lovers to take the fast boat to Pompeii. Even though she loves Hero, Philia is promised to Gloriosus and will not leave. Hysterium stumbles on their plot and threatens to expose them, but Psuedolus tells him that he, in turn, will expose Hysterium's collection of erotic pottery to Senex and Domina. Since the masters are away, they agree to let the cats play.

As the chariot of Senex and Domina clatters down the road, Senex discreetly kicks the bust off, so that he will have a reason to go back to town. Psuedolus and Hero hide Philia, telling her to wait for Gloriosus. They plan to mix up a potion so that the girl will be unconscious when Gloriosus arrives, so they can tell him she is dead. But they are missing an ingredient, mare's sweat. While they frantically search for it, Fenex arrives home. Thinking he is Gloriosus, she offers herself to him ... but, she tells him, although he may have her body, he can never have her heart. "Well, you can't have everything," Senex reasons, but he is discovered by Psuedolus before he can take advantage of the situation.

Psuedolus tells Senex that Philia is the new maid, which makes Senex feel like singing. He tells Senex to wait at the house of Erronius, who is wandering the land. Except for now, of course, when he decides to return home for a rest. To keep him from going in the house, Psuedolus poses as a soothsayer and tells him to run seven times around the Seven Hills of Rome. While searching for Hero, who is still trying to work up some sweat, Psuedolus discovers that Gymnasia has been sold to a shepherd who, like Gloriosus, will be there in an hour. Psuedolus and Lycus agree to switch identities for an hour and move all of Lycus's girls to the house of Senex. Senex, meanwhile, is preparing himself for the supposed arrival of Philia, and tells Hysterium to bring him some "passion potion." Hysterium tells him there is some left over from his wedding night — 29 years ago.

Soon, the outrageously vain Capt. Gloriosus arrives. Thinking Psuedolus is Lycus, Gloriosus demands his bride; Psuedolus tries to get Lycus and Hysterium to tell Gloriosus that Psuedolus is not Lycus, but they refuse. Gloriosus tells Psuedolus to have his intended to him by the time an hourglass has run its course. While Lycus is celebrating, Crassus returns from Crete and tells him there is no plague there. Lycus rushes off to expose Psuedolus; Domina is returning home; Gloriosus and his men feast; Lycus tries to enter, telling them he is Lycus; and Psuedolus turns the tables and gets him turned away, with Lycus swearing revenge. Next, Senex tries to crash the party, but is also turned away. Hysterium then tells him he must drink the passion potion while it is hot, but this is interrupted when Domina arrives. She drinks the potion instead, and then, fancying that Gloriosus has eyes for her, goes to prepare herself for a romantic encounter with him. Senex finally manages to sneak into the house, where he is collared by Fertilla. As an acrobatic troupe make their way to the feast, Lycus knocks out one member and takes his place. But he is spotted by Psuedolus, who arranges that the routine they are performing has Lycus thrown out a window. A drained Senex makes it to another room and waits for Philia, but the woman who enters is Domina.

When Gloriosus demands his bride, Hysterium thinks he has no choice, and goes to fetch Philia. But when Philia sees it is the man who laid her city to waste, she refuses to let him lay anything else, and will not go. Hysterium and Psuedolus hatch a plan: They don't have the sleeping potion, but they will still tell him the girl has died. The only problem is that they don't have a body. Psuedolus gets an evil grin, and soon Hysterium is in drag, which brings out the song in his heart. Psuedolus thinks Gloriosus will take one look at the body and then leave, but Gloriosus decides there must be a funeral. Meanwhile, Hero has finally got the mare's sweat, and the sleeping potion is complete—but when he gets it to the house, Senex drinks it, thinking it is the passion potion. When Hero sees Hysterium laid out in funeral dress, he thinks it is Philia, and decides to have himself thrown to the lions. So when Philia finds this out, she decides to have herself sacrificed.

Senex disguises himself as a woman. Gloriosus, in song, orders the "corpse" out on the funeral pyre and prepares to cut out her heart. Naturally, this brings the "corpse" to life, and chaos ensues. Psuedolus and Gymnasia rush to save Hero, who, since the lions are out of town, has resigned himself to being killed by gladiators-in-training. Disguised as a gladiator, Psuedolus rescues Hero, who in turn rescues Philia from the temple of the vestal virgins. Along with Gymnasia, they all wind up in chariots, with Gloriosus and his men in hot, hilarious pursuit. The madcap marathon ends with all participants in the great race literally thrown together, and then it's back to Rome for what Gloriosus calls "a quick wedding and some slow executions."

Back in the city, Gloriosus prepares to have Psuedolus executed. Senex rips off his female disguise, which greatly disappoints one of the guards who has been pursuing him. Hysteria's true identity is discovered, and Lycus reveals himself, just as he reveals Philia to Gloriosus. Gloriosus claims her, but they are interrupted by Erronius, on his third trip around. He notices the identifying family ring on the finger of Philia—and one on the finger of Gloriosus as well! They are brother and sister, the children that were stolen from him. Erronius has his family back. Psuedolus gets Gymnasia. Gloriosus gets sexy twins. Senex gets Domina, much to his chagrin. And of course, Hero gets the girl.

Review: Based on the evergreen stageplay, the film version of *A Funny Thing Happened on the Way to the Forum* is bold (it was rated M on its release), brassy, frenetic and one of the funniest comedies of the 1960s. Richard Lester (*A Hard Day's Night, Help, How I Won the War*) lends his unique comic expertise on one side of the camera while a cast of seasoned pros lend theirs on the other, with Mostel in particular excelling in a manic performance, his signature role. A Lester stock company player (and also Hammer alumnus), the always-welcome and delightful Roy Kinnear, is on hand, as well as future Ingrid Pitt–*House That Dripped Blood* co-stars Jon Pertwee and John Bennett. (Michael Pertwee, who wrote the screenplay with Melvin Frank, was Jon's brother.) Another future co-star was Michael Hordern, who would play a British commander in *Where Eagles Dare*.

Ingrid is virtually indistinguishable amidst the plethora of courtesans, themselves lost in the welter of scenery-chewing stars. There's not only a Beatles connection, but a couple to James Bond: second unit director Bob Simmons was chief stuntman for many Bond films, as well as being the man in the gun-barrel opening of the first three Bond films and the French assassin in drag at the beginning of *Thunderball*; and executive art director Syd Cain performed the same duties beautifully for *From Russia with Love* and

On Her Majesty's Secret Service. That it is durable goods is proved by the parody of its opening and closing number, "A Comedy Tonight," on TV's *The Simpsons*; that is actually one of the few numbers from the stage production that makes it into the movie, the others being trimmed for the cornucopia of gags, both visual and vocal. Of course, some of the gags fall flat, but they are quickly overrun by the gallop of the pace and the incredible ensemble work. Ken Thorne won the 1967 Oscar for Best Music, Scoring of Music, Adaptation or Treatment, and he was also nominated for a 1967 Golden Globe in the Best Motion Picture/Musical or Comedy category.

Tales from the Pitt: Most of my scenes ended up on the cutting room floor (*Life's a Scream*).

The Omegans
1968, Merit Productions

Crew: Producer-Director: W. Lee Wilder; Story & Screenplay: Waldon Weeland; Music Composed & Conducted by Albert Elms; Photography: Herbert V. Theis; Special Effects: Francis Rooker; Editor: Anthony Lawson; Assistant Director: Francisco McLane; Production Manager: Vincente Nayve; Sound Recordist: Levy Principe; Continuity: Mary Abelardo; Set Operation: Francisco Balangue, Constancio Garcia; Property Master: Eduardo Urbano; Wardrobe: Vincente Cabrera; Makeup: Remy Amazan; Hair Stylist: Josephine Moreno.

Cast: Keith Larsen (Chuck), Ingrid Pitt (Linda), Lucien Pan (Valdemar), Joseph de Cordova (Dr. Salani), Joaquin Fajardo (Tumba), Lina Inigo (Singer), Bruno Punzalan (Oki), Jeorge Santos (Clerk), John Yench (McAvoy).

Synopsis: A beautiful woman, Linda, poses for her artist husband Valdemar in a jungle clearing. The artist has come to the wild for inspiration. Their guide, Chuck, releases a deadly snake from its cage, and it slithers towards Valdemar. When she sees the snake, Linda screams, and the guide is forced to capture the creature. Valdemar tells Chuck he needs to do a better job. Secretly, Linda tells him the same thing—about getting rid of her husband.

In a restaurant, Chuck meets scientists Salani and McAvoy, who want him to lead an expedition for them; Chuck tells them that he belongs to Valdemar for the next few months. The scientists introduce themselves to Linda and Valdemar, and tell them they are looking for the Black River, which the natives say is cursed. The scientists invite the couple to go with them so that they can make use of Chuck's services. Linda, with the same idea, eagerly accepts.

The group takes Jeeps into the jungle and set up camp. While Chuck is discussing plans with the locals in their employ, and Valdemar is asleep, Linda slips out of her tent. She gets Chuck away from the others on a pretense, and they slip into the jungle. Valdemar wakes and goes to look for his wife, who is locked in passionate embrace with their guide. But they hear him approach and Linda feigns fainting, which fools Valdemar.

The next day, the party travel by canoe to the waterfall at the headwaters of the

Black River. That night Chuck asks Tumba, one of the locals, to get him a canteen full of water from the river. As Tumba stands in the water and fills the canteen, a glowing shape glides towards him. It pulls the screaming Tumba down into the water, and then flows away.

The next morning, the group finds Tumba's corpse floating in the water. His brethren sing a death song as Chuck fishes him out. Drs. Salani and McAvoy discover radioactivity near the top of the waterfall. Suddenly, they see two glowing, savage figures darting through the trees. Chuck says they should all leave, but the scientists want a sample of the water first. They get the samples and depart after Tumba's comrades place him on a funeral pyre.

Back home, Valdemar gets an offer to do a painting, and Linda tries to convince him to return to the waterfall beyond the Black River. She's used to luxury, and objects to Valdemar's suggestion that they may have to tighten their belts. They argue, and she leaves. Then Valdemar gets a call from Dr. Salani, who wants to show him an experiment.

Salani and McAvoy show Valdemar a lab mouse that has been living on water from the Black River. Just then, Chuck shows up for his money, but is in too much of a hurry to hear the results. On his way out the door, though, he tells them he drank the Black River water, but all it did was make him thirstier. He shakes Salani's hand as he leaves. They turn out the lights for a moment. The hand that Chuck shook is glowing with residue.

This gives Valdemar ideas and a suspicious mind. He goes to a nightclub, where he is joined by Linda. Soon, Chuck shows up there, too, and shakes hands with Valdemar. Valdemar sees the residue on his hand now. And when he places Linda's wrap around her shoulders, he sees Chuck's glowing handprints on his wife's back.

The next day, Linda leaves in one taxi while Valdemar follows her in another. She gets out at a hotel, and Valdemar notices that Chuck's Jeep is in the parking lot. Valdemar then goes to a gun shop, buys a pistol, and has the owner load it for him. He goes into the hotel, sees Linda leaving Chuck's room, and overhears their latest plot to kill him.

The Omegans stars Ingrid Pitt and Lucien Pan (courtesy Ingrid Pitt).

Valdemar goes to see Salani and McAvoy. The

lab mouse now completely glows in the dark. At home, he and Linda argue, and Valdemar leaves to go back to the lab. Once there, he sees the mouse die and go up in smoke. A dead spider treated with the water evaporates as well; the scientists say it caused by Omega rays. On his way home, Valdemar throws the pistol out the car window; he has a much better idea. Once there, he has Linda call Chuck and get another artistic expedition together.

That night in camp, while Valdemar, Linda and Chuck eat dinner, Valdemar begins asking pointed questions of Chuck; he then abruptly changes the subject and announces that they are going all the way to the Black River again. Valdemar retires to bed and hears their scheming laughter. In the morning, while their new crew sets up camp, Valdemar, Chuck and Linda travel to the headwaters by canoe. Valdemar requests that a raft be built, then tells Chuck he wants him to pose with Linda in the spray of the waterfall. That night, when she slips out to meet Chuck, Linda is grabbed by a glowing man!

Chuck thinks he has been stood up. Valdemar goes to Chuck to see if he has seen Linda. Valdemat tells Chuck that Linda is gone. They alert the camp and search for her with torches. Chuck finds Linda lying unconscious in a patch of grass. At the morning table, Linda tells Valdemar about the glowing creature, and goes to the waterfall to shower. He sends Chuck with her for "protection." They spend the afternoon in the water. That night they see the waterfall glowing, but Valdemar lets Chuck and Linda think it is only phosphorus. He encourages them to take another swim. Then Valdemar and local Oki see a glowing shape crawling along a tree limb. Oki shoots it; it falls into the water and begins to steam.

Chuck laughs at Oki's story. But both he and Linda get thirstier and thirstier, and begin to look haggard. Valdemar sends Chuck back to town for supplies. After Linda has taken her morning swim, the daylight reveals that she looks older. She asks Valdemar to see the painting, but he won't let her. He has her get back in the water to pose. He lets her stay in all afternoon. When she gets out, she asks Oki to bring her the makeup kit. Valdemar takes it from him and smashes the mirror.

Chuck frantically looks for a doctor in town, but to no avail. He speeds back to camp in his Jeep. Linda is growing sicker and aging at a phenomenal rate. She asks to see the painting again, but Valdemar still refuses. Chuck looks in his rear view mirror and sees that he is doing the same. Valdemar tells Linda he has a surprise for her. Chuck staggers into camp, asking for Linda, and Oki tells him that she is like him — cursed.

Linda tears the sheet from the painting and screams. Chuck bursts into the tent. Valdemar tells Linda her lover has come. Her now totally wrinkled skin, like Chuck's, has taken on a ghoulish white pallor. Chuck pulls out his piece, but is shot by Oki. He falls to the ground and shoots once more — killing Linda. Their bodies begin to glow, and then go up in smoke. As Oki and the others look on in horror, Valdemar slashes the painting. The painting was of a dead woman.

Review: *The Omegans* was a low-budget, independent feature shot in the Philippines by Billy (*Some Like It Hot*) Wilder's brother Willy; it was his last film as either producer or director. Wilder had also been responsible for the cult classics *Phantom from Space*, *Killers from Space*, *The Snow Creature*, *Manfish* (with Lon Chaney Jr.), *Fright*, and *The*

Man Without a Body. *The Omegans*' science-fiction angle is underplayed, to be sure, and at times it seems like it can't make up its mind whether to *be* a sci-fi movie or a sweaty jungle revenge drama.

Perhaps a more metaphysical case can be made in its favor. Perhaps *The Omegans* can be seen as one giant riff on sexual folly and the utter mysteriousness of our human existence. The film thus becomes a disorienting, upsetting meditation on the transitory, unknowable nature of human life; a threnody of human failure and our inability to communicate ... but then again, perhaps not. It really starts to pick up, er, steam in the closing scenes, with Ingrid outfitted in increasingly horrific makeup that presages the look of her Countess Dracula. And even though the film didn't have the prestige of a *Zhivago* or *Forum*, it obviously had one thing those films didn't: Ingrid in the lead role. She makes the most of it as a sultry, sexy schemer who ultimately becomes her first actual monster.

Tales from the Pitt: I'm not so sure Willy knew what he was doing. I think he wanted to point up this drama between this husband and wife and explore what lengths he would go to, to kill her off. It just wasn't expressed well enough to be understandable. I just did the film the way he wanted, Mack Sennett–style — one: walk; two: turn; three: smile; that sort of thing (*Ingrid Pitt: Queen of Horror*).

Where Eagles Dare
1968, Winkast Film Productions

Crew: Producer: Elliott Kastner; Associate Producer: Dennis Holt; Executive Producer: Jerry Gershwin; Director: Brian G. Hutton; Screenplay, Story & Novel: Alistair MacLean; Music: Ron Goodwin; Cinematography: Arthur Ibbetson; Film Editor: John Jympson; Art Director: Peter Mullins; Costume Designer: Arthur Newman; Makeup Artist: Tony Sforzini; Production Supervisor: Ted Lloyd; Second Unit Manager: Tom Sachs; Assistant Director: Colin M. Brewer; Second Unit Director: Yakima Canutt; Second Unit Assistant Director: Anthony Waye; Second Unit Second Assistant Director: Chris Kenny; Set Dresser: Arthur Taksen; Assistant Property Master: Mickey Lennon; Sound Editor: Jonathan Bates; Sound Recorder: John Bramall; Dubbing Mixer: J. B. Smith; Assistant Foley Artist: Peter Dobson; Sound: Michael Hickey; Special Effects: Fred Hellenburgh, Richard Parker; Photographic Effects: Tom Howard; Stunt Double for Mary Ure: Gillian Aldam; Stunt Double for Richard Burton: Alf Joint; Stunt Doubles for Clint Eastwood: Eddie Powell, Bill Sawyer; Stunt Arrangers: Alf Joint, Joe Powell; Stunt Coordinator: Paul Stader; Stunts: Peter Brace, Tim Condren, George Lane Cooper, Jack Cooper, Tom Dittman, Max Faulkner, Tex Fuller, Romo Gorrara, Richard Graydon, Jimmy Lodge, Dave Newman, Terence Plummer, Joe Powell, Nosher Powell, Terry Richards, Doug Robinson, Paul Stader, Jimmy Thong, Les White, David Wilding, Terry Yorke; Camera Operator: Paul Wilson; Second Unit Camera Operators: H.A.R. Thomson, Ginger Gemmel, Kelvin Pike; Gaffer: Bob Bremner; Grip: Dennis Fraser; Still Photographer: John Jay; Clapper Loaders: Graham Scaife, David Wynn-Jones; Assistant Editor: Alan Strachan; Conductor: Ron Goodwin; Continuity: Penny Daniels; Dialogue Coach: Alfredo (Al) Lettieri; Assistant to Producer: Marion Rosenberg; Production Assistant: Raymond Becket; Military Advisor: Brian L. Davis; Process Projectionist Trainee: Steve Pickard.

Cast: Richard Burton (Major Jonathan Smith), Clint Eastwood (Lt. Morris Schaffer), Mary Ure (Mary Elison), Patrick Wymark (Col. Wyatt Turner), Michael Hordern (Adm. Rolland), Donald Houston (Capt. James Christiansen), Peter Barkworth (Edward Berkeley), William Squire (Capt. Philip Thomas), Robert Beatty (Gen. George Carnaby), Brook Williams (Sgt. Harrod), Neil McCarthy (Sgt. Jock MacPherson), Vincent Ball (Carpenter), Anton Diffring (SS-Standartenfuhrer Kramer), Ferdy Mayne (Gen. Rosemeyer), Derren Nesbitt (SS-Sturmbannfuhrer Von Harpen), Victor Beaumont (Col. Weissner), Ingrid Pitt (Heidi), John G. Heller (German Major), Guy Deghy (Maj. Wilhelm Wilner), Olga Lowe (Lt. Anne-Marie Kernitser), Richard Beale (Telephone Orderly), Ivor Dean (Second German Officer), Max Faulkner (Sgt. Hartmann), Harry Fielder (German Soldier), Lyn Kennington (German Woman), Nigel Lambert (Young German Soldier), Ian McCulloch (German Officer), Anton Rodgers (German Officer — Airfield), Jack Silk (German Officer — Ammunition Shed), Philip Stone (Sky Tram Operator), Ernst Walder (Airport Control Officer).

Synopsis: During World War II, a tri-motored Junkers JU-52 soars over the mountains of Bavaria. On board are seven men dressed in Nazi winter uniforms. As the red drop light blinks, the scene flashes back to a briefing room in London. Led by Major Smith, the men are all British except for an American Ranger, Lt. Schaffer. They are told that an important American general's plane has crashed in the Alps; he has been captured by the Nazis and is being held in the "Castle of the Eagles" (the Nazi Secret Service HQ in that area). Their mission: to get General Carnaby out of the castle before the Nazis can extract any information from him. The scene returns to the plane, where the men make their drop. A few minutes later, a woman, Mary, also dressed in winter gear, comes out of hiding in the rear of the plane and she parachutes out of sight of the others.

The men rendezvous on the ground, except for one. They spread out to look for him and discover him dead — but he has not been killed by the fall. His neck has been broken by another member of the party as soon as they hit the ground. At least one of the men is a traitor. They make their way to an outpost, and unbeknownst to the others, makes

"I bid you ... welcome!" Ingrid serves up a round in a publicity shot from *Where Eagles Dare* (courtesy of Kim Holston).

Where Eagles Dare pressbook ad mat, with Ingrid pictured, rather prominently, in the foreground.

contact with Mary. She is also a British agent and his lover as well. Smith arranges to meet her at a woodshed in the village of Werfer the next night.

In the morning, the men head down a mountain and Smith gets his first glimpse of the castle that can only be reached by eagles — or a cable car system that connects it to the village. After Smith and Schaffer observe a Nazi general being flown in by helicopter, they commence to the tavern. Smith, disguised as a Nazi major, is attended to by barmaid Heidi, herself an Allied agent in disguise, and the top agent in the area since 1941. Mary is to infiltrate the castle posing as a domestic looking for work, and Heidi is to pose as her cousin. Smith gives her the required papers, and she speculates that the forgeries look too well-made to have been only processed since the plane crashed yesterday morning. Smith tells her that that they have been in preparation for some time, and that the crash was arranged. The man being held in the castle is not Gen. Carnaby at all, but an American corporal named Cartwright Jones. Now he tells her the mission is not really to rescue Carnaby, but get Jones out before the Nazis discover his true identity.

After Smith's rendezvous in the shed, he finds another of his men murdered. He goes back to the tavern, where Schaffer demands to know the facts. As Smith tells him, Mary enters the tavern and is greeted by Heidi. She is also noticed by a Gestapo officer who takes an immediate liking to her. He offers to escort her and Heidi to the castle in the cable car. As the women prepare to leave, troops that are looking for Smith, Schaffer, and the other three men burst into the tavern. Smith and Schaffer decide to take their chances by surrendering; they are taken in the officer's command car while the others are transported by truck. The women depart on the cable car.

Smith and Schaffer kill their captors and push the staff car over a cliff. Mary is accepted for work at the castle. When she is taken to her room, there is a heated exchange between the Gestapo man and Kramer, the commandant. Kramer has informed him that the five prisoners are British agents. Their ruse has been discovered.

Smith and Schaffer already suspect this, and when they contact HQ, Admiral Rolland tells them to pull out because now their security has been breached. Smith ignores him. Schaffer rigs a trip-wire explosive, and they exit the shed they've been hiding in. The Nazis enter the shed and trip the wire, setting off a domino-effect of explosions; Smith and Schaffer use the ensuing chaos to make their escape in a motorcycle with a sidecar. On their way to the cable car, they set a series of traps, and also break into a garage to make sure a bus with a snow plow is in working order. The men see the other male members of the team herded onto a cable car, and as it begins to ascend, they hop on top.

The cable car arrives at the station, and Smith and Schaffer leap onto the roof. They make their way up the side of the castle, aided by Mary. She gives them a floor plan of the castle, and they arm themselves with machine guns. After killing the helicopter pilot, they arrive at the main dining hall, where the Nazis are questioning the soldier acting as General Carnaby. He refuses to give them any information but his name, rank, and serial number. As Kramer prepares to have them tortured, he receives a radio phone call that three of the prisoners are being brought to him — and now they claim to be Nazi agents.

Mary is preparing a suitcase full of explosives when she is visited by the Gestapo major. She is supposed to be from Dusseldorf, and he was a student there, so he would

Where Eagles Dare pressbook ad mat.

like to talk about the place. Mary cannot remember details well, and he becomes suspicious.

Smith and Schaffer make their move, and get the drop on the Nazis. Then Smith gets the drop on Schaffer. He tells him to throw down his gun and sit down. Smith tells the assemblage that he is actually a Nazi agent, and exposes Jones' masquerade. He also reveals that Schaffer is actually not a Ranger, but an O.S.S. assassin. The reason for the Allies' ruse was twofold: to get the Nazis to torture the wrong information on a second front out of him, and to give the British a reason to send in a team of agents. Smith tells the Nazis that the other three men are really British agents, which they deny. He tells the Nazis to call Kesselring's HQ to verify his identity, which they do. Smith then tells Thomas, Christiansen, and Berkeley to write down the names and addresses of their contacts so they can compare them with his own list. Kramer looks through their lists, and then Smith hands Kramer his notebook. The pages are blank.

Smith shoots a guard, and Schaffer picks up the machine gun that Smith had him throw down. Now the truth is finally revealed: Smith is indeed a British agent, and the real reason for the mission is to find out what Nazis have infiltrated MI 6. Thomas, Berkeley, and Christiansen really are Nazi agents, and now they have revealed their contacts. Then the Gestapo officer bursts in. Smith tells him that he and Schaffer are Nazi agents that have just uncovered a plot to kill Hitler. He offers to show him a list of conspirators. Just then, Mary opens the door; Smith and Schaffer use the distraction to shoot the Gestapo officer, Kramer, the visiting general and the secretary.

Now they plan how to create confusion so they make their escape. They rig explosives in strategic places, timed to go off in sequence so that the Nazis will think they are being attacked by a division. They are soon discovered and engage in a pitched battle with the Nazis while trying to make radio contact for their pick-up. The explosives start to go off, and the group makes its way out of the castle. Schaffer starts the cable car in motion. One of the double agents has already been killed, and one of the remaining two fakes an injury in order to subdue Schaffer. Smith lets them escape in a cable car in exchange for Schaffer's life, and then leaps onto the roof. Smith battles them both, and sends one falling to his doom. Smith then plants an

ABC Film Review cover featuring Richard Burton and Ingrid Pitt in *Where Eagles Dare*.

50　　　　　　　　　Films: *Where Eagles Dare* (1968)

Where Eagles Dare promotion tour photograph with unidentified reporter from *Showbiz* (courtesy Ingrid Pitt).

explosive on the roof and leaps to an oncoming car. The other double agent perishes in the explosion, and the group piles into the remaining cable car.

In the village, Nazis see the smoke from the castle explosions and prepare to kill the group on arrival. Heidi, who has already gone back to the village, readies the snowplow bus. Schaffer places another bundle of TNT in the cable car, and the group leaps from the car into the river. When the cable car reaches the station, it explodes and delays the Nazis' pursuit. The same JU-52 that brought them returns to make the pickup. They rendezvous with Heidi at the bus; Smith takes the wheel and they smash through the garage door. As Mary and Schaffer fire at their Nazi pursuers, Smith rams the bus past the previously mined checkpoints, and one by one, the pursuers are taken out. They make it to the plane safely, but the battle is still not over. There is still one more Nazi agent to be revealed — the top Nazi agent in Britain. His identity is exposed on the plane. Rather than face the hangman and public trial and disgrace, he is permitted the alternative. A member of the group gets up and shuts the fuselage door; now they can truly rest easy.

Review: *Where Eagles Dare* was a box office smash upon release, which was good for Richard Burton, who was in sore need of one after having appeared in three straight flops (*Boom*, *The Comedians*, and *Doctor Faustus*). Burton had been mightily impressed by *The Guns of Navarone* and wanted to model his next film on it, so his friend, producer Elliot Kastner, appealed to *Navarone* author Alistair MacLean, who responded with this high-flying World War II spy thriller, his first screenplay. It was a smash with most of the critics as well, the *Variety* review being a good example: "*Where Eagles Dare* is so good for its genre that one must go back to *The Great Escape* for a worthy comparison." *Time*, however, complained, "[I]t is a little melancholy seeing Richard Burton reduced to playing cardboard parts like this one, but he at least manages to look as if he was having a good time." True, none of the characters are revelatory, but the film is fast-paced and well-mounted and fun; as much spy vs. spy as us vs. them, and serves as a reminder (like *The Spy Who Came in from the Cold*) as to what a wonderful James Bond Burton would have made. The whole cast performs with aplomb.

Ingrid Pitt certainly holds her own against heavyweights like Burton and Eastwood. She is beautiful and courageous as Heidi, central to the plot and action. Although prominently featured in the advertising for the film, she does not receive commensurate billing. Future *Vampire Lovers* co-star Ferdy Mayne is on hand as a German officer, as is fellow Hammer alumnus Anton (*The Man Who Could Cheat Death*) Diffring. And of course, Eastwood had gotten his start in horror films, appearing in bit parts in the classics *Revenge of the Creature* and *Tarantula* (both 1955). At one point, Clint says, "I'm an American; I don't even know what the hell I'm doin' here," and you fully expect Burton to reply, "Because you have box office appeal, dear boy." Although it was only director Hutton's fourth feature, he carries it off quite well, more than ably assisted by second unit director and stunt legend Yakima Canutt; Hutton would only make a few more, including the truly bizarre *Kelly's Heroes* (also starring Eastwood), before giving up both acting and directing to become a plumber. Legendary horror-punk band The Misfits paid tribute to Ingrid and the film with the song "Where Eagles Dare" on their 1979 *Night of the Living Dead* EP; 31 years later, Ingrid would return the favor by hosting "Stoker's

Inferno," which featured the reconstituted band as headliners for a night of music and mayhem.

Tales from the Pitt: Then Clint leaned forward. "Shall we tell her?" he asked Richard ... slumped in the corner, almost asleep. "Tell me what?" I asked. "Might as well," Richard mumbled. "What?" I demanded. Clint grinned. He had a mischievous sense of humor. "Richie and I had a bet," he said. "What sort of bet?" I was getting exasperated. "Who'd get you in the sack first," Richard said. "Who won?" I asked innocently (*Life's a Scream*).

The Vampire Lovers

See the chapter on Hammer's Karnstein Trilogy.

Countess Dracula
1971, Hammer Film Productions

Crew: Producer: Alexander Paal; Director: Peter Sasdy; Screenplay: Jeremy Paul; Story: Alexander Paal, Peter Sasdy; Idea: Gabriel Ronap; Novel: Valentine Penrose (*The Bloody Countess*); Music: Harry Robinson (Robertson); Additional Music-Music Supervisor: Philip Martell; Photography: Kenneth Talbot; Editor: Henry Richardson; Art Director: Philip Harrison; Costume Design: Raymond Hughes; Makeup Supervisor: Tom Smith; Hairdressing Supervisor: Patricia McDermott; Production Manager: Christopher Sutton; Assistant Director: Ariel Levy; Construction Manager: Arthur Banks; Set Designer: Tim Hutchinson; Dubbing Mixer: Ken Barker; Sound Recordists: Terry Poulton, Kevin Sutton; Sound Editor: Alban Streeter; Sound Re-Recording Mixers: Graham V. Hartstone, Otto Snel; Special Effects: Bert Luxford; Camera Operator: Kenneth J. Withers; Wardrobe Master: Brian Owen-Smith; Continuity: Gladys Goldsmith; Choreographer: Mia Nardi.

Cast: Ingrid Pitt (Countess Elizabeth Nadasdy), Nigel Green (Capt. Dobi), Sandor Eles (Lt. Imre Toth), Maurice Denham (Master Fabio), Patience Collier (Julie Sentash), Peter Jeffrey (Capt. Balogh), Lesley-Anne Down (Ilona Nadasdy), Leon Lissek (Sergeant of Bailiffs), Jessie Evans (Rosa), Andrea Lawrence (Ziza), Susan Brodrick (Teri), Ian Trigger (Clown), Nike Arrighi (Fortune Teller), Peter May (Janco), John Moore (Priest), Joan Haythorne (Cook), Marianne Stone (Kitchen Maid), Sally Adcock (Bertha), Anne Stallybrass (Pregnant Woman), Paddy Ryan (Man), Michael Cadman (Young Man), Hulya Babus (Belly Dancer), Lesley Anderson, Biddy Hearne, Diana Sawday (Gypsy Dancers), Andrew Burleigh, Gary Rich (Boys), Albert Wilkinson, Ismed Hassan (Circus Midgets).

Synopsis: A young Hussar, Lt. Toth, arrives late at the funeral of his former commander. The aged Countess Nadasdy, takes note of him and smiles. As the funeral party rides away from the service, a man leaps on their coach and clings to it, begging for help for his starving family. The castle steward, Capt. Dobi, beats the man off, and the coach runs him over.

Toth and the others arrive for the reading of the will. To Dobi, the late count has

Countess Dracula pressbook ad mat.

left his pistols and uniforms, but to Toth he leaves his stable and all of his horses. Dobi is outraged. The will also states that the countess must divide everything equally with her daughter Ilona, who is arriving at the castle soon. The countess is outraged. She invites Toth to dinner, and then watches him leave.

As Countess Nadasdy prepares to take a bath, she angrily strikes a chambermaid, cutting the girl's face. The blood splashes onto the countess, and when she wipes it away she finds her skin soft and youthful again, her former beauty restored. She summons Capt. Dobi and faithful nurse Julie, and orders them to bring the girl to her...

The next day, the chambermaid's mother is worried by the disappearance of the girl. Dobi tells her to look in the whorehouse. The countess calls for Dobi. When he opens the door, he falls to his knees and crosses himself. The countess stands before him, young and beautiful again. But Dobi, who has loved the countess for years, keeps her terrible secret. He is appalled by the means by which she has restored herself, but is hopelessly devoted to her. As the countess' young daughter is due to return to the castle, having been sent away when she was a child, her kidnapping is arranged by Dobi.

The countess passes herself off as her own daughter at dinner, taking in both the aged Fabio and Toth. She takes Toth away from the table and leads him on a merry chase through the house, which ends in her bedroom. Soon they are lovers. The next day, Fabio comments to Julie that he remembered Ilona as resembling her father, but now she is the picture of her mother. Julie tells him that he is confused. But that night, he not only observes "Ilona" and Toth entering her room, but Dobi consulting a book on the human body. Locked in passionate embrace, the countess looks in a mirror and finds she is no longer young; in fact, she looks older than before! She flees from the room before Imre can see the change, and screams for Julie.

A traveling gypsy circus arrives in the village. As the dancing girls whirl, the countess argues with Dobi. The countess tells Julie to bring her someone. Julie asks one of the gypsy girls to come to the castle and read the countess's fortune. The girl finishes, and the countess takes an ornate necklace from a chest. She places it about the girl's neck, and then stabs her in that neck with a hairpin.

Again the countess is radiantly beautiful. She meets with Toth at the stables, where they succumb to their passion. They go for a ride, and then again succumb to passion. Later, children playing in the woods discover the gypsy girl's corpse. The countess agrees to marry Toth. When she gives Dobi the task of making the arrangements, he is outraged. He takes Toth to the inn, where they are joined by Capt. Balogh. Balogh tells them that they have the gypsy girl's corpse; she has been drained of blood, and the villagers are growing suspicious. Then Balogh introduces Ziza the barmaid to Toth. At the castle, the countess awakes with a start and finds that she is soon old again. Dobi gets Toth drunk and offers Ziza money to accompany Imre back to the castle. Then he arranges for the countess to find them in bed. The countess is enraged. She tells Dobi to bring Ziza to her. Fabio overhears, locates the book that Dobi had consulted and finds a bookmark in the "Human Sacrifices" chapter. Naturally, Ziza becomes the next victim, but her blood has no effect. The reason is discovered by Fabio in the pages Dobi missed: only a virgin's blood will work.

This classic *Countess Dracula* portrait of Ingrid was used for her fan club Christmas cards in 2009.

Dobi goes to the village and buys a young woman. Toth, still unaware that the countess and her "daughter" are one and the same, goes to see the countess and she tells him that she approves of the marriage. Her real daughter has yet to escape from her kidnappers. Fabio secretly tells Toth to meet him in secret after supper. Julie burns Ziza's clothes. Toth goes to meet Fabio, but finds him hanging dead in the library. Dobi is there; he asks Toth if he would like to see his bride. Burning with jealousy, Dobi forces Imre to see the countess when she is bathing her nude body in blood. Imre is shocked and stunned. But Elizabeth confesses in a desperate bid to keep her young lover, and when he still seems unsure, she blackmails him into going ahead with the marriage by telling him that he murdered Ziza while he was drunk. Fabio's corpse is removed, and Balogh questions Dobi.

Captain Balogh and his men have discovered the nude bodies of three dead girls in the castle cellars. Dobi and Toth play chess, and Toth knocks the pieces from the board in a rage. Julie tells Dobi that the countess wants to see him. The countess tells Dobi to find her another girl. Dobi agrees, tells Julie the girl is ready, and takes her to where the girl is kept. There Julie discovers that the countess' latest victim is to be her very own daughter! Julie and Toth devise a plan for her escape during the wedding ceremony.

The morning of the wedding, the countess tells Dobi to invite the servants and the rest of the village to the ceremony. Dobi is to give the countess away, and walks her down the aisle. Julie slips away. The vicar begins to read the wedding vows. Julie tries to lead the countess's daughter away, but when Ilona hears the vicar speak, she insists on seeing what is happening.

Countess Dracula stars Ingrid Pitt and Sandor Eles.

Just as the vicar is about to pronounce them man and wife, the countess suddenly ages yet again; beneath her veil she is now a hideous hag! Screaming, she snatches Dobi's dagger and rushes up the stairs to stab Ilona, but Toth intervenes and the blade plunges into his chest instead. He tumbles down the stairs, dead, as the countess realizes what she has done.

Morning finds her in a dank cell, with the sun rising and the hangman near. As the crowd taunts her with cries of "Devil Woman" and "Countess Dracula," she stares out from behind the bars and awaits her fate.

Review: Like Universal's *Tower of London* (1939), which turned the real-life political intrigues surrounding Richard III into Grand Guignol, *Countess Dracula* takes the real-life atrocities performed by Countess Elisabeth (Erzebet) Bathory and shoehorns them into a Hammer Horror. But even though the title attempts to cash in on the drawing power of Hammer's most famous monster, to be fair, the movie doesn't try to rework the "Bloody Countess" story into traditional vampire fare. In fact, given the extent of Bathory's real-life deeds, *Countess Dracula*, which has its own copious share of plasma, perversion, and pulchritude, is actually rather tame (even more so by today's standards). These deeds included having women torn apart by beasts, frozen alive in the snow, thrusting hot needles beneath their fingernails, and having young girls suspended above her in an iron cage lined with spikes which, when closed, provided the (literal) blood bath described by Ingrid (below). Nigel Green is on hand to lend his steady, forceful presence, as he had done in fantasy classics besides this one (*Gorgo, Jason and the Argonauts,* and *The Masque of the Red Death*). Peter Jeffries' buffoonish policemen, *a la Dr. Phibes*, are always good for a laugh. But of course, the show is Ingrid's all the way. Her countess is as memorable as her Carmilla, but in a different way. Carmilla, for all her bloodlust, is a sympathetic character; wicked, but with a proviso. The countess shows no such restraints; she is a law unto herself and victim of nothing but her own vanity and the insane lengths which she

Countess Dracula paperback movie edition.

would go to, in order to keep it. Ingrid is regal, sensual and, above all, thoroughly evil and her portrayal still ranks as the finest among the many who have taken on the role of the countess. There had only been one before the Hammer version, *Necropolis*, starring Viva as Bathory, but the strength of the Hammer version and Ingrid's vivid portrayal of the character made the countess fair game for ever more bloody and sexual versions (*Countess Dracula's Orgy of Blood*, *The Erotic Rites of Countess Dracula*). The difference between the two was that what Le Fanu had only suggested could only become more overt and, in many cases, gratuitous, with the passage of time and the changing of social mores. *The Vampire Lovers*, although a faithful adaptation, was still extremely exploitative, albeit tastefully exploitative, but compared to current fare, almost tame. But, as already noted, Hammer's version of the Bathory tale literally pales in comparison to the real story, and so it would be all future versions could do to keep up in terms of blood spillage! The countess got off to a good start to that end later the very same year, in Paul Naschy's fourth film in his classic Waldemar Daninsky series, *La Noche de Walpurgis* (*The Werewolf vs. the Vampire Woman*), and appeared in three other films from that series, *El Retorno de Walpurgis* (*Curse of the Devil*), *El Retorno del Hombre Lobo* (*Night of the Werewolf*) and Naschy's return-farewell to the role, *Tomb of the Werewolf* (2004). In fact, the newest millennium has been quite the prolific decade for the Blood Countess: she appeared in almost twice as many features in those ten years as she had in the previous 30. A *Countess Dracula* tie-in paperback, novelized by Michel Parry, had movie photos on the front and back covers; it was later re-issued with a new cover model and nude photos inside.

Tales from the Pitt: There was always this conflict between the historical aspect of it (which Alexander Paal and Peter Sasdy tried very hard to emphasize), but somehow the idea of making a Hammer horror film got in the way. Sasdy wanted to make an Eisenstein type of film, which I think to a certain extent makes the film look very beautiful. Peter wanted to change the title, not to have a title like *Countess Dracula* but to have a greater significance, maybe even historical significance. He wasn't allowed to do that, which really upset him. In the end I was upset that everybody was upset, because there was a lot of acrimony on the set. I think when you make a film with Hammer and it is called *Countess Dracula*, it ought to be Countess Dracula! I think there were aspects of Sasdy's direction that I didn't agree with. For instance, the scene where the barmaid is murdered and there's no blood. I said to him, "Please, hang the girl up by her feet, cut her open, and let the blood flow from her body and let the countess wash the blood all over herself ... let her bathe in the girl's blood!" I'm quite bitter about the film really (*Ingrid Pitt: Queen of Horror*).

The House That Dripped Blood
1971, Amicus Productions

Crew: Producers: Milton Subotsky, Max J. Rosenberg; Executive Producers: Paul Ellisworth, Gordon Wescourt; Director: Peter Duffell; Stories & Screenplay: Robert Bloch; Music Composed & Conducted by Michael Dress; Photography: Ray Parslow; Editor: Peter Tanner; Casting:

Ronnie Curtis; Art Director: Tony Curtis; Makeup Artists: Harry Frampton, Peter Frampton; Hair Stylist: Joyce James; Production Manager: Teresa Bolland; First Assistant Director: Peter Beale; Set Dresser: Fred Carter; Draughtsman: Thomas Goswell; Scenic Artist: Peter Wood; Dubbing Editor: Michael P. Redbourn; Sound Mixer: Ken Ritchie; Dubbing Mixer: Nolan Roberts; Camera Operator: Gerry Anstiss; Wardrobe: Laurel Staffel; Continuity: Phyllis Townsend.

Cast: John Bennett (Detective Inspector Holloway), John Bryans (A.J. Stoker), John Malcolm (Sgt. Martin), Denholm Elliott (Charles Hillyer), Joanna Dunham (Alice Hillyer); Tom Adams (Richard/Dominic), Robert Lang (Dr. Andrews), Peter Cushing (Philip Grayson), Joss Ackland (Neville Rogers), Wolfe Morris (Waxworks Proprietor), Christopher Lee (John Reid), Nyree Dawn Porter (Jane Reid), Jon Pertwee (Paul Henderson), Ingrid Pitt (Carla Lynde), Geoffrey Bayldon (Theo von Hartmann), Richard Coe (Film Director), Roy Evans (Hunchback), Carleton Hobbs (Doctor), Bernard Hopkins, Joanna Lumley (Film Crew Members), Jonathan Lynn (Set Designer), Hugh Manning (Psychiatrist), Winifred Sabine (Tea Trolley Woman).

Synopsis: Actor Paul Henderson has disappeared, and Scotland Yard sends Detective Inspector Holloway to investigate. After Holloway rudely tells the local police sergeant that he has better things to do than look for actors, the sergeant reveals that the house Henderson vanished from has a recent strange history of unexplained, tragic occurrences. It had sat empty until a writer named Charles Hillyer and his wife Alice came to look at it...

In flashbacks, we see the agent, a Mr. Stoker, show the couple around the house; Alice is very disapproving. But then Charles discovers a skull and a fantastic collection of first edition horror novels and stories; as Charles himself specializes in horror stories, he feels the house will be just what he needs to inspire him. Alice reluctantly agrees, with the proviso that it only be for a few months. There Hillyer creates Dominic, an insane strangler. As Hillyer becomes more obsessed with the character, Dominic seems to become more real. He sees Dominic at the head of the stairs, laughing, and then discovers the sketch he made of him is missing. When he finds it back in the drawer, he crumbles it up, goes outside, and throws it in a stream — but a laughing Dominic fishes it out!

Alice convinces Hillyer to see a psychiatrist. The doctor tells him that an author is like an actor playing a role, and sometimes the role takes over. This is nearly tragically proved when Hillyer thinks he sees Dominic strangling Alice, only to be told it was himself. He goes to see the doctor again. As he lies on the psychiatrist's couch, the door behind the doctor opens and reveals Dominic. He strangles the doctor. But was it Dominic or Charles? As Alice paces the floor, Dominic creeps in. He takes off his fright mask, and he and his lover Alice begin to make plans to go away. But then she receives a call from the police. Not only is the doctor dead, but Charles too. Alice tells him that the plan was only to make it look as if Hillyer were insane, and now the police will be looking for a killer; perhaps her lover, whom she calls Richard. To which he replies: "Richard? I don't know anyone named Richard. My name is Dominic!"

The sergeant tells Holloway that the police found Dominic standing over her body, while laughing maniacally. He continues to insist there is something wrong with the house itself, but Holloway says he's interested in facts, not fantasy. The sergeant then asks him to consider the case of the next tenant...

A quiet and lonely retired stockbroker, Philip Grayson, moves in. He tells Stoker that he has never been married, and won't lack for want of things to do. While going through old photographs, he comes across one of a beautiful woman, but memories make him want to take the air. Visiting a wax museum, he is fascinated by the figure of Salome, bearing the head of John the Baptist on a tray. Her face looks like a woman once loved by both Philip and his best friend, Neville Rogers. The museum's proprietor explains that Salome was modeled on his dead wife, after she had paid the final penalty for murdering his best friend.

The House That Dripped Blood pressbook ad mat.

At the house, Grayson imagines himself back in the Museum of Horrors. His reverie is interrupted by Rogers, whom he has not seen in years. As he tells Rogers that everything is in the past, he discovers Rogers looking at the photo of the woman. He tells Grayson she is dead. When he gives Grayson a lift to town, he spots the house of wax and insists they go in, despite Grayson's protestations. Of course, he sees the Salome figure. The next day, Neville cuts short his visit with Grayson, but after he has left, Grayson is drawn back to the museum, where he sees Rogers' car. When he returns to the house, Rogers is there. He tells Grayson he is leaving town, but next morning, he calls from a hotel and tells Grayson he cannot leave, that he must go to the museum. Grayson, after not finding him at the hotel, rushes to the wax museum and sees Rogers's head on Salome's platter. As the proprietor bars Philip's exit with an axe, he tells Grayson that his wife did not murder his best friend — he himself did, and made sure she paid for the crime, so that his friend and other men could no longer admire her. But even after death, men still admire her, and so each time a new patron becomes entranced by the figure of Salome...

Holloway is not convinced, and goes to see Stoker. Stoker asks him if he hasn't guessed the secret of the house yet, and then, oddly, asks him if his flat is cold. Holloway dismisses the question, and asks Stoker about the tenant in between Grayson and Henderson. Stoker tells him it was a man named John Reid, who was quiet, but dangerous — to himself.

The house is leased by widower Reid and his eight-year-old daughter Jane; Reid is inexplicably cruel to his daughter. While Stoker shows them the house, he lights a fire in the fireplace, which causes the girl to run in fright. Reid arranges for a governess for the girl, a Mrs. Norton. She asks him why Jane isn't in school, and he tells her to find out for herself. At first, Jane is uncommunicative, but soon the governess seems to win her over. She finds out that Reid will not let the girl have friends or toys. When the governess buys her a doll, Reid throws it into the fireplace, but will not explain why.

The next day, Mrs. Norton and Jane walk through the woods, and Mrs. Norton is surprised when Jane identifies a tree as a symbol of evil. She tells Mrs. Norton she read it in a book. Mrs. Norton discovers that it is a book on witchcraft, and expresses her concerns to Reid. Shortly, the power fails. Reid looks for candles,

The House That Dripped Blood's Jon Pertwee and Ingrid in "The Cloak" (courtesy Ingrid Pitt).

and when he finds them, he discovers that some are missing. He demands to know what Jane did with them and slaps her. The day after, Reid is in town, making a business arrangement. Jane goes in the bathroom and gathers whiskers from Reid's electric razor. Suddenly, in the middle of the meeting, Reid is seized by a stabbing pain. It stops when Mrs. Norton takes Jane out for a walk. That night, Reid lies staring at the clock. He begins to convulse again, and Mrs. Norton calls the doctor. Jane appears in the doorway, holding a wax doll with a hatpin stuck in it. Reid tells Mrs. Norton that he is cruel to Jane because he is afraid of her; that her mother was evil and so is the child. He tells her she must get the doll. Mrs. Norton catches up to Jane, and tries to talk her down, but the girl throws the doll into the fire. Reid screams...

The House That Dripped Blood's Jon Pertwee and Ingrid in "The Cloak" (courtesy Ingrid Pitt).

This brings Holloway to Henderson's disappearance: Stoker tells him that he tried to dissuade Henderson from the deal, but the vainglorious ham would not hear of it. His co-star, the beautiful Carla, also liked the place. Henderson is a horror film star and expert on the supernatural, and was currently shooting a low-budget vampire film, *Curse of the Bloodsuckers*. He doesn't like anything about the film, even the wardrobe, so he buys a cloak from the strange proprietor of a musty old costume shop. When Henderson dons the cloak, he feels a chill; the old man tells him that it will be 13 shillings and his for life. After Henderson leaves the shop, the old man says that now he can rest in peace. The cloak has strange effects on Paul; while in his dressing room, he casts no reflection in a mirror, and while filming a scene, he bites Carla. After midnight that night, he levitates and grows fangs. The next day, he apologizes to Carla, and invites her to dinner. After they dine, Henderson reads in a newspaper that the costume shop has burned down; in the basement they found a coffin containing the body of an elderly man. Henderson tells Carla he knows he is a vampire. Carla laughs as he tells her of the cloak's effect. She dares him to put it on at midnight, but nothing happens to him — because he does not have the real cloak. Carla does. She puts it on and bares her fangs, telling him that they have enjoyed his films so much, they wanted him to join them. "Welcome to the club!" she laughs, as she flies up towards him...

Holloway thinks the story is rubbish, and he decides to go to the house and look around. Stoker tries to talk him out of the notion by posing more cryptic questions, but Holloway isn't having it. There's no electricity in the house, so Holloway lights a cande-

The cover for the eighth issue of this late, lamented monster magazine featured this magnificent portrait of Ingrid from *The House That Dripped Blood* by the legendary Basil Gogos.

labra. In the basement he sees a coffin. The door behind him slams shut, and the clock chimes at midnight. Henderson, now a true vampire, rises from his coffin and attacks Holloway. Holloway dispatches him with a stake—and then Carla rises from another coffin, changing into a bat. There are no stakes left....

Review: Although considered by some to be the poor country mouse compared to Hammer Films' Giant Rat of Sumatra, Amicus was not merely a cheap imitation. The company had a style all their own, and nowhere is this style displayed to better effect than in what may be their finest anthology film; it invokes the twisted spirit of E.C. Comics even more so than the company's official E.C. anthologies *Tales from the Crypt* and *The Vault of Horror*. The first segment "Method for Murder" features Denholm Elliot as the writer who's being driven mad, and Peter Cushing is entirely sympathetic in "Waxworks" as the lonely man who loses his head over an old flame. Christopher Lee is at his cold, unsympathetic best as the man who doesn't understand what the little girl knows, in "Sweets to the Sweet." But it is Ingrid and Jon Pertwee, both hamming it up to the hilt in the exceedingly well-realized "The Cloak," who steal the movie.

By far the most delightful moment in "The Cloak" occurs when Henderson, having poked his cane through the scenery and complained loudly about the quality of the film itself and the crew involved, proceeds to give the crew a lecture about "the classic horror films, like *Frankenstein*, or *The Phantom of the Opera*, or *Dracula*—the 1931 version, of course, not the one with that new fellow." Especially since that new fellow was also in the same film. It also recalls those films when Ingrid takes flight, *a la* Carroll Borland in *Mark of the Vampire*. But "The Cloak" is far and away the best story of the four, and not just because Ingrid is in it, but precisely because of that element of wit. *Variety*, in its March 3, 1971, edition, agreed: "It fits perfectly—no jarring of the sensibilities and so tongue-in-cheek in its jibes at spook film clichés that it is wisely saved until the windup of the four-story feature.... This omnibus ... is one of the most entertaining of its genre to come along in several years. The title is misleading, as there's no gore and all the evil is suggested, not graphically depicted. But even for filmgoers who don't usually follow the shocker market, this one is worthwhile." And of course, it is the film from which *that* photo, *the* iconic Ingrid Pitt pose, is taken, although, as with many great publicity photos, it does not exactly correspond with an actual scene (and it is somewhat ironic that her most famous vampire photo is not from *The Vampire Lovers*). Who cares? It's the "Marilyn's skirt blowing up around her waist" of horror films. And was there ever a better visual audition for Vampirella? When Hammer announced they were making a Vampi film and had cast Barbara Leigh as Vampirella, what were they thinking? Actually, the same question could be asked of the designers of the first Hammer Horror trading card set, as the box containing the packs of cards features photos of Hammer's most famous monsters — Peter Cushing as Dr. Frankenstein, Christopher Lee as Dracula, Frankenstein's Creature and Rasputin, Jacqueline Pearce as the Reptile, Oliver Reed as the cursed Werewolf, David Prowse from *Horror of Frankenstein*, and Ingrid Pitt—from the Amicus film *The House That Dripped Blood*!

Tales from the Pitt: Originally I was going to do the first of the four-story compendium. Then I talked to Peter Duffell, the director, and Jon Pertwee and they convinced

Ingrid in *the* photograph from *The House That Dripped Blood*.

me I should do the final episode, "The Cloak." It was a fairly serious piece, but Jon and Peter soon fixed that. We all gathered round at Jon's house in Castlenau and kicked the film around over lunch until it finished up the way you see it now. One of my favorite films (*The Ingrid Pitt Bedside Companion for Vampire Lovers*).

Nobody Ordered Love
1972, World Arts Media

Crew: Supervising Producer: John Lightfoot; Associate Producers: Robert Shearer, David Tringham; Director: Robert Hartford-Davis; Screenplay: Robert Shearer; Music: Tony Osborne; Cinematography: Desmond Dickinson; Editor: Alan Pattillo; Art Director: Hayden Pearce; Assistant Director: David Tringham; Sound Recordist: Peter Pardo; Sound Re-Recording Mixer: Ken Barker; Camera Operator: Norman Jones.

Cast: Ingrid Pitt (Alice Allison), Judy Huxtable (Caroline Johnson), John Ronane (Paul Medbury), Tony Selby (Peter Triman), Peter Arne (Leo Richardstone), Mark Eden (Charles),

David Weston (Jacques Legrand), Janet Lynn (Valerie), David Lodge (Sergeant), Frank Jarvis (Corporal), Barry Meteyard (Lieutenant), Larry Taylor (Camera Operator), Heather Barbour (Janet), Tricia Barnes (Continuity Girl), Charles Houston (Assistant), Carolyn Wilde (Virginia), John Glyn-Jones (Harry), Pauline Pearl.

Synopsis: In this film, Ingrid was cast as a has-been sex symbol whose role in a big-budget movie is jeopardized by her alcoholism. What little anyone knows about the film is mostly limited to Ingrid's recollections (see below).

Tales from the Pitt: Nobody Ordered Love is a film I've become obsessed with. It's obviously a case of absence makes the heart grow nostalgic. I've never seen the finished version, and the more time passes, the more I want to see it. It was quite a nice story about a past-it actress try-

Stills exist, yes; the movie *Nobody Ordered Love*, no (courtesy Ingrid Pitt).

ing to do away with her up-and-coming rival. Played out on a film set about World War I, it had a nice Truffaut atmosphere to it. Then the money man pulled out for reasons unknown. A film was cobbled together and put out on the Rank circuit. Now it gets a little murky. The director, Robert Hartford-Davis, got a bit of wind in his water, stuck the tins of film under his arm and headed west. There he married and tried to keep a low profile — not low enough, it seems. He died in mysterious circumstances and the tins of film went missing. Since then, I've tried on every occasion to find the movie, but, like a couple of other films of mine, it seems to have gone beyond recall (*The Ingrid Pitt Bedside Companion for Vampire Lovers*).

The Wicker Man
1973, British Lion Film Corporation

Crew: Producer: Peter Snell; Director: Robin Hardy; Screenplay: Anthony Shaffer; Based (without credit) on the Novel *Ritual* by David Pinner; Music: Paul Giovanni; Photography:

66 Films: *The Wicker Man* (1973)

Harry Waxman; Editor: Eric Boyd-Perkins; Casting: Maggie Cartier; Art Director: Seamus Flannery; Costume Design: Sue Yelland; Makeup Artist: W. T. (Billy) Partleton; Hair Stylist: Jan Dorman; Unit Manager: Mike Gowans; Production Manager: Ted Morley; Assistant Director: Jake Wright; Second Assistant Director: Brian W. Cook; Third Assistant Director: Vic Smith; Assistant Art Director: Richard Rambaut; Sound: Robin Gregory, Bob Jones; Sound Editor: Vernon Messenger; Second Unit Photography: Peter Allwork; Still Photographer: John Brown; Camera Operators: James (Jimmy) Devis, Ken Worringham; Focus Puller: Mike Drew; Wardrobe Supervisor: Masada Wilmot; Assistant Editor: Denis Whitehouse; Associate Musical Director: Gary Carpenter; Musicians: Magnet; Production Secretary: Beryl Harvey; Choreographer: Stewart Hopps; Publicist: Frank Law; Continuity: Susanna (Sue) Merry; Location Manager: Jilda Smith; Marketing Consultant: Craig Miller.

Cast: Edward Woodward (Sgt. Howie), Christopher Lee (Lord Summerisle), Diane Cilento (Miss Rose), Britt Ekland (Willow), Ingrid Pitt (Registrar/Librarian), Lindsay Kemp (Alder MacGregor), Russell Waters (Harbor Master), Aubrey Morris (Gardener/Gravedigger), Irene Sunter (May Morrison), Walter Carr (Schoolmaster), Ian Campbell (Oak), Leslie Blackater (Hairdresser), Roy Boyd (Broome), Peter Brewis, Michael John Cole, Michael Cole, Ian Cutler, Bernard Murray, Andrew Tompkins, Paul Giovanni (Musicians), Barbara Ann Brown (Rafferty)

Ingrid is in no mood for cutting remarks in this tense moment from *The Wicker Man*'s May Day celebration.

(Woman with Baby), Juliet [Juliette] Cadzow, Helen Norman, Elizabeth Sinclair (Villagers), Ross Campbell, Ian Wilson (Communicants), Penny Cluer (Gillie), Kevin Collins (Old Fisherman), Geraldine Cowper (Rowan Morrison), Donald Eccles (T. H. Lennox), Myra Forsyth (Mrs. Grimmond), John Hallam (P.C. McTaggert), Alison Hughes (Fiancée), Charles Kearney (Butcher), Fiona Kennedy (Holly), John MacGregor (Baker), Jimmy MacKenzie (Briar), Lesley [Leslie] Mackie (Daisy), Jennifer Martin (Myrtle Morrison), Lorraine Peters (Grave Girl), Tony Roper (Postman), John Sharp (Dr. Ewan), Richard Wren (Ash Buchanan), John Young (Fishmonger), S Newton Anderson (Landers), Robin Hardy (Minister), Annie Ross (Willow's Voice).

Synopsis: A plane bearing a Scottish policeman, Sgt. Howie, lands on the island of Summerisle. He has received an anonymous letter recommending that he investigate the disappearance of a young girl, Rowan Morrison. None of the men who meet him at the dock seem to recognize the photo, and even the girl's own mother denies her disappearance. She tells Howie that her daughter is in the back room, and takes him to meet her. When Mrs. Morrison leaves the room, Howie asks the little girl if she knows Rowan, and she says she does. He then asks if she knows where she is, and she says she does. Howie then asks if Rowan will be back in time for tea, to which the girl laughingly replies "Tea? Hares don't have tea, silly."

At the local inn, the landlord directs his beautiful daughter Willow to take Howie to his room, and the crowd breaks out into a lusty shanty, "The Landlord's Daughter." The policeman, a chaste and virtuous man, is offended and makes them stop. He asks the inn crowd about the missing girl, but they all profess ignorance. He notices the row of Spring Harvest photos on the wall, and notes that one is missing. "Broken," the landlord tells him. After Howie finishes his supper, he goes out for a walk and sees couples copulating in the churchyard, as well as a nude girl sobbing onto a gravestone. Shocked and stunned, he returns to his room to pray. As he tries to sleep, the music from below begins to penetrate the walls, as do the knocks and exhortations of Willow, who is dancing nude in the next room. Howie refuses to give in to temptation.

The next morning, Howie visits the local school and observes the male students dancing around the maypole, singing a fertility song. Headmistress Miss Rose tells the small girls that the maypole represents the penis. Howie tells the woman he is going to report her, and asks the girls if they've seen Rowan. They and the teacher deny knowing her, but then Howie spots an empty desk. He seizes the school register and discovers her name. He calls the girls and the headmistress liars. The woman tells Howie that Rowan is what he would call dead, buried in the forsaken churchyard. Howie goes to the churchyard and discovers a girl nursing her baby at her breast, holding an egg in one hand. Disgusted, he knocks two apple crates from atop a crypt, fashioning a cross from the slats, and placing it on the crypt.

He discovers a fresh grave with a tree, but no headstone. The gravedigger tells him it is Rowan's grave. Howie says that it looks as though skin is hanging from the tree, and the gravedigger nonchalantly informs him that it is Rowan's natal cord.

Reeling from the continuous assault on his Christian sensibilities, Howie returns to Mrs. Morrison's and observes her putting a frog in her daughter's mouth to cure a sore

Christopher Lee and the title character in *The Wicker Man*.

throat. He tells the woman that they're all mad. When he visits the registrar to see their index of deaths, the beautiful, mysterious woman tells him that he must have authorization from Lord Summerisle. When threatened with arrest, she shows him the book. There is no record of Rowan's death. But when he asks if she knew the girl, the woman says yes, and when he shows her the girl's photograph, the woman identifies it as Rowan Morrison, but says she knows nothing else.

On his way to see Lord Summerisle, Howie sees the headmistress conducting a fertility rite with nude young girls. He is greeted warmly by Summerisle, and voices his objections. He scoffs at the idea of the girls being impregnated by the fire god, and Summerisle merely compares it to the Immaculate Conception. Howie asks for permission to exhume Rowan's body, and Summerisle gives it willingly, because he believes there was no murder; he tells Howie that they are a deeply religious people. Howie is incredulous at the claim after what he's seen, but they are not religious in the Christian sense; they believe in the old gods. Howie leaves to exhume Rowan's body. When he opens the casket, he finds a hare.

He bursts in on Lord Summerisle and Miss Rose, who are engaged in drinking and song. When he throws the dead hare at Rose's feet, she tells him that it is Rowan. Enraged and frustrated, Howie tells them that he is going to the mainland in the morning; Summerisle tells him that this is good, so that he won't be offended by their May

Day celebration. When Howie is shown out, Summerisle and Rose resume their singing.

That night, Howie breaks into the photographer's shop. He finds the Spring Harvest photo negatives, and discovers that the missing photo from the wall at the inn was that of Rowan. In the morning, he goes to the library and studies a book on May Day festivals. He finds that when the harvest is good, produce and animals are offered up to the gods, but if the harvest fails, a human is sacrificed. Then he realizes: Rowan is not dead, but being held for sacrifice at the May Day festival!

People in animal masks begin to appear about town. Howie attempts to leave for help, but his plane will not start. He is led on a merry chase through the streets by a man dressed as a horse (the leader of the May Day procession). Howie observes Summerisle instructing the villagers that the procession will begin at three that afternoon, and that a sacrifice is to be made. Howie confronts Mrs. Morrison, who tells him that he does not understand the concept of sacrifice. He replies that he will search every house in town. He does, and finds ever more bizarre sights and scenes — nude Registrars in the bath, dolls copulating, etc. A dead-looking girl tumbles out of a closet, only to begin laughing at

The Wicker Man stars (from left) Ingrid Pitt, Diane Cilento, Britt Eklund, and Edward Woodward.

him. He goes back to the inn to rest, only to overhear Willow and her father making plans to keep him away from the celebration. After Willow leaves, Howie knocks out her father and dons his Punch the Fool costume.

The drums beat, the horns blow, and the procession begins. Summerisle exhorts Punch to play the fool. Miss Rose, Willow and the Registrar dance about him with pointed sticks, while he smacks them on the bum. Young men in kilts form "the star of swords," a grim game of chance that is a prelude to the real sacrifice, and the celebrants dance through one by one while the others chant "Chop! Chop!" They then head to the beach, where they offer up ale to the god of the sea. Summerisle announces it is time for the sacrifice. Howie turns to see Rowan standing at the mouth of a cave. He bounds up the stairs to the cave and frees her from her bonds. She thanks him, and says she knows a way to escape through the cave. They emerge a few minutes later into the sunlight. There sit Summerisle, Willow, and the Registrar. Rowan runs into Summerisle's arms as he compliments her on a job well done.

In disbelief, Howie looks at Summerisle, who tells him that the game is over. It was never Rowan who was to be sacrificed, but Howie himself. Summerisle tells him that in particularly fallow times, in order to appease the gods, animals and children will do, but what is really needed is "the right kind of adult." After careful research, they concluded that Howie was that kind of adult, and lured him to the island with the story of the missing girl. So he came of his own free will, he came as a man who represented the law; he came as a virgin, and a man who has now come as a fool. And since the fool is king for a day, he is told he will be revered and anointed as a king. He is anointed by Willow and the Registrar and dressed in a white robe. He continues to proclaim his Christian faith as he is led away. He tells Summerisle that if the crops fail, that the next year Summerisle will be the sacrifice, but to no avail. Then he sees the huge effigy of the Wicker Man. Screaming, he is placed inside, and the Wicker Man is set aflame. While the villagers hold hands and sing "Sumer Is Icumen In," Howie recites the 23rd Psalm....

Review: *The Wicker Man* is considered by many critics and fans to be one of the most genuinely haunting, atmospheric and terrifying examples of the horror genre. Not respected author William K. Everson, who in the "Re-Assessments" chapter of his book *More Classics of the Horror Film* opines, "*The Wicker Man* is certainly one of the most over-rated of all 'intelligent' horror films, and deserves to be put in its place at least once. It is a cold and lifeless film, although not an uninteresting one.... [U]nfortunately, the film is relentlessly aware of its own intelligence and resolutely refuses to diminish it by creating any real excitement. It is funereal in its pacing, static in its photography, and dull in its performances." This seems a somewhat puzzling argument from Mr. Everson, who generally valued intelligence very highly in horror films. He notes the irony of the fact that, had Howie succumbed to Willow's seduction ploy, he would have lost the "purity" required for the sacrifice — but had Summerisle not also known that he would *not* succumb, Howie would not have been chosen in the first place; not to mention the fact that there also would have been no story. Rather than being cold and lifeless, the film is filled with local color and natural splendor and, on the whole, makes the concept of paganism seem rather appealing ... all except for the frog-eating and sacrificing parts, that is. It does not create any "excitement" of the red-eyed, fangs-bared vampire type, no, but utilizing familiar Hammer stars such as Christopher Lee and Ingrid Pitt and totally eschewing the typical Hammer blood-and-thunder style, it pulls the viewer in with a spell created by few other horror films before or since, especially including the ludicrous 2006 remake. The pace is languid, but then again, so is the pace of many mysteries, and really, the film is as much that as it is a horror film.

Most of the performances are very naturalistic, in some cases creepily so. Lee is obviously enjoying playing away from his Dracula stereotype. The only performance that can be said to be dull is that of Britt Ekland, an absolutely hopeless actress who was one of the most talked-about and photographed celebrities of the '70s, due to her very public social life. But to say that her performance is compensated for by the fact that she dances in the nude would be to reduce the argument to the same level as that of the author who postulated that Ingrid Pitt's popularity was only due to her "willingness to disrobe for the camera." (Many of Ekland's dancing scenes are done by a double, and all of her lines were dubbed due to her accent.) As for Ingrid's performance, well, she does disrobe for the camera, but only briefly, and unlike Ekland, this was not her chief asset. She manages to subtly shift the viewer's attention in her scenes by inventing little bits of business; she is both properly reserved and mysterious as the Registrar, and equally as properly full of life during the May Day celebration. Ingrid may not have made as many film appearances as some actresses, but quality beats out quantity every time.

Tales from the Pitt: The nasty bottom line to *The Wicker Man* was that George [Pinches] refused even to look at the film, claiming it was not commercial. The Rank Cinema circuit therefore wouldn't show it. Later ... he said that any other film that I might manage to make would suffer the same fate. He subsequently showed that he was a man of bitter action (*Life's a Scream*).

Click
1975

Crew: Producer-Director: Michael Cort; Screenplay: Steve Moore, Michael Cort; Photography: Allan More; Music: Geoff Britton.

Cast: Tom Adams, Ingrid Pitt, Irfan Atasoy, Gordon Mitchell, Geoff Britton

Synopsis/Review: Poster art for this Turkish-made film appeared in the March 19, 1975, *Variety*, but the film was never produced. Composer Geoff Britton was a member of Paul McCartney's band Wings for a year, and was announced on the poster as making a "Guest Appearance in a fighting role"— presumably based on his experience at rehearsals.

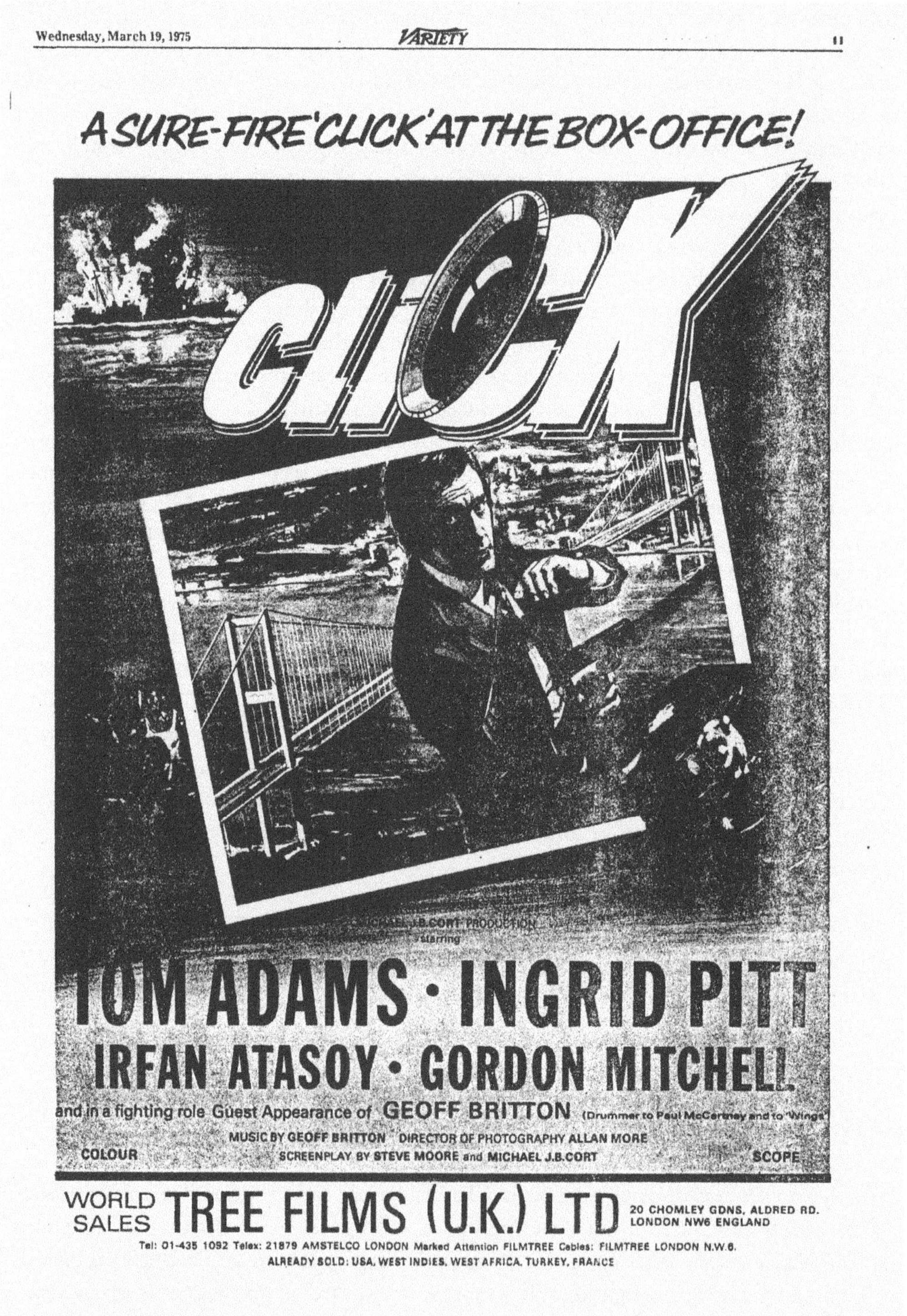

Posters are often created for films before the film is actually made, which was the case with this cancelled production from 1975 (courtesy Kim Holston).

Left: Ingrid in a scene from the little-seen Argentinean film *El Ultimo Enemigo* made in 1976 (courtesy Ingrid Pitt). *Right:* Ingrid's "Z Book" portrait for 1977.

Argentina, 1976 — Ingrid and husband Tony meet with members of Cine Internationale Latino Americano at the Circulo Italiano in Buenos Aires to announce that, with the backing of *El Pais* (leading newspaper of Uruguay), they would make six features and a television series, which unfortunately never came to pass. From left to right: Producer Orlando de Benedetti, director Gunter Jeanee, Tony Rudlin, Ingrid, co-producer Juan Sires, and *El Pais* co-producer Emilio Perina (courtesy Ingrid Pitt).

Who Dares Wins
(a.k.a. *The Final Option*)
1982, Richmond Light Horse Productions

Crew: Producer: Euan Lloyd; Executive Producer: Chris Chrisafis; Associate Producer: Raymond Menmuir; Director: Ian Sharp; Screenplay: Reginald Rose; Original Story Outline: George Markstein; Based on the Novel *The Tiptoe Boys* by James Follett; Music: Roy Budd; Photography: Phil Meheux; Editor: John Grover; Casting: Esta Charkham; Production Design: Syd Cain; Art Director: Maurice (Mo) Cain; Assistant Art Director: Jim Morahan; Makeup Artist: Neville Smallwood; Makeup Assistants: Eddie Knight, Tommy Manderson; Hair Stylist: Jeannette Freeman; Production Manager: Ron Purdie; Assistant Director: Bill Westley; Second Assistant Director: Michael Murray; Third Assistant Director: Chris Brock; Graphic Artist: Maurice Binder; Carpenter: Trevor Nicol; Buyer: Sid Palmer; Construction Manager: Michael Redding; Prop Dresser: Bob Sherwood; Set Dresser: Robin Tarsnane; Property Master: Arthur Wicks; Sound Recordist: David Crozier; Sound Assistant: Guido Reidy; Boom Operator: Colin Dandridge; Chief Dubbing Mixer: Gordon K. McCallum; Dubbing Mixers: John Hayward, Richard Langford; Dubbing Editors: Derek Holding, Colin Miller; Assistant Dubbing Editors: Christopher Lloyd, Bob Mullen; Special Effects Supervisor: Nick Allder; Assistant Special Effects Supervisor: John McGoldrick; Visual Effects Supervisor: Nick Allder; Action Arranger: Bob Simmons; Stunts: Terry Cade, Terry Forestal, Martin Grace, Greg Powell, Joe Powell, Denise Ryan, Bob Simmons, Stuart St. Paul, Tip Tipping, Malcolm Weaver; Camera Operator: Bob Smith; Still Photographers: Graham Attwood, Peter Kernot; Video Assistant: Kevin Brookner; Clapper Loader: John Ignatius; Grip: John Payne; Gaffer: John Tythe; Focus Puller: Derek Worley; Wardrobe: David Murphy; Wardrobe Assistants: Gloria Barnes, John Hilling; Assembly Editor: Peter Davies; Assistant Editor: Matthew Glen; Armorer: Simon Atherton; Technical Research Advisor: Ian Black; Location Manager: Peter Carter; Assistants to Producer: Mo Coppitters, Helene Theill; Choreographer: Anthony Van Laast; Continuity: Alison Thorne; Publicist: Derek Robbins; Production Accountant: Carolyn Hall; Assistant Production Accountants: Penny Forrester, Pauline Granby; Floor Runner: Kevin Westley.

Cast: Lewis Collins (Capt. Peter Skellen), Judy Davis (Frankie Leith), Richard Widmark (Secretary of State Arthur Currie), Edward Woodward (Commander Powell), Robert Webber (Gen. Ira Potter), Tony Doyle (Col. Hadley), John Duttine (Rod Walker), Kenneth Griffith (Bishop Crick), Rosalind Lloyd (Jenny Skellen), Ingrid Pitt (Helga), Norman Rodway (Ryan), Maurice Roeves (Major Steele), Bob Sherman (Hagen), Albert Fortell (Freund), Mark Ryan (Mac), Patrick Allen (Police Commissioner), Aharon Ipale (Malek), Paul Freeman (Sir Richard), Briony Elliott (Baby Samantha), Jerry Donahue, Mark Donahue, Gerry Conway, Dave Pegg (Pop Group), Alan Mitchell (Harkness), Richard Coleman (Mr. Martin), Nigel Humphreys (Sgt. Pope), Stephen Bent (Neil), Martyn Jacobs (Mews Policeman), Raymond Brody (Bank Manager), Andrew McLachlan (Immigration Officer), Oz Clarke (Special Branch Man), Peter Geddis (Butler), Jon Morrison (Dennis), Trevor "Ziggy" Byfield (Baker), Michael Forrest (Pickley), Don Fellows (Ambassador Franklin), Alan Gifford (Sen. Kohoskie), John Woodnutt (Harold Staunton), Nick Brimble (Williamson), Michael Godley (M.P.), Meg Davies (Mary Tinker), Lynne Miller (Melissa), Christopher Muncke (U.S. Security Man), Anna Ford, Bill Hamilton (Newscasters), Alan Polonsky, Martin Grace (U.S. Marine Guards), Tarig Yunus, Bruce White, Patrick Gordon, Niall Padden, Tony Osoba, Glyn Baker, Ben Howard, Alyn Renwick, Peter Turner, Simon Heywood, Ralph Arliss, Ewan Stewart, Billy McBain (Terrorists), Martin Denning (SAS Technician, Harry Fielder (Policeman).

Ingrid Pitt (bottom) and Rosalind Lloyd mix it up in *Who Dares Wins* (courtesy Ingrid

Synopsis: At a large anti-nuclear rally, a marcher is hit by a crossbow bolt fired from a window. High officials discuss how terrorists are using the peace movement as cover. An American Ranger, Hagen, and a German officer, Freund, are taken to SAS (Special Air Services) training grounds to learn their methods. They meet squad leader Skellen and embark on a training mission. At their mountain rendezvous point, Skellen begins to accuse the two of being terrorists and savagely tortures them. He is booted out of the SAS.

But it is merely a ruse: His contact, Bradley, tells him that the "Peoples' Lobby" is planning something, as yet unknown, and Skellen's mission is to go undercover and infiltrate the organization. A man named Malek gets a passport, telling immigration that he is in Britain for pleasure, with a lot of money to spend. His pleasure is to give the money to various radical groups, including a large sum to the Peoples' Lobby. While Skellen spends time with his wife and child, Helga is training new recruits at the terrorists' training grounds.

At a guerilla theater performance, Skellen meets the attractive Frankie Leith, leader of the Peoples' Lobby. She takes him back to her sumptuous apartment, and then to bed. He tells her he has been kicked out of SAS. She takes him back to Peoples' Lobby HQ, which immediately raises the ire of her lover Rod. He thinks Skellen is a plant, but Frankie asks him to join them.

Skellen meets with Bradley on a ferry, a rendezvous which Helga reports to Rod. At the SAS training grounds, Hagen and Freund are given Skellen's London address. They are waiting to ambush him upon his return, and he is convincingly beaten. Skellen meets with Hadley to tell him that another ruse has worked, and it has bolstered his credibility with Frankie. Bradley reports to SAS, and is seen doing so by Helga.

After a rock group plays at an anti-nuke rally, a priest tries to speak to the crowd, but skinheads cause a riot. It has been staged by Malek and Rod, who cannot wait to see the headlines. Skellen meets with his wife in the park, and is photographed kissing her. Frankie is shown the photos, but insists she will destroy him before he can destroy them. She has Skellen sleep on the couch that night; she says she has a big day coming up.

That next day, Skellen meets with Bradley on the buses, and tells him whatever is going to happen is going down that day. But before Hadley can report, Helga takes a seat on the bus and kills Bradley with poison from her spray perfume bottle. The radicals hijack a bus carrying a military band and kill the singer. The terrorists now take their places. Skellen is dropped off by Helga, and Frankie gives him a uniform.

Security officials cannot determine where the Peoples' Lobby will strike. Frankie informs the group they will strike at a reception given at the residence of the American ambassador, attended by the American Secretary of State Currie and other diplomatic and military luminaries. They will take them hostage, and if their demands are not met, they will kill them. She also informs Skellen that his wife and child have been taken hostage.

Helga and another terrorist break into Skellen's home and take his wife and child hostage, but they are already under observation by the police. The terrorist band arrives at the residence, and after being ushered in by security, they put their plan into action. They kill a Marine guard and then crash the dinner party, holding the dignitaries at bay. Frankie calls Commander Powell and tells him that they want a nuclear missile fired at a spot in Scotland — in the name of peace. She gives him until three the next day to comply. She says that they want the world to see what nuclear devastation is really like.

The servants and women are taken to another room. Currie and Frankie have an ideological argument. As the SAS puts their plan into operation, the police set up surveillance in the apartment next to the Skellens'. Frankie tells Powell they want full press coverage. Powell asks her to release the servants; she agrees, but will not release the wives. She allows Powell to tap the phone for instant communication.

As all concerned parties watch the television coverage, Powell tries stalling tactics, but Frankie refuses to cooperate. Frankie tells a comrade to watch Skellen. Skellen goes into a bathroom and signals SAS with a mirror; they arrange a time of attack. The police watching Skellen's family also prepare to make their move.

General Potter goes for a terrorist's gun and is shot down. Frankie says she is sorry, and Powell calls to inquire about the shots. Frankie tells him it was just someone's nerves, but she is not believed. Powell gives him the order to begin. The SAS moves in with swift efficiency. At Skellen's home, the baby's crying upsets Helga, and she gets into a catfight with Mrs. Skellen. Just as she is ready to shoot them both, the police blow a hole in the wall and holes in the terrorists.

Frankie hears the copters, but Skellen tells her it's only aerial observation. He grabs a machine gun and kills all the terrorists in the room. The SAS comes in through the windows and methodically begin to pick off their targets. The hostages are freed, and the

SAS finds Skellen. They go after Frankie. When she appears in a doorway, Skellen hesitates, and she is gunned down by another. Secretary Currie comments that his host throws one hell of a party. Elsewhere, a Sir Richard meets with Mr. Malek, who tells him that the operation was a success, if only because it caused a glorious uproar. Malek promises Sir Richard that there will be many more, as they walk away arm-in-arm to the strains of "Oh, Christmas Tree."

Review: The film was based on a true story (the Iranian Embassy siege in 1980 by Britain's SAS; "Who Dares Wins" is the group motto). Its politics make the *Dirty Harry* and *Death Wish* series look like *Hair*. Although it is an accurate depiction of the methods of the SAS, it is rather risible in many other respects. Australian Judy Davis is an embarrassingly caricatured spoiled rich-kid revolutionary who jumps into bed with Collins at the drop of a macho pick-up line. Davis is normally a fine actress but here, all of her dramatic pauses seem given to figuring out how to say her lines with an American accent, which wavers from annoyingly flat to a semi–Southern drawl.

But it's not just the hardcore radicals that are ridiculed; it seems that anyone who even vaguely believes in the concept of "peace" is considered to be an uninformed fool, or at best a dupe, although both the authorities and those who question them are shown to be dupes in the hands of money. Ingrid lends a suitable and convincing air of menace to her role as beautiful-but-deadly Helga the terrorist, and her ideologically rigid character seems much more suited to a position of leadership within the group than the naïve Frankie Leith. Producer Euan Lloyd was also responsible for the *Wild Geese* movies (as well as being responsible for Rosalind Lloyd), and crew members like Syd Cain, Maurice Binder, and Bob Simmons had long and honorable association with the Bond series, so the production is well-mounted, and the action sequences are adroitly handled. Ubiquitous character actor Robert Webber, who plays General Potter, was also featured in Lloyd's *Wild Geese II* (see below); he starred in Hammer's *Hysteria* in 1964. Edward Woodward and Ingrid were on opposite sides in *The Wicker Man*. Ingrid was re-teamed with two other co-stars from the past on this picture; Aharon Ipale appeared with her in the *Zoo Gang* episode "Mindless Murder" and Norman Rodway played Hotspur in *Chimes at Midnight*. Richard Widmark is also part of the Hammer legacy, starring with Christopher Lee in *To the Devil a Daughter*.

Tales from the Pitt: The SAS guys impressed me to the bone. The only sad bit was that Euan was determined to use Judy Davis when he could have had Jane Fonda for the main lead. The Americans didn't like an Australian imitating a Yankee terrorist, and the film didn't do all that well in America, where it was called *The Final Option* (*"Life's a Scream"*).

Octopussy
1983, United Artists

Crew: Producer & Presenter: Albert R. Broccoli; Executive Producer: Michael G. Wilson; Associate Producer: Thomas Pevsner; Director: John Glen; Story & Screenplay: George Mac-

German one-sheet poster design for *Octopussy*.

Donald Fraser, Richard Maibaum, Michael G. Wilson; Original Stories: "Octopussy" and "The Property of a Lady" by Ian Fleming; Music Composed & Conducted by John Barry; Composer of James Bond Theme: Monty Norman; Photography: Alan Hume; Editors: Peter Davies, Henry Richardson; Production Designer: Peter Lamont; Art Director: John Fenner; Assistant Art Directors: Ernest Archer, Fred Hole, Jim Morahan; Additional Art Directors: Ken Court, Michael Lamont, Jan Schlubach, Ram Yedekar; Set Decorator: Jack Stephens; Costume Design: Emma Porteus; Makeup Supervisor: George Frost; Makeup Artists: Eric Allright, Peter Robb-King; Hairdressing Supervisor: Christopher Taylor; Hairdresser: Jeanette Freeman; Production Managers: Leonhard Gmur, Philip Kohler, Gerry Levy, Barrie (M) Osborne; Production Supervisor: Hugh Harlow; Assistant Directors: Anthony Waye, Barbara Broccoli, James Devis; Second Assistant Directors: Tony Broccoli, Terry Madden, Andrew Warren, Michael Zimbrich, Dilip Roy; Additional Assistant Directors: Don French, Baba Shaikh; Second Unit Director: Arthur Wooster; Second Unit Assistant Director: Gerry Gavigan; Property Master: David Jordan; Production Buyer: Ron Quelch; Construction Manager: Michael Redding; India Set Dresser: Crispian Sallis; Scenic Artists: Ernest Smith, Jacqueline Stears; Carpenters: Duncan Guest, Robert Jackson; Prop Man: John Chisholm; Props: Wesley Peppiatt; Dressing Prop: Bob Sherwood; Stand-By Prop: John Wells; Sound Recordist: Derek Ball; Sound Re-Recording Mixers: Ken Barker, Gordon McCallum, Graham V. Hartstone, John Hayward, Nicolas Le Messurier; Dubbing Editors: Derek Holding, Michael Hopkins; Sound Effects: Jean-Pierre Lelong; Sound Editor: Colin Miller; Boom Operator: Ken Nightingall; Special Effects Supervisor: John Richardson; Special Effects: David Domeyer; Second Unit Effects Supervisor: John Evans; Model Photographer: Leslie Dear; Model Effects Supervisor: Front Projection: Charles Staffell; Model Unit: Julian Parry; Stunt Team Supervisors: William H. Burton, Martin Grace, Paul Weston; Stunt Engineers: Dave Bickers, Dan Peterson; Stunt Team: Del Baker, Pat Banta, Clive Curtis, Jim Dowdall, Dorothy Ford, Nick Hobbs, Jazzer Jeyes, Wayne Michaels, Rocky Taylor, Malcolm Weaver, Christopher Webb, Bill Weston; Stunts: Terry Cade, Terry Forestal, Richard Graydon, Reg Harding, Nosher Powell, Nick Wilkinson; Additional Stunts: Roy Alon, Ken Barker, Marc Boyle, David Brandon, William H. Burton, George Lane Cooper, Eddie Eddon, Steve Emerson, Stuart Fell, Alan Gold, Fred Haggerty, Frank Henson, Buddy Joe Hooker, Arthur Howell, Tommy J. Huff, Jimmy Lodge, Eddie Powell, R. A. Rondell, Michael Runyard, Jack Sholomir, Colin Skeaping, Tony Smart, Stuart St. Paul, Roy Street, Tip Tipping, Dick Ziker; Driving Stunts Arranger: Remy Julienne; Action Sequences Arranger: Bob Simmons; Stunt Doubles for Roger Moore: Jim Dowdall, Martin Grace, Norman Howell, Jake Lombard, Rocky Taylor, Paul Weston; Stunt Pilot: J. W. "Corky" Fornof; Stunt Performer: Dave Holland; Explosion Stunt Driver: George Leech; Twin Stunt Double: Wayne Michaels; Louis Jourdan Stunt Double: Bill Weston; Kabir Bedj Stunt Double: B. J. Worth; Motorcycle Stunt Driver: Henri Trautman; Camera Operator: Alec Mills; Second Unit Camera Operators: Jack Lowin, David B. Nowell, Malcolm Vinson; Assistant Camera: Nick Schlesinger; Second Assistant Camera: Nigel Seal; Camera Grips: W. C. "Chunky" Huse, Colin Manning; Still Photographers: Frank Connor, George Whitear; Additional Photographers: Robert E. Collins, James Devis; Second Unit Photographer: Arthur Wooster; Electrical Supervisor: John Tythe; Clapper Loader: Ian Foster; Electrician: Vince Goddard; Aerial Camera Operator: Geoff Mulligan; Casting: Jane Jenkins; Costume Supervisor: Tiny Nicholls; Supervising Editor: John Grover; Assistant Editor: Nigel Galt; First Assistant Editor: Matthew Glen; Music Mixer: John Richards; Music Contractor: Sidney Margo; Location Manager: Rashid Abassi; Production Assistants: Mohini Banerji, Sheila Barnes, May Capsaskis, Iris Rose, Joyce Turner, Robin Melville; Production Secretaries: Joanna Brown, Eleanor Chaudhuri, Mary Stellar; Production Controller: Reginald A. Barkshire; Location Manager: Peter Bennett; Main Title Designer: Maurice Binder; Executive Assistant: Barbara

Broccoli; Continuity: Elaine Schreyeck; Second Unit Continuity: Penny Daniels, Doreen Soan; Aerial Team: Beech 18: Rande DeLuca, Jake Lombard, Joe Taylor, B. J. Worth; Acro Star Jet Pilots: J. W. "Corky" Fornof, Richard Holley; Helicopter Pilot: Marc Wolff; Aerial Team Director: Philip Wrestler; Aerial Team Coordinator: Clay Lacy; Unit Publicist: Geoff Freeman; Production Advisor in India: Shama Habibullah; Director of Publicity: Charles Juroe; Boat Master: Michael Turk; Crane Technician: Adam Samuelson; Assistant to Roger Moore: Doris Spriggs; Production Accountant: Douglas Noakes; Location Accountants: Jane Meagher, Marge Rowland, Ursula Schlieper; Assistant Accountant: Sarah Lucraft.

Cast: Roger Moore (James Bond), Maud Adams (Octopussy), Louis Jourdan (Kamal Khan), Kristina Wayborn (Magda), Kabir Bedi (Gobinda), Steven Berkoff (Gen. Orlov), David Myer (Twin One), Tony Meyer (Twin Two), Desmond Llewelyn ("Q"), Robert Brown ("M"), Lois Maxwell (Miss Moneypenny), Michaela Clavell (Penelope Smallbone), Walter Gotell (Gen. Gogol), Vijay Amritraj (Vijay), Albert Moses (Sadruddin), Geoffrey Keen (Sir Frederick Gray), Douglas Wilmer (Jim Fanning), Andy Bradford (009), Philip Voss (Auctioneer), Bruce Boa (U. S. General), Richard Le Parmentier (U. S. Aide), Paul Hardwick (Soviet Chairman), Suzanna Jerome (Gwendolyn), Cherry Gillespie (Midge), Dermot Crowley (Kamp), Eva Reuber-Staier (Rublevitch), Jeremy Bulloch (Smithers), Tina Hudson (Bianca), William Derrick (Yo-yo Saw Thug), Stuart Sanders (Major Clive), Patrick Barr (British Ambassador), Gabor Vernon (Borchoi), Hugo Bower (Karl), Ken Norris (Col. Toro), Tony Arjuna (Mufti), Gertan Klauber (Bubi), Brenda Cowling (Schatzi), David Grahame (Pump Attendant), Brian Coburn (South American VIP), Michael Halphie (South American Officer); Mary Stavin, Carolyn Seaward, Carole Ashby, Cheryl Anne, Jani-Z, Julie Martin, Joni Flynn, Julie Barth, Kathy Davies, Helene Hunt, Gillian De Terville, Safira Afzal, Louise King, Tina Robinson, Alison Worth, Janine Andrews, Lynda Knight (Octopussy Girls); Susanne Dando (Gymnast Supervisor); Teresa Craddock, Kirsten Harrison, Christine Cullers, Lisa Jackman, Jane Aldridge, Christine Gibson, Tracy Llewellyn, Ruth Flynn (Gymnasts); Roberto Germains (Ringmaster), Richard Graydon (Francisco the Fearless), The Hassani Troupe, The Flying Cherokees (Circus Performers), Carol Richter, Josef Richter, Vera Fossett, Shirley Fossett, Barrie Winship (Circus Personnel); Ravinder Singh Reyett, Gurdial Sira, Michael Moor, Sven Surtees, Peter Edmund, Raymond Charles, Talib Johnny (Thugs); Ingrid Pitt (Galley Mistress' Voice), R. J. Bell (Man), Ken Burns (Bodyguard), Ishaq Bux (Fakir), Sally Dewhurst (Circus Personnel), Reg Harding (Fisherman), Eugene Lipinski (Head VOPO), Derek Lyons (USAF Officer), Lenny Rabin (Sotheby's Bidder), Gary Russell (Teen), Nicola Stapleton (Girl), Michael G. Wilson (Soviet Security Council Member/Tour Boat Man).

Synopsis: A horse trainer arrives at a show near a military base in Cuba. The trainer is really James Bond, who quickly changes his disguise to that of a military officer. He infiltrates the base, but is discovered by the officer he is impersonating. As Bond is taken away in a truck, his female contact drives the horse trainers rig beside them and shows the guards her legs. Bond overpowers his captors and leaps into the other vehicle. He unhitches the horse trailer and climbs in as the girl drives away. The back of the horse and trailer open up to reveal a miniature jet plane, in which Bond escapes. He is then attacked with missiles, which he manages to dodge, even leading the last one into the hangar in which he was discovered. After the resulting explosion, he does a victory roll for the horse-show spectators, but then discovers that his fuel gauge reads EMPTY...

East Berlin: A clown runs from the circus grounds pursued by knife-throwing twin brothers. One of their knives finds the clown's back, and he falls into a waterway where he is carried towards the British Embassy. He crawls from the muck and falls through a door, dead. From his hand rolls a Faberge Egg.

London: Bond, after the customary byplay with Moneypenny (and her new assistant), is shown the Egg. But it is a fake, as are several others which have already been sold that year. The Russians are implicated, and Bond is assigned to the case, replacing 009 — the dead clown.

In Moscow, the insanely aggressive General Orlov is behind the fake Eggs. When he is informed that the fake Egg is missing, he demands the real one back, but it is up for auction at Sotheby's. While driving up the bidding against a man named Khan, Bond switches the fake for the real one, and Khan buys the fake. Bond is instructed to follow him to India and learn what his connection to the case is.

Dehli: Bond meets his contact Vijay, who tells him that Khan plays high-stakes backgammon at the very hotel where Bond is registered. Bond goes to the casino that night and discovers Khan wins by using loaded dice. Using the real Egg as collateral, Bond beats Khan at his own game, enraging him and making sure that they will have another meeting in the very near future. As soon as they leave the hotel, Bond and Vijay are set upon by Khan's men, whom they lead on a dangerous chase. Eluding them, Bond and Vijay go to a secret location where they are greeted by Q.

Bond returns to the hotel, where he finds Khan's mistress Magda waiting for him at a table. She suggests trading the Egg for his life, and Bond suggests something else. Bond notices the tattoo of an octopus on her shoulder; he remembers that it is the same design as on the flag of the Roman-style galley on which she had arrived. In the morning, Bond permits her to escape into Khan's waiting car. As he goes back into the room, is knocked unconscious by Khan's bodyguard.

The octopus is the symbol of Octopussy, a notorious jewel smuggler with whom Khan is in league. She tells Khan to bring Bond to her. After taunting Khan twice at dinner, Bond escapes from his room in time to see Khan meet with Gen. Orlov. Orlov has underlings create the fakes, which Khan sells; Khan gets the originals, and Orlov gets the money to feed his mad dreams of Russian domination of the world. Orlov smashes the fake, and Khan finds the homing device secreted within. Now he uses it to hunt down Bond like a jungle animal, mounting a full safari. After a perilous chase through the jungle, Bond escapes.

Bond makes his way to Octopussy's fabulous floating palace, but discovers she knows nothing of 009 or his murder; she invites Bond to be her guest. When Khan discovers he is there, he sends a team of assassins to the palace. They kill Vijay on their way there, and apparently are successful in dispatching Bond as well.

But Bond is not dead, and he attends Octopussy's circus in East Berlin. He sees Octopussy with Khan and Gen. Orlov. Octopussy thinks it simply another smuggling operation, but Khan has double-crossed her, and Orlov's plan is far more sinister. A cache of jewels is sealed in a case on one of the circus' train cars, but is switched for an identical car and case — and this one contains an atom bomb. Bond confronts Orlov, who reveals his plan: The circus' next stop is at a U.S. Air Force base, where the bomb will explode, but no one will know that it has come from Russia. They will think one of the U.S.

bombs has malfunctioned, and NATO will insist on the unilateral disarmament of Europe, therefore leaving it with its defenses down and making it easy for Orlov's divisions to conquer. A furious fight follows, and Orlov is killed, but Bond cannot stop the train or the performance.

Infiltrating the circus disguised as a clown, Bond battles assassins and authorities before he can deactivate the bomb at the last second. Bond tells Octopussy of Khan's double-cross, and she intercepts Khan while he is trying to get away. Her all-girl army has mounted an assault on Khan's stately dome; Bond and Q arrive by balloon, but cannot prevent Khan from grabbing Octopussy and fleeing by plane. Bond is able to leap from horseback and grab the wing. Khan cannot shake Bond loose, and sends his henchman out to battle him, but Bond sends him hurtling to his doom. Bond and Octopussy leap from the plane as it skims the ground, but Khan cannot control it, and the plane goes over the cliff, where it crashes and explodes. The world saved once more, Bond will need time to recuperate on Octopussy's galley....

Review: Alas, Ingrid Pitt is only heard as the voice of the "Galley Mistress" in Roger Moore's next-to-last cinematic fling as James Bond (exhorting, "In, out, in, out," to the all-female crew), which only makes her a "Bond Girl" in the loosest sense of the term. Certainly other "Hammer Heroines" had made the transition, like Caroline Munro, Martine Beswick, Valerie Leon, Julie Ege and Madeline Smith. Ingrid was as well-suited for those parts as her counterparts; one can easily imagine her in a number of key roles in the series: Domino or Fiona in *Thunderball*; Helga in *You Only Live Twice*; Tracy in *On Her Majesty's Secret Service* (especially in the context of her role in *Where Eagles Dare*); Solitaire in *Live and Let Die* (where she could have been re-teamed with Maddy Smith); Andrea or *particularly* Mary Goodnight in *The Man with the Golden Gun* (can anyone forget Britt Eklund's sheer helplessness in that latter role?); Anya in *The Spy Who Loved Me*; so many, up to and including this one (Maud Adams *again?*). Moore's the pity...

There are moments of hope in the Moore Bonds; certainly the hiring of Christopher Lee as a villain was wise, but putting him in a sweatsuit was not. But *The Man with the Golden Gun* is the Gospel According to Fleming compared to *Octopussy*. As was the case with most of the Moore films, the spectacle overwhelms any and all in its path, and even composer John Barry cannot enliven the action. His score is certainly competent, but we are so used to him being so much more than that, and the soundtrack, with its many echoes of *Goldfinger*, only makes us remember how much better that film and score were.

And so it goes with the rest of the movie, the theory seemingly being that if it worked before (even if in films not even of the Bond series), it would work again. Instead of Pussy Galore's Flying Circus, we get Octopussy's Regular Circus. Bond's mini-jet is an updated "Little Nellie" (*You Only Live Twice*). Bond escapes his pursuers by driving tipped over on two wheels in *Diamonds Are Forever*? Right, it's been 12 years; let's have a go again (and let's not even wait for another film to do basically the same thing in an airplane). And it's been even longer since *Thunderball*, so let's trot out the "doing it for Queen and country" gag. Bond amuses the audience by having his opened parachute reveal a Union Jack in *The Spy Who Loved Me*? Well, this time, why don't we have "Q" and Bond float into battle by means of a Union Jack–emblazoned hot-air balloon? Sean Connery in

Goldfinger disarms an atomic device with only seconds to go? Right, then, we'll have Roger Moore do the same thing in this one, only dressed as a clown! And if they think he's amusing in the clown suit, just wait 'til they see him in the gorilla suit! In *Goldfinger*, Oddjob uses his bare hands to crush the golf ball with which Bond has just beaten his boss; in *Octopussy*, Khan's bodyguard performs the same function after a high-stakes game of backgammon, with Khan's loaded dice. When Bond gives an Indian agent a share of his winnings from Khan, he tells the man, "That'll keep you in curry for a few weeks," unfortunately echoing similar comments in *The Man Who Shot Liberty Valance* when Jimmy Stewart gives Woody Strode some "pork chop money." The face-hugging *Alien* gives inspiration to a face-hugging octopus. Bond gives the pre-recorded Tarzan yell from the Johnny Weissmuller movies during the *Most Dangerous Game*–style safari-manhunt. A cliffhanging scene is taken directly from *North by Northwest* (itself somewhat of a distaff Bond). The laws of aerodynamics (or at least storytelling dynamics) have also apparently changed since *Goldfinger*: In that film, a broken window in a small plane is enough to depressurize the plane and suck Goldfinger out through it. In *Octopussy*, Louis Jourdan's Sikh henchman rips the entire door of the fuselage off its hinges in order to crawl out onto the wing to engage Bond, and Maud Adams remains seated a few feet from the now very large hole in the plane with her sari barely ruffled. She tells Bond that she was given the nickname Octopussy by her father, which is frankly rather disturbing. Admittedly, Adams was still quite a beautiful woman, and indeed, hardly seems to have advanced in age at all in the years between this film and *The Man with the Golden Gun*. Unfortunately, the same can also be said of her acting ability, which, to bring the discussion full circle, only shows how much more suited, say, Ingrid would have been for the part. Adams in no way suggests the depth of experience the part calls for. Douglas Wilmer, Ingrid's co-star from *The Vampire Lovers*, is present in a bit role, and perhaps it is Llewelyn who sums up best the audience's viewpoint at this juncture in the series: "Oh, Bond, will you stop all this adolescent nonsense?"

Tales from the Pitt: Never was a Bond girl. But—I was having dinner at the home of producer Chris Chrisaphis one evening, and I was sitting next to Bond director John Glen. He asked me what Bond film I had been in. When I told him nary a one, he said, "Come to Pinewood in the morning, we have to rectify that." That surprised me. I knew the filming was over and in the editing suite. But I turned out anyway. If you listen carefully to the end of *Octopussy*, you will hear me say something like, "All together, girls—in, out, in, out...." But I don't think that qualifies (*The Pitt of Horror* website).

Parker
(a.k.a. *Bones*)
1984, Moving Picture Company

Crew: Producer: Nigel Stafford-Clark; Associate Producer: Peter Jaques; Director: Jim Goddard; Writer: Trevor Preston; Music: Richard Hartley; Cinematography: Peter Jessop; Editor:

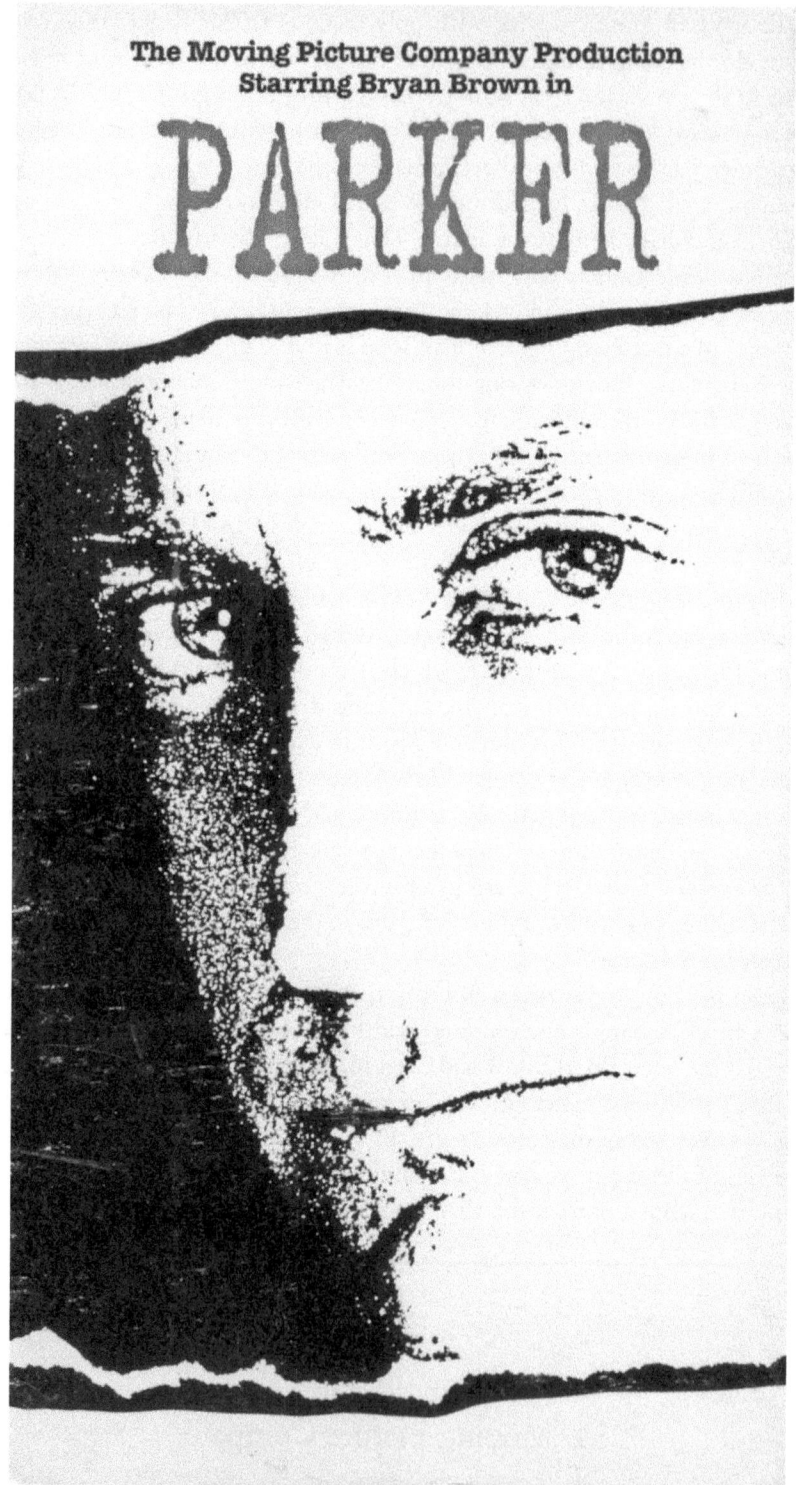

Promotional poster for *Parker*.

Ralph Sheldon; Production Designer: Andrew McAlpine; Costume Design: Catherine Cook; Makeup Artist: Stella Morris; Hair Stylist: Stephanie Hall; Production Managers: Peter Jaques, John Oldknow; Assistant Director: Gino Marotta; Assistant Director in Germany: Michael Zens; Best Boy: Brian Kemp; Transportation Captain: Richard Booz; Helicopter Pilot: Al Cerullo.

Cast: Bryan Brown (David Parker), Cherie Lunghi (Jenny Parker); Kurt Raab (Haag), Frank Mills (Mr. Epps), Elizabeth Spriggs (Mrs. Epps), Bob Peck (Rohl), Beate Finckh (Sister), Gwyneth Strong (Andrea), Simon Rouse (Richard), Uwe Ochsenknecht (Boots Man), Micha Lampert (Tall Man), Dana Gillespie (Monika), Ingrid Pitt (Widow), Phil Smeeton (Reich), Tom Wilkinson (Tom), Hannelore Elsner (Jillian Schelm), Achim Geissler, Jurgen Kuehn (Cowboys), Klaus Fuchs (Bald Man), Colin Gilder (Driver), Marie-Charlotte Schuler (Groupie), Alexander Duda (Taufer), Klaus Menzer (Taxi Driver), Jane Bertish (Officer), John Huth (Wild Boy), Udo Weinberger (Fat Man), Thomas Goode (Joe), Rebecca Goode (Eva), Virginia Goode (Sophie), John Blundell (Salesman), Mandy More (Singer), Robert Goodale (Blind Man), Osman Ragheb (Barz), Peter Jaques (Priest).

Synopsis: As a group of modern-day German cowboys gather around a campfire, a man with a dazed look on his face walks out of the woods. They take the man into town, and the police are called. The man is Parker, a toy manufacturer who claims he has been kidnapped and held hostage for 12 days. On his way to the police station, his mind flashes back to the events leading up to the kidnapping. He dresses for the opera, in the presence of the prostitute he has been keeping company with for two years. "An Australian businessman who lives in England taking a German whore to a French opera—how cosmopolitan," she comments acidly. She refuses to go with him. When she leaves, he follows her and sees her with another woman, but does not confront her. Then he goes to the opera. He hails a taxi when he leaves, but complains that the driver is taking him the wrong way. The driver turns onto a darkened street where Parker is pulled from the car.

No ransom was ever demanded, so the detective assigned to his case is skeptical. Parker recounts more details for the detective: The masked kidnappers never said a word to him, but they took his picture. He even knows that one of them was a young female due to the look of her hands. But the detective says that no one ever received the picture, and he cannot understand why they would release Parker unharmed. Parker recalls how the kidnappers took him to the woods, performed a mock execution, and then left him there. As he stumbled through the woods, he was found by a feral boy and his savage dog. The boy and his dog freed Parker from his bonds and then disappeared back into the woods. The doubting detective sends him to a hotel where he will be met by his wife.

He is met not only by his wife, but a horde of paparazzi, whom he tells to buzz off. The detective questions Mrs. Parker, but also plants seeds of doubt in her mind. After the flight home, Parker gets sick and then begins to see things. He imagines he sees the taxi from which he was abducted; he imagines he sees the dog from the woods. He goes to a used-car lot, sits in a car just like the taxi and then bolts from it. He then goes and buys two cars from a beautiful widow who attempts to seduce him, but the only ride he's interested in is a Mercedes. While he is out, his wife begins to receive constant phone calls from a female who asks if he is there. She believes it to be his mistress, and they have a terrible row.

Parker goes to visit a psychic who has had visions of his kidnappers and done drawings of them. When Parker sees the drawing of the female kidnapper, he realizes that it is the same woman he saw with his mistress.

The girl keeps a photo of herself and the mistress on her table. She receives a phone call, and is picked up by car by one of the other kidnappers. They drive to a downtown theater, where she goes backstage and delivers a package to the lead actress. The package contains smack, which the woman immediately shoots up. The girl then makes another connection at a John Wayne film festival, with a blind man who has memorized every line of the film onscreen. When they return to her flat, they are set upon by men without hats, in suits. Now it is the turn of the kidnappers to be terrorized. The girl gives one of the men a bundle of money, but he wants to know where the rest is, and where the rest of the heroin is. She spits in his face. He kills her, and her partner is shot by the other man.

The detective examines the corpses. He knows that they are the kidnappers, and suspects Parker. Meanwhile Parker has bought a dog that looks just like the dog in the woods. Parker's wife tells him she thinks he is going mad, and leaves him.

Another kidnapper is walking through an alley when he is grabbed by the men in suits. They leave him hanging on a meat hook. A man in a car tells them to talk to the whore, who soon meets the same fate as the kidnappers. The detective finds a photo of Parker and another man in her purse. The detective deduces that it must be Parker's brother, and also determines that the mistress and the female kidnapper were sisters.

Parker gets in his car, and a girl pops up in the back seat. She has the photo that the kidnappers took. When he asks her how she got it, she has him drive to a remote estate. He finds his brother, very sick. He tells Parker that the kidnappers found him through the prostitute, and Parker learns that she and the female kidnapper were sisters. They told the prostitute that they would kill Parker if she didn't cooperate. As the girl prepares a fix, she tells him not to look so disgusted; heroin bought his life. Parker's brother reveals that he deals in heroin. Parker's kidnappers (small-time dealers trying to make it big) stole the heroin from him. As Parker leaves to get the money that his brother owes, the girl reveals to him that she is his brother's wife. Parker gets stuck in traffic, and the skag baron's killers arrive at the house. First they grab the girl, and then enter the room where Parker's brother is in bed. They wake him, bind him, douse him with liquor, and then set him on fire. They bring his wife into the room to watch him burn and hear his screams. Then they kill her. Parker gets back too late.

Time passes. Parker's Mercedes is on the scrap-heap. His home is deserted. At another sumptuous estate, the skag baron's killers enjoy the fruits of their labors, lounging nude by a pool. Parker, now with a beard, hides in the bushes. He walks up calmly and shoots one of the killers; the other jumps in the pool, but within seconds, he too is dead. As Parker stands by the side of the pool surveying his bloody handiwork, he is joined by his dog. Later, at the same restaurant where he was taken when he was found by the cowboys, he puts money in the jukebox and sits quietly at a table. The detective walks in, and neither says a word. Parker simply looks up at him and ever so slightly smiles.

Review: Parker is a grim and gritty crime thriller. The mystery is engrossing, although

Bryan Brown's Parker is decidedly unsympathetic, and only heroic when compared to the rest of the characters. Ingrid's part is small but sexy; she plays the widow on the make who sells Parker the cars, and has a wonderful line with, "So, you are interested in ... tropical fish?" Australian Brown was just coming off of his Emmy-nominated role in *The Thorn Birds*; he's best-known to genre audience for his role in *F/X* and its sequel. Striking Dana Gillespie appeared in two "lost race" movies, Hammer's *The Lost Continent* and Amicus' *The People That Time Forgot*, as well as Peter Cook and Dudley Moore's comic *The Hound of the Baskervilles* (1978).

Tales from the Pitt: There were a few other films about at this time. *Parker, Transmutations,* and *The House* ... and *Hanna's War* ... but we don't talk about these... (*The Ingrid Pitt Bedside Companion for Vampire Lovers*).

Wild Geese II
1985, Frontier Films

Crew: Producer: Euan Lloyd; Executive Producer: Chris Chrisafis; Co-Producer: A. Eric Scotoni; Director: Peter Hunt; Screenplay: Reginald Rose; Based on the Novel *The Square Circle* by Daniel Carney; Music Composed & Conducted by Roy Budd; Cinematography: Michael Reed; Editor: Keith Palmer; Casting: Allan Foenander; Production Designer: Syd Cain; Art Director: Peter Williams; Assistant Art Director: Thomas Riccabona; Costume Design: Diane Holmes; Makeup Artists: Karin Bauer-Hurst, Hasso von Hugo; Hairdressers: Karin Bauer-Hurst, Hasso von Hugo; Executive in Charge of Production: Willy Egger; Unit Manager: Ralf Blankenburg; Assistant Unit Manager: Rolf Wappenschmitt; Unit Production Manager: Jochen Feldhoff; Production Supervisor: Norman Foster; First Assistant Directors: Ken Baker, Eva-Maria Schonecker; Second Assistant Directors: Peter Bennett, Stefan Diepenbrock; Second Unit Director: James Devis; Props: Mario Stock; Sound Recordist: Chris Munro; Sound Editor: Graham Harris; Dubbing Mixer: Gerry Humphreys; Dubbing Editor: Jim Roddan; Second Unit Sound Recordist: Don Brown; Special Effects: Richard Richtsfeld; Optical Camera: Alan Church; Action Arranger: Dickey Beer; Stunts: Frank Henson, Nick Hobbs, Billy Horrigan, Wayne Michaels, Gareth Milne, Valentino Musetti, Denise Ryan, Bill Weston, Jason White; Camera Operators: James Bawden, Herbie Smith; Gaffer: Berndt Hubner; Grips: Brian Osborn, Peer Menke; Still Photographer: Laurie Ridley; Focus Pullers: Keith Thomas, Anthony Woodcock; Clapper Loader: Tim Dodd; Electrician: Joachim Scholz; Wardrobe Master: Philippe Pickford; Assistant Editor: Joe Illing; Music Recording Mixer: Dave Hunt; Technical Advisor at Spandau Prison: Col. Eugene K. Bird; Production Controller: Carolyn Hall; Personal Assistant to Director: Nikos Kourtis; Publicist: Doreen Landry; Supplier of "Faulkner's Survivor Rifle": Don McNabb; Technical Advisor on Weapons: Capt. James P. Monaghan; Titles: Tom Pullinger; Armorer: Gunther Schaidt; Production Coordinator: Elisabeth Schwartzer; Script Supervisor: Doreen Soan; Dialogue Coach: Brook Williams; Pre-Production Location Manager: Wolfgang Bajorat; Dedicatee: Richard Burton.

Cast: Scott Glenn (John Haddad), Barbara Carrera (Kathy Lucas), Edward Fox (Alex Faulkner), Laurence Olivier (Rudolph Hess), Robert Webber (Robert McCann), Robert Frietag (Stroebling), Kenneth Haigh (Col. Reed-Henry), Stratford Johns (Mustapha El Ali), Derek Thompson (Hourigan), Paul Antrim (Murphy), John Terry (Michael Lucas), Ingrid Pitt

(Hooker), Patrick Stewart (Russian General), Michael Harbour (KGB Man), David Lumsden (Joseph), Frederick Warder (Jamil), Malcolm Jamieson (Pierre), Billy Boyle (Devenish), David Sullivan (EBC Commentator), Dan van Husen (Stroebling's Driver), James Monaghan, Michael Buttner (Heavies), Herbert Chwoika (Ali's Man), Carl Price (British Corporal), Ronald Nitschke (East German Soldier), Wilfried Gronau (Immigration Official), Shaun Lawton (Intelligence Man), Peter Kybart (Hunter), Amelie zur Muhlen (Russian Woman), Gabriele Kastner (East German Tour Guide), Tom Deiniger (Nightclub Artist).

Synopsis: The Eagle Broadcasting Company wants the biggest news story ever, and they don't care if they start a war to get it. They want to kidnap the only surviving Nazi leader in captivity, Rudolph Hess, from Spandau Prison, so that he can reveal his secrets to the world. They attempt to hire Allen Faulkner's brother Alex, who is also a mercenary; he turns them down but suggests a friend who just might be insane enough to try such a job: John Haddad. On his way to met with them, Haddad shows what he is made of when he is attacked in a men's room. Siblings Michael and Kathy Lucas, Eagle's representatives in London, meet with Haddad, but he tells them that he won't accept the job unless he thinks he can succeed. Haddad flies to Berlin the next day, and Cathy the day after that.

Haddad is under surveillance from the time he arrives. The next day, he goes for a jog around the prison and is photographed from concealment. He meets with Kathy to tell her that he knows how the changing of the guards works, as least for the American troops. He then infiltrates the grounds disguised as a workman to get a better idea of the layout. As he leaves with the other workers, he is approached by a hooker. Haddad declines, but she insists on giving him her card, which turns out to be an automatic pistol. He is then forced into a waiting car. He is questioned by a bearded man, and beaten and nearly suffocated by the man's thugs. They know who he is, and that he has a price on his head in Palestine. They manage to discover that Haddad is after Hess, but then he throws himself from the car.

Later, in the hospital, he is visited by British Colonel Reed-Henry of MI 6. Reed-Henry shows him photos of the men who attacked him, but Haddad denies having ever seen them. Reed-Henry tells Haddad that the bearded man is Stroebling, who works for the Soviets, supplying urban terrorist groups. They also know who Haddad is, but he denies him any more details. When Haddad gets out of the hospital, he meets Kathy and tells her that even if he doesn't take the job, he still needs help, which means that Alex Faulkner will be in on the job after all. Haddad and Kathy go to a hotel outside of Munich, posing as a married couple, and from there he contacts Faulkner, who is performing an assassination of his own.

Haddad is out for his morning run, along with the unwanted company of Kathy on a bike, when shots ring out. They are not intended for either of the couple, though; it is only a man boar-hunting. Nonetheless, Kathy is terribly shaken, and they return to the inn, where they make love. Before they can finish, in walks Alex with champagne, much to Kathy's fury and Haddad's amusement. He tells Faulkner to find him a safe house and cover his back. Then he is visited by a British soldier who tells him that he has been invited out for the evening by Col. Reed-Henry.

Haddad meets Reed-Henry at a nightclub. He knows that Haddad is after Hess, and would actually like him to perform the same secret service on behalf of Her Majesty; Hess in Spandau gives the Russians the right to station troops in the British sector of Berlin, which the British don't like. Reed-Henry tells Haddad that the weak link in the chain is when Hess is taken to routine medical checkup by military convoy, and so Haddad begins by surveying the territory. Kathy wants him to survey her territory; he refuses her advances, but accepts the mission. He then gets a call from Faulkner, who informs him that his apartment is being watched by two men. When Haddad goes downstairs, those two are joined by another man in a car and the hooker, and they follow him to a dead-end street, but the only people who wind up dying on this dead-end street are the original two men and the hooker. Haddad surprises the driver of the car, putting him in a headlock and handing him a message to give to Stroebling. He also gives him a deep cut on the cheek with his switchblade.

Ingrid takes a walk on the *Wild Geese 2* side (courtesy Ingrid Pitt).

Haddad and Reed-Henry meet in a graveyard. Reed-Henry tells him he can provide him with the rest of his wild geese, as well as with an escape route out of Berlin; but there's nothing he can do about Stroebling, nor will he tell Haddad what the British intend to do with Hess. Haddad and Kathy attend a carnival to meet one of Haddad's contacts, Pierre. Afterwards, he tells Stroebling that he has found a way to kidnap Hess. Naturally, Stroebling wants Hess, too, and Haddad tells him that he's prepared to give Hess to Stroebling, if Stroebling will not only call off his dogs, but have the Palestinian price on John's head lifted. Stroebling agrees to his terms.

Haddad meets with Murphy, a former member of the Irish Guard and the man who will train Haddad's men to impersonate British troops, and also with Pierre, who will cause the traffic accident that will delay the convoy transporting Hess. As he finishes with Pierre, they are alerted to the presence of armed men in a car by Alex, who shoots them and blows up the car. Stroebling tells Haddad he knows nothing about it, but soon afterwards, he has Kathy kidnapped. Stroebling calls Haddad and tells him and tells him he is responsible, arranging a meeting by the Berlin Wall.

Stroebling tells Haddad to call off Faulkner; Haddad refuses. When Stroebling tells him it's either his life or Kathy's, Haddad tells him to kill her. He then shows Stroebling a switchblade and tells him he doesn't mind dying. He tells Stroebling he wants Kathy for Hess, or Hess dies. Stroebling tells him he is placing a man with Haddad to see that he keeps his end of the bargain. Haddad asks him why he wants Hess. Stroebling tells him that Hess knows secrets of cataclysmic betrayals that would wreck England and Russia forever, and nothing could make Stroebling happier, because even though he works for the Soviets, he's still a proud German, stung by his country's defeats in two world wars.

The man Stroebling assigns to Haddad is an ex–Irish Republican Army man, Hourigan. When the other wild geese, including Michael Lucas, gather, Haddad details sleeping arrangements, but Hourigan says he won't share a room with wogs. Alex pretends he is Italian, and when Hourigan agrees to share his room, he then informs him he is British, much to the amusement of the others. When Murphy arrives to begin the training as troops, there is an instant hatred between the Protestant and the Catholic.

Stroebling permits Kathy to speak to Haddad and Michael on the phone, but when Michael asks her where she is, Stroebling hangs up. Faulkner tells Haddad that Hourigan thinks he's been slipping him LSD in booze, and then when he thinks Alex is tripping, he sneaks out to make his report to Stroebling. But that night, Faulkner has one of his recurring attacks from having had malaria, and Hourigan gives him the LSD instead of the pills Alex asks for. With Haddad's help, Alex makes it through the bad trip, and when Hourigan returns, Haddad nearly breaks his neck. But that is nothing compared to the next day. Murphy finishes his training, and is then called out by Hourigan. Murphy responds by calling him an IRA scum, and then shoots him in the knees and the head.

To help Kathy escape, Haddad offers Michael as a second hostage. Michael is wearing an explosive overcoat. He is able to pull off the necessary deception, but is killed in the ensuing chaos. Pierre is also killed when he causes the crash in the convoy, but Hess is successfully taken. Haddad and one of the men go to meet Stroebling, but tell him that to get Hess, they must go to the Kaiser Wilhelm Memorial disguised as British soldiers. When Stroebling and the men arrive, they are gunned down by Reed-Henry, thinking it is Hess. He shoots Murphy in the head. He is working with the Russians, and when they find out he has shot Stroebling by mistake, they shoot him in the head.

The one factor they have not figured into the equation is Hess himself. He has neither the desire nor the will to reveal any secrets; he only wants to die in the prison that has become his home. They return him to Spandau. It has all been for nothing. A newspaper article informs us that the plot to kidnap Hess was only a rumor, and the story has no substance whatsoever.

Review: Yes, too bad about that final headline, eh wot? It's a sequel in name only to *The Wild Geese* (1978), which starred Richard Burton, Roger Moore and Richard Harris, itself sort of a third-order simulation of *Where Eagles Dare*. Of course, there is a James Bond connection; Peter Hunt had directed *On Her Majesty's Secret Service*, and production designer Syd Cain worked on that film as well, but it's something else, a thematic (unintended, one hopes) connection, both tangible and intangible. On the surface, both are stories about hired killers (secret agents, mercenaries) involved in high-stakes intrigue, but in both cases, the high-explosive action sequences and set pieces are linked by a leading man with a limited acting range, leading one to suspect that the play, and not the players, was the thing to Hunt. As such, the action sequences are competently staged, but lacking the star power and acting ability displayed in the original *Wild Geese*, the film becomes no better or worse than a thousand other thick-eared *policiers*. Laurence Olivier's attitude towards the film is probably best summed up in his lines, "What am I doing here? Who are you people?"

Ingrid Pitt is only in a couple of scenes, but she handles her brief screen time with aplomb, and when she coos to Haddad that she could do things "you wouldn't believe," well, she's entirely believable. She certainly looks a lot more comfortable than Barbara (*Island of Dr. Moreau*) Carrera, who seems rather embarrassed to be part of it all, or Edward (*Skullduggery*) Fox, who seems to be just having a laugh. Fox replaced Richard Burton; and the film is dedicated to Burton, which perhaps made him roll over in his grave.

Tales from the Pitt: To be in Berlin was horrific for me. We were filming near the border and I was paranoid. I felt binoculars were trained on me, rifles aimed at me, I even imagined I could hear gunfire. I wondered if the tormenting images imprinted on my brain in my youth would ever fade and leave me in peace (*Life's a Scream*).

Underworld
(a.k.a. *Transmutations*)
1985, Alpine

Crew: Producers: Kevin Attew, Don Hawkins; Executive Producers: Al Burgess, Paul Gwynn, Charles Band; Co-Producer: Graham Ford; Director: George Pavlou; Story & Screenplay: Clive Barker; Writer: James Caplin; Music: Freur; Cinematography: Sydney Macartney; Editor: Chris Ridsdale; Art Director: Len Huntingford; Costume Designer: Geoff Sharpe; Chief of Makeup: Vivian Placks; Prosthetic Makeup: Peter Litton; Key Hair Stylist: Jeanette Freeman; First Assistant Director: Simon Hinkly; Second Assistant Director: Paul Frift; Third Assistant Director: Peter Freeman; Property Masters: Terry Wells, Andreas Marschall; Sound Mixer: Bill Burgess; Boom Operator: David Sutton; Special Effects Supervisor: Malcolm King; Stunt Coordinator: Jim Dowdall; Stunts: Tracey Eddon, Nick Hobbs, Gareth Milne, Tip Tipping; Camera Operator: Steve Alcorn; Clapper Loader: Grant Cameron; Focus Puller: Jeremy Hiles; Best Boy: Steve McLeod; Post-Production: Juliet Avola; Continuity: Sarah Hayward; Production Coordinator: Caroline Hill; Assistant Unit Publicist: Catherine O'Brien; Choreographer: Radford Quist; Location Manager: Adam Sedgwick.

Cast: Denholm Elliott (Dr. Savary), Steven Berkoff (Hugo Motherskille), Larry Lam (Roy Bain), Nicola Cowper (Nicole), Irina Brook (Bianca), Art Malik (Fluke), Brian Croucher (Darling), Ingrid Pitt (Pepperdine), Trevor Thomas (Ricardo), Clive Panto (Abbott), Sean Chapman (Buchanan), Candy Davis (Barmaid), Karen Gould, Jeanette Landry, Mark West (Dancers), Gary Olsen (Red Dog), Paul Bown (Nygaard), Philip Davis (Lazarus), Miranda Richardson (Oriel), Paul Mari (Dudu), Philip Tan (Tung), Tina Maskell (Chevron); Jim Dowdall, Mathew Zajac, Guy Dartnell (Underworlders).

Synopsis: Night. A group of masked figures make their way across the cityscape. In another section of town, a man goes to a high-class brothel. He mentions a name, but the madam, Pepperdine, refuses him entrance, backed up by Ricardo. The disgusted man

One-sheet design for *Transmutations*, the film originally titled *Underworld*.

lingers until he sees one of the masked men. Inside the mansion, Pepperdine calls for Nicole, her most popular girl. She tells the girl that the client is new and important, and to let her know if he shows any violent impulses. After receiving a vial of white fluid, Nicole lies in wait for her john, but instead, two of the masked men enter stealthily. As one of them chloroforms her, Pepperdine catches him in the act and calls for Ricardo. The other masked marauder, growling like an animal, throws him across the room and draws a knife, while the other escapes with Nicole down the fire escape. Ricardo leaps at his attacker and rips off his mask. It is a red-eyed, fanged monster! The creature easily subdues Ricardo and escapes.

Roy Bain, artist and action man, is working on a painting when he is visited by two strong-arm men, Fluke and Darling. They tell him that their boss, Hugo Motherskille, wants to see him, but Bain says he doesn't run in their circle any more. Fluke says Nicole needs him, which quickly changes his mind. Fluke and Darling take Bain to a high-rise office building, Palladium, Inc. Motherskille tells Bain that their former lover Nicole has been kidnapped and he wants him to go after her. Bain refuses until Hugo says that she was kidnapped by men who will chop her up and film it.

Bain goes to see Pepperdine, who claims she saw nothing. Bain searches Nicole's room and finds the vial of white stuff. Pepperdine tells him he doesn't know what he's getting into. Bain encounters Bianca, another old flame who is also employed by Pepperdine. He tells her that they're all lying to him. He asks her about the vial, and she tells him to go see a Dr. Savary. As he gets in his car, he sees Darling, who has been assigned to shadow him. He invites Darling to the pub for a few pints, and quizzes him about the vial. Darling tells Bain that Dr. Savary invents things and Motherskille makes them. They leave the pub and separate, but then Darling gets right back on Bain's trail.

Savary has just injected a subject with the white liquid in his lab, and goes to the main part of the house to admit Bain. Savary denies knowledge of Nicole or what's in the vial; but then they hear the sound of breaking glass. Savary tells Bain to wait and rushes off to the lab, so Bain takes the opportunity to search his desk. Savary soon returns and tells Bain to leave. He then returns to the lab, where he surveys the damage and begins to pick up vials from the floor.

In an underground lab, Nicole is a guinea pig for the mutating monsters. They talk of her seeming immunity, that the "dreams" haven't affected her. It seems that the white liquid is a powerful hallucinogenic and addictive drug, which also turns them into mutants. But Nicole is an addict too, and they want to find out why she is unaffected. The damage at Savary's was caused by the mutants, one of whom reports back to their leader that not only did they fail to get Savary, but that his partner went rogue because "the dreams had taken over."

The partner, "Red Dog," throws open the gates to the brothel and creeps up the fire escape, where he watches Bianca put on her stockings. But before he can pounce, Bianca is distracted by a commotion in the yard; it is Pepperdine being roughed up by Fluke and Darling. They tell her to fix Bain or they'll fix her. Bianca puts on a wrap and leaves, followed by Red Dog. She goes to Bain's apartment and goes to sleep in his bed. Bain leaves. When Red Dog enters the room, Bianca awakens with a scream.

Bain has not yet left the building, and comes back to battle the beast. The bestial bastard has Bain in a brutal grip, but Bianca brains the beast with a bottle, breaking Bain free. But Bain is bested, and Bianca is backed into the lift; the beast is barred by the doors of the cage. But Bain bounces back with a bullet, and the badly wounded beast breaks free, dropping a vial in the process. Red Dog bumbles into a back alley, where he bounces to the brick. He's back to brief life as Bain beholds the body, but bites the big bone as he tries to best Bain with bitter bile. As Bain begins back down the alley, a mutant appears from a sewer hole and stares at Bain a bit before dragging the body back into the underground whence it came.

Motherskille, Fluke and Darling are taking in an exotic dance routine when Bain walks in and demands to talk to Hugo alone. Bain shows him the vial; when Motherskille denies a connection, Bain roughs him up and leaves to see Savary on the sly. He gets on Savary's computer and sees video of Savary's subjects which shows their progressive degeneration from the effects of the drug; they crave it even as they beg for death. Savary appears with a pistol and he leads Bain by gunpoint to his lab. He intends to inject Bain. Savary has unintentionally created a small army of dependents, who also hate him, but need him to manufacture the drug while he ostensibly works on a cure for their conditions and addiction. When Bain asks him why, Savary admits to his own addiction—for Nicole. Bain knocks the gun from his hand and makes his escape. He returns to the alley where Red Dog died and enters the underworld.

The underworlders need a fix badly, and Nicole offers to get it and Savary for them. She calls Savary and tells him that she wants and needs him. While exploring, Bain hears music from a neon-lit room. When he enters, it is empty—but it is soon occupied by the underworlders, who take Bain prisoner. Nicole intervenes on his behalf, but must leave Bain hanging to go meet Savary. Fluke appears and tells Bain that Motherskille never cared about Nicole; he just wanted Bain to find the underworlders for him so he could kill them all. He injects Bain and laughingly makes his exit.

Fluke calls Motherskille and informs him where the mutants and Savary will meet. Savary arrives there and is cornered by his creations, which are intent on taking him back to the underworld. But just as they are about to inject Savary, Motherskille and his men arrive and open fire. The mutants think Savary has set them up. They grab him and the drugs, and engage the Motherskillers in battle. Below, Bain breaks his bonds and makes his way to the surface world. He garrotes one thug and puts the torch to another. He makes it to the besieged beasts, and with his added brains and brawn, they escape the exploding building and return to their underworld.

The heroic mutants decide to take a stand and try to spare Bain and Nicole the coming battle, but Bain is besieged by guilt and cannot leave his bestial buddies to be battered. When the head scientist stabs one of Motherskille's men, Hugo orders the mutants to be executed with poisonous gas. He gets the drop on Bain, but the man with the gas unexpectedly flails into the room, and Motherskille frantically shoots him. Bain uses the opportunity to grab Motherskille and yank off his mask. Motherskille dies from his own gas.

Nicole is discovered by Savary, who advances on her with a machine gun. She offers to make his dreams real. She tells him to show her his dreams, and quickly he falls under her power. Her eyes begin to glow red; the atmosphere crackles, and Savary explodes in flames. Bain sees this. She asks him if he is afraid, and says he used to love her. He shows her he still does with a kiss, and tells her she can't stay there; that everybody's dead and it's all over. But she tells him that it is just the beginning, and returns to the underworld, the world that is now hers.

Review: Transmutations is a disappointing film for Clive Barker fans who are expecting something more along the lines of *Hellraiser*, which is the primary reason that Barker directed the latter film himself. There are good performances in it; for the first time in a horror movie since *The Sound of Horror*, Ingrid is on the side of ... well, if not the angels, she's not the monster.

Ingrid's *House That Dripped Blood* co-star Denholm Elliott, primarily remembered by modern audiences for his role as Marcus in the Indiana Jones series, had a long and honorable association with the fantasy genre, appearing in the Jack Palance *Dr. Jekyll & Mr. Hyde*, *The Vault of Horror*, *To the Devil a Daughter*, and two versions of *The Hound of the Baskervilles*. Steven Birkoff, like Ingrid, was also recently in the cast of *Octopussy*; his C.V. includes *The Flesh and the Fiends*, Hammer's *Prehistoric Women*, and the brilliant *A Clockwork Orange*.

Like *The Omegans*, the film's ultimate problem is that it can't quite decide what it wants to be, action or horror-science fiction. That isn't to say the two genres can't be combined to great effect (*Aliens* and *Predator* immediately spring to mind), but this movie comes nowhere close to achieving that balance. Important plot points are raised and then forgotten; Nicole is immune to the "Whitemare" drug, and the whole point of the mutants kidnapping her is to discover why, but it is never explained why she is. Bain is injected with the drug, but absolutely nothing happens to him. Director Pavlou apparently hopes to emulate the style of Dario Argento by bathing his scenes in lurid colors, but this, combined with some incredibly bad '80s fashions, at times gives the sense that one is watching an extended Human League video, only it's not that horrifying.

Hanna's War
1988, Golan-Globus Productions

Crew: Producers: Yoram Globus, Menahem Golan; Associate Producers: Carlos Gil, Otto Plaschkes; Director: Menahem Golan; Writers: Menahem Golan, Stanley Mann; Music: D. Seltzer; Cinematography: Elemer Ragalyi; Editors: Alain Jakubowicz, Dory Lubliner; Casting: Noel Davis, Jeremy Zimmerman; Art Directors: Tivadar Bertalan, Michal Japhet, Tibor Nell; Set Decoration: Fred Carter; Costume Design: John Mollo; Makeup Supervisor: Vered Hochman; Makeup Artists: Christine Allsop, Judith Toros; Hair Stylist: Linda Peterson; Assistant Hair Stylists: Janosne Horvath, Tami Levi; Unit Managers: Jozsef Ahel, Imre Bodo, Julia Popa; Post-Production Supervisor in Los Angeles: Michael Alden; Post-Production Supervisor in London: Stephen Barker; Production Supervisor: Zoli Ben Chorin; Production Managers: Andras Elek, Asher Gat; Executives in Charge of Production: Itzik Kol, Rony Yacov; First Assistant Directors: Miguel Gil, Gabor Varadi; Second Assistant Directors: Gabor Gaidos, Yael Golan,

Petra Simko; Second Unit Director: Carlos Gil; Assistant Second Unit Director: Hajnisch; Set Dressers: Shachar Baradan, Rami Baruch, Zoltan Horvath, Miklos Molnar, Micha Tzuri; Property Masters: Bert Gadsden, Sandor Kirsch; Production Designer in Israel: Kuli Sander; Sound: Ron Hitchcock; Sound Mixer: Cyril Collick; Sound Editors: Jim Bryan, Jeff Burman, Richard Burton, Albert Glasser, Jean-Paul Jones, Godfrey Maras, Richard Raderman, Bill Van Daalen, Dick Vandenberg; Sound Re-Recording Mixers: Patrick Cyccone Jr., Ron Hitchcock, Frank A. Montano; Supervising Sound Editor: Tony Garber; Assistant Sound Editor: Kurt Nicholas Forshager; Sound Effects Editor: Andy Newell; First Assistant Sound Editor: Tesa Laviolette; Apprentice Sound Editors: Mark Sebastian Capolla, Kathy Siegel, Jon Varady; Additional Sound: Andras Vamosi; Boom Operator: Sam Morris; Foley Artist: Jerry Trent; Foley Mixers: Tommy Goodwin, Preston Oliver; Foley Recordist: Dean St. John; ADR Mixer in L.A.: Tommy Goodwin; ADR Recordist: Dean St. John; ADR Supervisor in London: Louis Elman; Special Effects: Gabor Budahazi, Ferenc Habetler, Moshe Klugman, Alon Meir, Nany Rosenstein; Stunts: Sandor Boros, Gyorgy Kives; Grips: Effi Agami, Casaba Bankhardt, Miki Grinboim, Shaul Nagar; Key Grip: Reuven Ajami; Electricians: Moshe Alon, Avi Avrahami, Haim Fletcher; Camera Operator: Geza Pasztor; First Assistant Camera: Geza Gonda, Gabor Hamvas; Assistant Camera: Jozsef Takacs; Additional Camera Operator: Tibor Variasi; Second Unit Camera Operator: Gabor Szabo; Still Photographers: Egon Endrenyi, Yoni Hamenachem; Gaffers: Miklos Hajdu, Avraham Leibman, Peter Sidlo; Clapper Loaders: Deva Melman, Ronen Shechner; Second Camera Focus Puller: Avi Koren; Casting in Israel: Riki Shelach Nissimoff; Casting in Hungary: Peter Vajda; Wardrobe Supervisor: Buki Shiff; Wardrobe Mistress: Hagit Farber; Wardrobe Master: Imre Orosz; Wardrobe: Shuli Silberberg, Ora Stikovski; Assistant Costume Designer: Barbara Rutter; Post-Production Coordinator: Omneya "Nini" Mazen; Associate Editor: Dory Lubliner; First Associate Editor: Marcelo Sansevieri; Second Associate Editors: Julie Doyle, Alexander Garcia, Beth Jochem, Sloan Klevin, Vincent Laino, Jeanine Schaack, Steve Schwalbe; Assistant Editor: Teodora Honti; Apprentice Editor: Doron Regey; Music Editor: Virginia S. Ellsworth; Assistant Music Editor: Lisa Walker; Transportation Managers: Haim Rinsk, Jon Varady; Truck Driver: Amnon Nachumovski; Script Girl: Julia Bettic; Secretary: Emma Boxhall; Armorers: Gabor Csakovics, Pini Klavir; Continuity: Renee Glynne, Naomi Golan; Unit Publicists: Ellen Levene, Chen Sadan; Production Secretaries: Vera Loosz, Vered Safir; Location Managers: Helena Toth, Sandorne Toth; Production Coordinator: Naomi Mayberg; Production Administrator: Felicity Newton; Production Assistant: Prosper Saul; Fight Arranger: Gabor Piroch; Secretary to M. Golan: Jill Samueles; ADR Group Coordinator: Burton Sharp; Production Accountants: Maty Einav, Joe Straw, Lothar Zielinski.

Cast: Maruschka Detmers (Hanna Senesh), Ellen Burstyn (Katalina Senesh), Anthony Andrews (McCormack), Donald Pleasence (Capt. Thomas Rosza), David Warner (Capt. Julian Simon), Vincenzo [Vincent] Riotta (Yoel), Christopher Fairbank (Ruven), Rob Jacks (Peretz), Serge El-Baz (Tony), Eli Gorenstein (Aba), Joe El Dror (Yonah), Ingrid Pitt (Margit), Jon Rumney (Uncle Egon), Magda Faluhelyi (Aunt Ella), Emma Lewis (Cousin Evi), Dorota Stalinska (Maritza), Yehuda Efroni (Sandor), George Dillon (Milenko), Nigel Hastings (Jancsi), John Stride (Dr. Komoly), Patsy Byrne (Rosie), Rade Serbedzija (Capt. Ivan), Miodrag Krivokapic (Col. Ilya), Agi Margittay (Prof. Ravas), Patrick Monkton (Kalosh), Istvan Hunyadkurthy (Smuggler), Teri Tordai (Baroness Hatvany), Barry Langford (Air Commodore Hadley), Jeff Gerner (Lt. Col. Simmonds), Shimon Finkel (Ben Gurion), Rami Baruch (Enzo Sireni), Avi Korein (Eliyahu Golomb), Mordechai Tenenbaum (Avigur), Peter Czajowski (Andy), Tamas Philippovich (Andras), Josef Lakky (Ticket Clerk), Terez Varhegyi (Marietta), Gabor Varadi (Sgt.), Jozcef Incze (Hungarian Policeman), Gyorgy Gonda (German Officer), Miklos Nagy, Istvan Lakatos (Detectives), Tamas Farkas (Hotel Clerk), Zsuzsa Palos, Magda Darvis, Laura Bokonyi (Prison-

Films: *Hanna's War* (1988)

Hanna's War with Ingrid Pitt and Donald Pleasence (courtesy Ingrid Pitt).

ers), Jon Varady (Guard), Balazs Blasko (Male Secretary), Arpad Ladanyi (Refugee), Casaba Pethes (Porter), Imre Szalai (Sergeant).

Synopsis: Lake Balaton, Hungary, 1937: In a pastoral idyll beside the seaside, young Hanna Senesh plays ping-pong with her boyfriend. He proposes marriage and she refuses, saying they're too young and she does not love him. He asks her if it is because he is not Jewish. Her family and friends discuss Hitler's treatment of Jews, and their future plans. Her brother will go to school in France; Hanna wants to become a writer like her father.

The Baar-Madas Gymnasium, October 15, 1938: At the election of the secretary of Hanna's school's literary society, the proceedings are interrupted by a youthful, black-shirted, special police unit. Their captain says he is very interested in the election results. Hanna wins. The black-shirted youth tells her she cannot hold the post because she is a Jew. Her boyfriend will not intervene on her behalf. She runs from the hall in tears. Hanna decides to go to Palestine to study agriculture and write poetry.

September 13, 1939: Germany invades Poland. As Hanna leaves on the train, she sees that her now-former boyfriend has become one of the black-shirted thugs. She doesn't acknowledge him. She is gloriously happy in Palestine, learning to farm, becoming a fisherwoman, and writing poetry. Months turn into years.

Kibbutz Sdot-Yam, November 22, 1943: During a furious storm, a RAF Jeep arrives at Hanna's fishing village. The officer, Yoel, is also Hungarian, and he tells Hanna that the RAF wants her as part of a group that will infiltrate Hungary to join partisan groups. He tells her it might be a suicide mission; she asks him when they leave. Although she encounters resistance due to her gender, Hanna soon becomes a pilot-officer. Her superior officers learn in the final briefing that she understands her mission — to rescue and establish escape routes for British airmen first; to help her countrymen, even family, second. Upon leaving the meeting, she receives news that her brother is in a refugee camp, and she can visit him.

Atlit, Palestine; February 1, 1944: Hanna reunites with her brother, and they promise to meet at their school reunion after the war is over. As they walk along the beach, she recites her poetry. But soon it is time for the mission to begin. As they make their preparations for departure, Hanna's squad is joined by their training officer, who informs them that they will not be parachuting into their home countries; they will be dropped in Yugoslavia and then spread out. When Hanna protests, the officer reminds her of her priorities as an RAF officer.

Yugoslavia, March 14, 1944: When the squad members make their jump, they are spotted by Nazis; Hanna gets stuck in a tree and is cut down by a partisan. The partisans take the squad to a village, where they meet the resistance leader, Col. Ilya. He immediately accepts Hanna as a soul in solidarity.

Yugoslavia, March 19, 1944: Hanna wakes to news of the occupation of Hungary by Hitler's forces. When reminded that her first priority is the rescue of British airmen, Hanna appeals to Col. Ilya. She tells him that they must cross the Hungarian border that day. He reluctantly agrees to take them to a remote spot on the border that may not be as well-guarded, but is far from Budapest. On the way to the border, the partisans and RAF squad intercept a Nazi train that they think is loaded with ammunition. But after the bridge is blown up and the doors of the freight car are opened, they find not ammunition, but refugees headed for the concentration camps. As the prisoners escape, Hanna's c.o. is killed; as he dies, he tells her to go to Budapest. The group splits. A smuggler takes Hanna and her comrades to Budapest. In the hold of the ship, Hanna convinces a pair of freedom fighters to form a Hungarian resistance. They agree to meet the next morning. But as Hanna and her partner attempt to catch a train, they are set upon by Nazi troops; they were betrayed by the smuggler. Hanna makes it to the train, but the man with her is cornered on a rooftop and commits suicide. Hanna considers it herself for a moment, but is captured by the Nazis and turned over to Hungarian police.

Conti-Prison, Budapest; June 7, 1944: Hanna is not imprisoned long before the brutal torture sessions under Capt. Rosza begin, but she will tell them nothing other than her name, rank, and serial number. From her cell, she hears the bells of the town. The other partisans discover Hanna has been captured. After more torture sessions, Hanna is visited by State Security officer Capt. Julian Simon, who tells her that she must decide whether she is to be tried for espionage, but again she refuses to cooperate. But finally she reveals her real name. Rosza and other officers break in on Mrs. Senesh and her friends and family having lunch. They take Mrs. Senesh away over the protestations of Margit, a famous stage actress who also lives in the house, and Rosza tells her mother's cousins that they had better get to the ghetto. Capt. Simon questions Mrs. Senesh, and reveals that Hanna is there in the prison. After a tearful reunion, Rosza taunts them, and Hanna attacks him. They take her mother to a cell. They tell Hanna that if she does not reveal her contacts and the code, they will kill her mother. Hanna attempts suicide in her cell, but is stopped by the jailer. A battle rages outside the prison. Mrs. Senesh awakens in her cell, and attempts suicide as well, but is saved, and is told the war will be over soon. Capt. Simon asks Hanna if there is one person in the world who would have her choose her mother's death over giving up the information. Hanna says yes, there is one; her mother. The next day, the jailer tells her that the Russians have reached the border, and that the torture will stop. Hanna sees from a newspaper that it is June 22, her mother's birthday. She makes a flower from the paper for the jailer to give to her mother.

Conti-Prison, Budapest; October 4, 1944: In her cell, Hanna sees Morse code signals reflected onto her wall from a mirror. She finds out that her comrades have been captured too, and are at the same prison. She signals them back. Hanna is taken to see Rosza, who tells her that she is to be turned over to the Gestapo. He also tells her that they are releasing her mother. Before Mrs. Senesh leaves, she tells Hanna that it will be a week before she is turned over, and that she will speak to some people in the meantime. That night, the jailer tells her that an armistice is being signed, and that tomorrow they will be free. Cheers break out throughout the compound.

Parliament Square, Budapest; October 10, 1944: The armistice deal is undone by treachery, and the Nazis arrive and install a new Fascist leader. The prisoners are herded out of their cells, to be taken away in trucks. Capt. Simon informs Mrs. Senesh that he has just been appointed state prosecutor for Hanna's case. She is to be brought to trial for treason. Simon places a quick call to Rosza, and Hanna is taken from the trucks.

High Court, Budapest; October 29, 1944: The court finds Hanna guilty of treason, and permits her to speak to the court. She tells them that Israel is her home now; shames the officials for their collaboration with the Nazis; and tells them that soon they will be standing where she is. The judges declare that sentence will be passed a week from that day.

High Court, Budapest; November 7, 1944: As Russian bombs fall, Simon reminds Rosza of Hanna's words, and in the absence of the judges, decides that Hanna should be executed at once. He

Ingrid's photograph in the 1987 "Z Book."

tells Hanna that she has been sentenced to death, unless she asks for a pardon. She says no. He will not permit her to see her mother, but Rosza lets Hanna write a note to her. Mrs. Senesh and Margit arrive at the prison. They think they are going to see Hanna, but she is already being led to her execution. As Mrs. Senesh tells Margit that Hanna's speech to the judges reminded her of when Margit played Joan of Arc, Hanna is shot by the firing squad. Simon rushes into his office and breaks the news to Mrs. Senesh. He gives her the note that Hanna wrote, tells her that Hanna was very brave, and rushes out. Mrs. Senesh and Margit leave the prison; Margit reads her the note as Russian tanks roll down the main street.

Review: A moving and beautifully mounted film, based on the true story of Hanna Senesh (Szenes), a Hungarian Jew who became a national heroine of Israel; she was recruited by the British Army in World War II to parachute into Yugoslavia to save Hungarian Jews about to be deported to Auschwitz. She was indeed a poet and playwright, and most of her most famous work is incorporated into the film, including the last lines she wrote before parachuting into Yugoslavia.

Maruschka Detmers, of *Mambo Kings* fame, paints a fine portrait of Hanna, smart and brave beyond her years. Ingrid puts in a stately appearance as a famous actress, and although her part is small, she is there for the closing scene, a moving reading of Hanna's last note to her mother which segues into Hanna's voice; she certainly holds her own with Oscar winner Ellen (*The Exorcist*) Burstyn. Genre veteran Donald Pleasence (*1984, The Flesh and the Fiends, You Only Live Twice, Halloween* series to name but a few), an actor who is unfortunately creepy even when he's playing a detective or doctor, is right at home as the torturer, as is David Warner (*The Omen, Time After Time, Time Bandits*), playing a man who, in real life, even thirty years after the events did not show one ounce of regret for his actions.

Tales from the Pitt: Hanna's War ... was a grueling story, but I was glad to be part of it. Peter Weir was going to direct it, but in the end he couldn't stand [producer Menahem Golan's] insistence on changes to the script and he told him to direct it himself. Luckily I had no scenes to do which would give me nightmares (*Life's a Scream*).

The Asylum
2000, Nunhead Films

Crew: Producer: Carol Lemon; Associate Producer: Harry F. Rushton; Director-Writer: John Stewart; Music Composer–Orchestrator: Christopher Slaski; Cinematography: Nathan Sheppard; Editor: Paul Green; Production Designer: Philip Blowers; Chief Makeup Artist: Kath Rayner; Prosthetic Makeup Artist: Rob Mayor; Makeup–Hair Stylist: Fay de Bremaeker; Sound Recordist: Mike Donald; Sound Designer: Christopher Ackland; ADR Mixer: Sandy Buchanan; Sound Re-Recording Mixer: Gareth Bull; Sound Consultant: Alex Hudd; Boom Operator: John Lewis; Digital Artist: Tom Hocking; Stunt Coordinator: Rod Woodruff; Stunt Double for Jenny: Darrell Parker; Gaffer: Joe Allen; Camera Operator: Perry Barwick; Electricians: Mark Clayton; James Gilligan, Dan Lowe; Second Assistant Camera: Pier Hausemer; Wardrobe Assistant: Michelle Wraight; Script Supervisor: Renee Glynne.

Films: *The Asylum* (2000)

Cast: Steffanie Pitt (Jenny), Nick Waring (William), Ingrid Pitt (Isobella), Patrick Mower (Dr. Adams), Robin Askwith (Neville), Colin Baker (Arbuthnot), Chloe Annett (Rose), Paul Reynolds (Snape), Dennis Huett (Mr. Brindle), Jean Boht (Mrs. Brindle), Jane Shakespeare (Emma Brindle), Robin Parkinson (Arthur), Kevin Ashley (Orderly), Hanna Bridges (Little Jenny), Antonia Corrigan (Little Rose), Carolina Giametta (Tessa), Dan Jeiphes (Inmate), Penn Linfield (Sandra), Sadie Nine (Mrs. Adams), Terry Taplin (Fr. Matthew), Christopher Whitehouse (Warden).

In *The Asylum*, Ingrid had one of her finest latter-day roles as well as the chance to star with her daughter Steffanie (courtesy Ingrid Pitt).

Synopsis: A beautiful woman in lingerie and a robe enters a room. She adjusts her robe when she sees someone else in the room. It is her young daughter Jenny, who savagely stabs her to death.

Jenny, now a woman, awakes from the nightmare with a scream. She is comforted by her sister Rose. Jenny also dreams of leaping from a clock tower. Her psychiatrist is her own father, Dr. Adams, a cold man who treats Jenny as if she were just another patient. Dr. Adams tells her that her mother's murder was never solved by the police, who attributed it to one of the inmates at the asylum which her father ran and where the family lived.

Isobella conducts a fake séance. After her clients, the Brindles, leave in a huff, she begins to see the same visions as Jenny in the crystal ball. When William, a patient of Dr. Adams, comes for his appointment, Jenny gets him to agree to take her to the asylum, to see if what she remembers is real. William, who has a crush on Jenny, agrees. Neville, a junkie, needs to score. As he looks at an empty syringe in disgust, he sees the same visions as Jenny and Isobella and bolts from his room. A priest is at a baptismal font. He screams as he, too, sees the visions.

When Jenny and William arrive at the dilapidated asylum, they find the doors unlocked. William plays with the switchboard, which activates a red flashing light. Jenny looks through paintings she did as a child; she is frightened to find that some of the paintings are scenes from her dreams. They explore the darkened corridors and come upon the room where the murder took place. Voices begin to explode in Jenny's head, and she runs until they stop. She screams as she sees an old man, but it is only the caretaker, Arthur, who was alerted by the alarm that William triggered. Jenny asks Arthur if he remembers her mother's death, and shows him the painting. Arthur tells her she couldn't have done it, because he discovered the body and she wasn't there. He tells her that Dr. Adams acted as if he had something to hide.

Arthur goes to check the furnace. He is not alone. His tea water reaches a boil, and he is stabbed to death. As William and Jenny lie on the asylum beds, she is again tormented by her nightmares. She awakes and screams at him to leave, so he wanders the corridors. He goes to the furnace room, where he discovers Arthur's corpse. He runs, but is trapped by the killer, who stabs him to death. By the time Jenny goes to look for him, his body has disappeared.

The next morning, developer Arbuthnot and his assistant Snape look over the asylum, with the intent of turning it into a luxury hotel. Snape takes notes while Arbuthnot tries to get the inside track with the real estate agent. As Arbuthnot gives the agent a bribe, they hear Snape scream. Arbuthnot investigates, and slips on bloody stairs. Then the bank notes he has just given the real estate agent begin to flutter down on him. He retrieves the money as he makes it back up the stairs, even pulling the last note from the agent's cold, dead hands. But soon he is lying in his own pool of blood.

In one of the rooms of the asylum, Jenny discovers Isobella. Isobella was an inmate there, who was released when they decided to sell the asylum, but she has returned because of the shared visions. Isobella tells her that she has turned the voices in her head into big business as a psychic. Then she tells Jenny that she murdered her mother, and runs screaming from the room. Jenny goes to look for her, and enters the chapel. The organ plays, and she sits in a confessional. The priest is the one who shares her visions, and tells her that he has seen himself, her, and the "others" in the flames of eternal damnation, helpless in the hands of the father — her father.

Jenny stumbles upon the lab, where she finds Neville looking for drugs. As he tries to shoot up, it causes Jenny to recall herself as a young girl injected by her father. She knocks the syringe from his hand and forces him into the room that haunts them all. There she uncovers the very chair in which Dr. Adams injected her. She also discovers a lot of projectors, the room from which they are controlled, and William's corpse. As she backs away, she is seized by a hand — her father's. He tells her that it is the last chance to rid her of her fears. He straps her in the chair and turns on all of the projectors. Jenny has the same nightmare as before, only now it is repeated over and over — with a different killer every time.

Neville cuts through the screen and helps her escape. She runs to the chapel, where the priest is conducting a service — with the corpses of Arbuthnot, Snape, and the real estate agent. Her father chases her to the top of the clock tower. He tells her that the other deaths couldn't be helped. She slips, and he pulls her back up. She asks him what really happened when she was a child.

He tells her about experiments with drugs and hypnosis and audio-visual stimulation, to try and determine what mental illness really is. This was the reason he didn't cooperate with the police, and why all of the test subjects believed they had killed Mrs. Adams. He begs for forgiveness from Jenny, Isobella, Neville and the priest. He tells them that they may all be guiltless, for there is one person who was part of the experiments who is not there.

Then he is stabbed from behind by that person — Jenny's sister Rose. Rose stabs him twice more and they fall from the roof to their deaths. Isobella says that solves everything, but Jenny says that all it proves is that Rose killed their father. They still don't know if she killed their mother, or any of the others. Of the four standing there, one could still be the murderer — or they all could be innocent. Now they are stuck together, and just have to trust one another....

Review: While not really a Hammer tribute *per se*, this tense low-budget thriller recalls the company's psychological thrillers like *Paranoiac* and overall lives up to that standard, although the performances truly make it what it is. Ingrid is absolutely nuts in this film (both literally and figuratively), completely over the top and making the most of every minute of it; she is both hilarious (the fake séance scene) and chilling (when she tells Jenny that she murdered her mother). Ingrid's daughter Steffanie is quite good in a role that some might see as some sort of vanity project because of Ingrid, but no, Steff is a working actress, since 1985, and in some of her other roles, she even gets to smile! Not so much here, except briefly; she is harried and harassed throughout, not so much a case of "Does she or doesn't she?" but "Did she or didn't she?" Other familiar and welcome faces include Patrick Mower (*The Devil Rides Out, Cry of the Banshee*, the "Nadine" episode of *Jason King* that also featured Ingrid), Robin Askwith (*The Flesh and Blood Show, Horror Hospital, Queen Kong, Let's Get Laid*), Colin Baker (*Dr. Who*), and Robin Parkinson (the Douglas Wilmer *Sherlock Holmes* TV series).

Tales from the Pitt: It was actually filmed in an old asylum, and the atmosphere was overpowering. Everyone was aware that it was essential to finish on time. Not for the usual reasons, but a much more important one. Steffie was scheduled to get married in Venice the weekend after filming finished. (*Darkness Before Dawn*) This film holds a very special place in Ingrid's heart because it features her daughter Steffanie in the lead role. She is very proud of Steffanie (and her grandchild) and hopes that they will have the opportunity to work together again. Unlike some genre actresses, Ingrid has an acute sense of fan loyalty. As a result of the film, Ingrid is eager to reunite with other Hammer actresses and hopes that they'll be involved in other projects that might also feature Stef.

Green Fingers
2000, Big H Productions

Crew: Producer: Harry F. Rushton; Executive Producers: Ian Bellerby, Mark Cotgrove, Bob Horner, Kevin Oaten; Director-Adaptation: Paul Cotgrove; Screenplay: Paul Cotgrove & Ingrid Pitt; Adapted from a Short Story by R.C. Cook; Script Consultant: Olwen Wymark; Original Music Composer: James Bernard; Editor: David Scott; Production Assistant: John Roy; Production Manager: Susan Lord; Photography: David Byrne; Makeup Artist: Rita Payel; Hair Stylist: Janene Hawkins; Assistant Director: Ian Neale; Art Director–Wardrobe: Don Fearney; Sound Recordist: Liz Courtenay; Boom Operator: Beth Wall; Focus Puller-Clapper Loader: Kevin Oaten; Still Photography: Rik Snowley; Gaffer: Mark Outen; Props-Models: Arthur Payn; Continuity: Geraldine Higgins; Catering: Bryan Garrett; Unit Drivers: Geoff Dove,

Simon Foxen; Nursing Advisor: Tina Cotgrove; Negative Cutters: Tru-Cut; Opticals: Filmoptic; Rostrum Camera: Terry Handley; Titles: Spectra Titles; Laboratory Liaison: Bob Rodger; Garden Set Dressers: Dave Simpson, Peter Ball, Dave "One Bounce" Thompson; Arriflex Cameras: Technovision; Michael Samuelson Lighting: Eddie Diaz; Laboratory Processing: Bucks Laboratories Ltd.; Original Music Performer: Paul Bateman; Original Music Engineer: Pat Grueber; Original Music Recorder: Gemini Recording Studio; Song "The Goona God": Henry Hill and His Orchestra; Song "Shout 'Em, Aunt Tillie": The West Jesmond Rhythm Kings; Cat Supplier: Nick White; Bicycle Repairman: Erik Richardson.

Cast: Ingrid Pitt (Mrs. Bowen), Janina Faye (Nurse Foley), Robin Parkinson (Sam), Rosie (The Cat).

Synopsis: Mrs. Bowen cleans her windows and looks out over her beautiful garden. She sees a black cat come through the fence, and goes down and offers it a saucer of milk. Then she grabs the hatchet beside the door. The next thing we see is the blood-spattered bowl.

Old Sam rides his bike up the lane and stops to see Mrs. Bowen; he tells her he'd rather work for her than for the miser up on the hill, and she tells him that if it weren't for that man, she wouldn't have her garden. Sam gives her some plants that won't bloom, to see if she can do anything with them since she has "green fingers." After he leaves, she buries the black cat.

The next day, when Sam brings her some more plants, she shows him that the dead plants he brought the day before have already bloomed. When he expresses his disbelief, she tells him she can make *anything* grow. He toddles off on his bike again, and she goes to the burial spot of the black cat. She sees that a plant is already rising out of the ground — as well as a cat's tail!

Mrs. Bowen is trimming a vine when she hears a cat's meow. She angrily hacks away at the plant growing over the grave, and she is attacked by a black cat. Sam arrives in the nick of time and gets a doctor. Mrs. Bowen awakes from a fitful sleep and is horrified to see that half her index finger is missing. Nurse Foley gives her a sedative after they argue, and sends Sam away.

Mrs. Bowen waken again and gets out of bed. She stumbles outside and crawls around the spot where she was attacked. She finds the finger and plants it. The next day, she walks to the garden and finds a hand growing from the ground! She throws a sheet over it and goes inside, where she sinks into her chair with despair. Nurse Foley stops by and argues with Mrs. Bowen again; Mrs. Bowen tells her to stop interfering and just to leave her alone; she gets Nurse Foley to leave by telling her she will go to visit her sister.

That night, Sam stops by and gets no answer to his knocks. He calls through the mail slot, but still no response. But Mrs. Bowen is still in her rocker, asleep. Out in the garden, the hand starts to reach out from under the sheet. Soon a fully formed figure stands in the moonlight. It grabs the hatchet by the door, and goes inside to where Mrs. Bowen sleeps. It brings the hatchet down again and again...

The next day, Sam stops by again. He chats a bit with Mrs. Bowen, who looks fit but acts subdued. She is in the garden when Nurse Foley arrives and tells her about the murder the night before — a woman found chopped to pieces, beyond recognition. Mrs. Bowen tells her to leave again and again, and Nurse Foley goes on until Mrs. Bowen grabs the hatchet, which is the last thing Nurse Foley sees...

Review: This is a very enjoyable semi-remake of an episode of *Rod Serling's Night Gallery* of the same name ("Green Fingers," January 15, 1972). Ingrid follows in the footsteps of Elsa Lanchester, who played Mrs. Bowen in the original. In that episode, Mrs. Bowen can make *anything* grow, but she is not the beneficiary of a miser; rather, a rich industrialist wants her farm (he already owns all the land around it) but she refuses to sell. The running dog capitalist pig, who will stop at nothing to get what he wants, finds out to his horror that she *can* make *anything* grow. Ingrid's Mrs. Bowen shares that trait, certainly, but she is much less the victim, as seen only a minute into the film (but it *is* a short film, so things rather do have to get moving straight away) — to think, she kills a cat, and may I say, not in a shy way! Both takes on the story are well-done, and very creepy and eerie. The only things missing from Ingrid's version are the three other stories that would make up the anthology it should have (and originally was, in *Night Gallery*) been part of. James Bernard's last score is wonderful, and gives it an air of Hammer, but it really seems more like a chapter of a great lost Amicus anthology. The best part is that, even though it's only 13 minutes long, it's pretty much all Ingrid all the time, much more satisfying (and more screen time) than her bits in movies ten times as long, plus she's got a role with some substance (which she in part was responsible for; see below); this can hardly be said about her parts as a hooker or a horny widow. And it's even more of a yeoman performance considering the circumstances; but Ingrid has been a super trouper her whole life.

Tales from the Pitt: I promised to do it if I could work on the script. Director Paul Cotgrove gave his blessing and I got stuck in. I wasn't at my best ... it was all I could do to keep focused on what I was doing (*Darkness Before Dawn*).

Dominator
2003, Renga Media–Sci-Fi Channel

Crew: Producer: Jim Brathwaite; Executive Producer: Doug Bradley; Executive Producer for the Sci-Fi Channel: Jason Thorp; Director: Tony Luke; Screenplay: Alan Grant; Additional Dialogue: Mark Radcliffe, Mark Riley; Score: Peter Haycock; Title Music: Cradle of Filth; Lady Violator Design: Yasushi Nirasawa; Animation–Visual Effects: Renga Animation Studios; Editors: Doug Bradley, Tony Luke; Production Accountant: Nick Wilson; Storyboard Artist: Dan Woods; Assistant Animators: Tim Synthetic, Amanda Berenyi; Principal Animation Director & Supervisor: Tony Luke; Title Sequence Designer: Mandy Gilholme; Software: Curious Labs, Apple Computer, Alien Skin Software; Hardware: Mach One Design Equipment, Cancom, Solutions, Inc; Webmaster: Carl Hadler; Original Publicity Art: Liam Sharpe, Steve Pugh; Series Editor for Comic Afternoon: Hiro Morita; Special Assistants: Kimiko Nirasawa, Megumi Sakai; Dialogue Recording: Crocodile Studios in London, AVT in Brighton, Soundhouse in Manchester; Sound Mixing: Renga Studios; Special Music Effects: Synthetic; Manga Series: "Dominator"/Alan

Grant, Tony Luke; Publishers: Kodansha Company; Thanks: Fay Woolven, Vanessa Warwick, Salvation Films, Sue Grant of Bad Press, Jonathon Clements, Glenn Fabry, Bradley Warner, Buichi Terasawa, Junco Ito, Mike Lake, Tony James, John Coulthart, Matthew Barnard, Art Storm of Fewture, Mick Wall, Greg Swann, Guy & Dave/SFX, Simon Powell, M.J. Simpson, Mick Mercer, John & Christine Luke, Monster Distributes, Ross Pelling, Zomba Records, Universal Music, Chris Leach, Berenice Baker, Can Can Studios, PBJ Management, London Management, Carrington Residential; Very Special Thanks: Liam Sharpe.

Voice Cast: Dani Filth (Dominator), Ingrid Pitt (Lady Violator), Seera Backhouse (Hellkatt), Doug Bradley (Dr. Payne/Lord Desecrator), Alex Cox (Bishop), Liza Goddard (Fina), Tara Harley (Tara), Marc & Lard (Extricator & Decimator), Sam Synthetic (Molly), Billie Godfrey (Lendra), Doug Devaney (Prime Minister), Mandy Gilholme (Judith), Robert Rankin (Narrator/Shagg).

Disclaimer: No ghosts, demons, zombies, or other non-human entities were harmed during the making of this film.

Synopsis: A dark war has erupted in Hell, where Lord Desecrator has challenged Lucifer for his crown and the key to Hell. But Lord Desecrator's own general, Dominator, steals the key for himself. Lord Desecrator sends an army of demons after Dominator, but Dominator defeats them. In desperation, Lord Desecrator sends three other warriors to destroy Dominator: Decimator, Extricator, and Dominator's former flame, Lady Violator.

London: In the basement of the Happy Passage Funeral Home. Dr. Payne and his assistant Stan are attending to a corpse when it is possessed by a demon. Payne decapitates the corpse and banishes the demon with the aid of a cross.

Payne's daughters, Tara, Fina, and Molly, have a band called Crowcut. One day before practice, they steal one of their father's occult books, *The Lost Chord*. When they play the chord, they unwittingly open up a passageway to Darkadia, the Sonic Region of Hell. The passageway opens just as Dominator is doing battle with skeletal demons, and both he and the demons are pulled through the rip in time. He defeats the demons with the aid of his Hell-spawned guitar.

Dominator cannot go back the way he came, so he must stay in this world until Dr. Payne can discover a reverse spell. In return for Payne's aid, Dominator agrees to battle anything else that comes through the portal. Soon Lady Violator, Decimator, and Extricator enter, and Dominator summons his Hell-spawned motorcycle for aid. A spectacular battle takes place in the air over London. Dominator is able to teleport his opponents away by using the key.

While Decimator and Extricator get drunk, Dominator joins with the band at their rehearsal space. Dr. Payne takes Dominator to Number Ten Downing, and is delayed by a battle with a minor demon. Dr. Payne introduces Dominator to the prime minister and advises him of the situation. The news of Dominator's deal to protect the Earth does not sit well with the PM's aide, Mr. Bishop.

The next day, when Crowcut premieres their new video, a horde of demons appears in Charing Cross, and Dominator flies to battle in his Hell-train. Dominator dispatches the demons, but is then attacked by the half-human, half-demon Hellkatt, a mercenary who has been hired by Bishop. Hellkatt is a demon on her father's side, and her father is

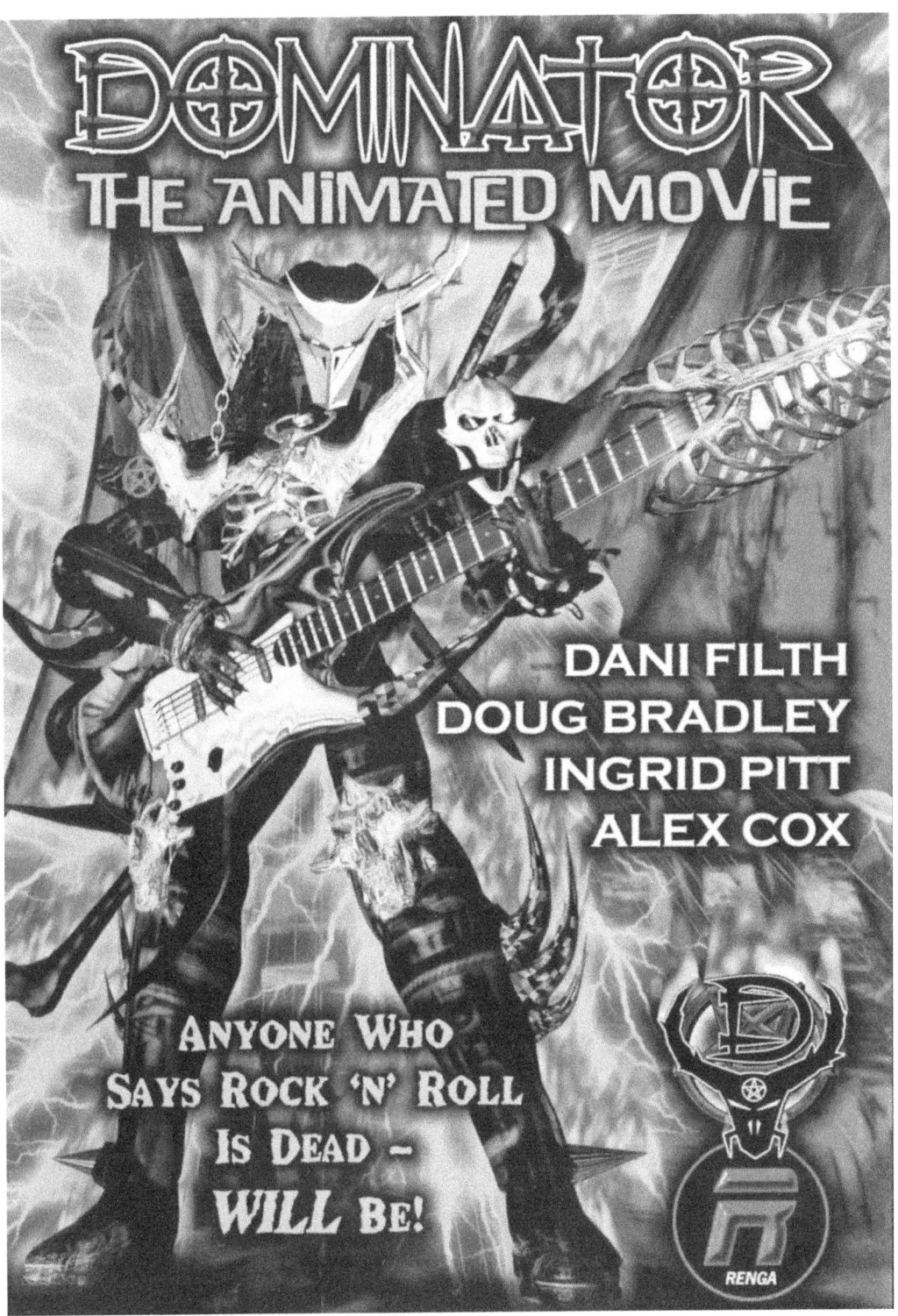

Promotional poster for *Dominator*.

none other than Lord Desecrator. As they begin to form an alliance, Dominator receives a call from Tara, who wants him to join with the band for a press conference at the Savoy.

Lord Desecrator confronts the drunken demons, banishing them from his service, and then pays a call on Bishop, who is really in his employ. By now, Dominator has arrived at the Savoy, and the band is hotter than hell, but the gig is interrupted by Lady Violator, who possesses Tara's body and once again engages in battle with Dominator. Dominator blasts Lady Violator's spirit from Tara, but her body and powers remain. Dominator appreciates Tara's makeover.

In the funeral parlor basement, Tara's jealous sister uses a ouija board to summon Lord Desecrator. She will get him the key, if he promises her Dominator. Meanwhile, Dr. Payne and Dominator survey a desolate part of town where over 200 homeless people have vanished over the last week. They uncover government involvement in the disappearances. After they return to the funeral parlor, sister's blood is mixed with Dominator's drink, weaving a spell over him. After they make love, she steals the key and turns it over to Lord Desecrator, whose powers become even more terrible. Tara sees Dominator and her sister together and runs away, heartbroken.

Decimator and Extricator offer their services to Dominator, who accepts. The government kidnaps Tara and takes her to a research facility near St. Paul's Cathedral. Bishop means to discover the secret of Lady Violator's powers; Dominator, Decimator, Extricator, and Hellkatt mean to stop him. They arrive in time to save Tara, but cannot prevent Lord Desecrator from taking advantage of the weakened fabric of the dimensions between Hell and Earth, ready to assume the mantle of Master of Reality. He devours Bishop, then assumes gigantic proportions as the cathedral explodes. The sky over London is again filled with horror: the tentacled skull of Lord Desecrator. London is burning.

Dr. Payne devises a plan: Since Lord Desecrator, after raping Hellkatt's mother, was able to return to Hell by means of a sacrifice, Payne will now, in effect, sacrifice Desecrator. Payne performs an exorcism while Dominator plays the Last Chord in reverse, and Lord Desecrator explodes in a hail of flame. The morning sun bathes London in its warm rays as Dominator and Tara go to Hell. And then Dominator's Hell-spawned cat-beast finds the Key....

Review: Depending on your view of anime and Heavy Black Death Speed Monster Chiller Horror Speed Metal, this animated British madness is either loads of fun or a right load of bollocks. For instance, as the narrator describes Hell as the place where "the beings in life who have committed atrocities are tortured for eternity," the camera pans across the gravestones of Alice Cooper, Ozzy Osbourne, Marilyn Manson, and Keith Richards. A character quaffs a bottle of Fabry Beer, in reference to British comic artist Glenn Fabry. At any rate, it's a historic achievement: the UK's first CGI-anime film. Dominator is voiced by Dani Filth, lead singer of British metal lords Cradle of Filth. This movie was not Ingrid's first voice work with the band; in 1998, Cradle of Filth released *Cruelty and the Beast*, a concept album based on the legend of the Blood Countess Elizabeth Bathory; Ingrid provided guest narration as, of course, the countess, and vocals for other songs.

More than anything else, the movie can be seen as a direct result of the influence of the horror genre in general and Ingrid Pitt in particular on Metal, Punk, and Goth; the fans who grew up loving Basil Gogos' covers for *Famous Monsters* or Ingrid Pitt in *The Vampire Lovers* are now the producers, directors, and actors who often, in turn, hire their heroes and expose them to whole new generations of fans.

Tales from the Pitt: I was to front three numbers on an album for a heavy metal group called Cradle of Filth, led by Dani Filth. I was a bit put off by the name of the group and the fact that they had more metal hanging from their appendages than your average knight in rusted armour. [Ingrid found the boys to be "quite sweet," nonetheless, upon completion of the job] For once I didn't rush around kissing everyone. With that much sharp metal on display it could have been fatal (*Darkness Before Dawn*).

Minotaur
2006, First Look International

Crew: Producers: Kimberly Barnes, Jonathan English, John Evangelides, Tom Reeve; Co-Producers: Mark Abela, Roberto Bessi, Charles Gassot, Antonio Guadalupi, Eda Kowan, Denise O'Dell, Christoph Meyer-Weil; Executive Producers: Jeff Abberly, Evan Astrowsky, Julia Blackman, Andrew J. Curtis, Romain Schroeder, Bob Sheng, Bjorg Veland, Daniel J. Walker; Assistant Producers: Sara Janasz, James Pass; Line Producer: Andrew Warren; Director: Jonathan English; Writers: Nick Green, Steven McDool; Music: Martin Todsharow; Cinematography: Nic Morris; Editor: Eddie Hamilton; Casting: Dave Hall; Production Design-Set Decoration: Anja Muller; Art Director: Keith Slote; Costume Design: Suzie Harman; Makeup Artists: Helen Speyer, Beatrice Stephany; Makeup Assistants: Fabienne Adam, Dunja Pflugfelder, Frederic Roeser, Sophie van der Windt; Makeup Designer: Lorraine Hill; Hair Stylists: Helen Speyer, Stephany; Hair Assistants: Dunja Pflugfelder, Frederic Roeser; Post-Production Supervisor: Sara Janasz; Executive in Charge of Production: Christopher P. Kibbey; Production Manager: Rozenn Le Pape; First Assistant Director: Robert Fabbri; Second Assistant Director: Ralph Eisenmann; Second Unit Director: James Pass; Assistant Art Director: Steve Summersgill; Art Department Coordinator: Michelle Bevilaqua; Art Department Assistant: Tanja Frank; Stagehands: Luc Arcisyewski. Julio Viega; Carpenters: Michael Bernardy, Thomas Bernardy, Alistair Overbrook; Painters: Angela Castro, Tilo Dries; Construction Manager: Bruno Zenatello; Construction Runner: Amilcar DeMatos Cadete; Prop Maker: Stephanie Rass; Assistant Props Men: Jose Mendes, Olivier Nunniger, Walter Oliveira; ADR Recordists: Dicken Berglund, Robert Edwards, Andy Thompson; ADR Mixer: Andy Thompson; Sound Re-Recording Mixers: Gareth Bull, Richard Straker; Supervising Sound Editors: Matthew Collingue, Danny Sheehan; Sound Recordist: Nick Stocker; Consultant on Dolby Film Sound: Mark Kenna; Boom Operator: Justin Smith; Dialogue Editor: Richard Todman; Key Animatronics Designers: Phil Ashton, Joshua Lee; Animatronics Designer: Guy Stevens; Animatronics Art Finishers: Astrig Akseralian, Melissa Lenihan; Animatronics Mold Makers: Barry Best, Giancomo Iovino; Animatronics Fabricators: Abbie Jones, Valerie Jones-Mendosa; Head Mold Maker: Barry Best; Animatronics Key Foamer: Andy Lee; Animatronics Workshop Technician: Alan Marshall; Special Animatronics Effects: Gary Pollard; Special Makeup Effects Supervisor for Hybrid Enterprises: Mike H. G. Bates; Special Effects Makeup for Hybrid Enterprises: Mark Kilburn, Dawn Whitehead-Binns; Prosthetic Effects Designer for Hybrid Enterprises: Mike Stringer; Special Effects Coordinator:

Edward Wiessenhaan; Special Effects Technicians: Roland Goddijn, Patrick Rappard, Rob Siepers; Lead Animator-Digital Compositor-Matte Artist: Tal Peleg; Lead Compositor-Matte Painter: August Coleman; CG Supervisor: Neil Atkins; Compositors: Nicholas Caramonta, Diego Galtieri, Wing Kwok, Jeremy Nelson; Visual Effects Production Coordinator: Chih-Min Chang; Visual Effects Executive Producer: John Follmer; Visual Effects Producers: Jennifer Glezer, Robert W. Morgenroth; Visual Effects Supervisor: David Kucklish; Co-Visual Effects Supervisor for DED Taiepai: Buddy Gheen; Visual Effects Editor: Aaron Paterson; Visual Effects Production Manager: Steve Woo; Titles: Thomas Diesselhorst; Digital Artist: Dirk Frischmuth; DI Supervisor: Frank Hellman; Lead Matte Painter: Dark Hoffman; Digital Compositors: Robyn Marie Kralick, Andre Taft; Technical Supervisor for Double Edge: Keith Lackey; Lighting & Effects: Arthur Sarkisian; Creature Animator: Jason Thielen; Matchmove and Visual Effects Artist: Panat Thamrongsombutsakul; Stunts: Rob De Groot, Suri Petonilia, Rick Wiessenhaan; Camera Operator: Ricardo Besantini; Second Camera Operator: Benny Ashoff; "A" Camera Operator: Martin Perry; Still Photographer: Etienne Braun; Electricians: Pascal Charlier; Gilbert Degrand, Pierre Dermience, Kevin Dresse, Arnout Glas, Oliver Krupke, David Alexander Trunk; Assistant Electricians: Philippe Lussagnet, Jacco Toufexis; Gaffer: Mick Durlacher; Second Unit Focus Puller: Pier Hausemer; Key Grip: Stephane Thiry; Grips: Nunes Neto Omei, Jean-Francois Roqueplo; Video Assistant: David Morais Rocas; Best Boy: Gregoor van de Kamp; Casting/USA: Marisa Ross, Matthew Skrobalak; Casting/Luxembourg: Monique Durlacher; Extras Casting: Katja Wolf; Costume Supervisor/Costumer: Lara Walker; Assistant Costume Designer: Alice Wolfbauer; Wardrobe Assistants: Angela Egan, Pierre Reichert, Peggy Wurth; Wardrobe Daily: Magdalena Marczynska, Francoise Meyer; Wardrobe Seamstress: Isadora Steyaert; Assistant Editor: Robert Hall; Colorist: Ronnie Afortu; Orchestrator: Maurus Ronner; Conductor: Joris Bartsch Buhle; Score Engineer: Rene Moller.

Cast: Tom Hardy (Theo), Michelle Van Der Water (Raphaella), Tony Todd (Deucalion), Lex Shrapnel (Tyro), Jonathan Readwin (Danu), Rutger Hauer (Cyrnan), Maimie McCoy (Morna), Lucy Brown (Didi), James Bradshaw (Ziko), Fiona Maclaine (Vena), Claire Murphy (Nan), Ingrid Pitt (The Leper), Ciaran Murtagh (Turag), Angela Furtado (Handmaiden), Donata Janeitz (Ffion), Shiva Gholamianzadeh (The Queen), Stefan Weinart (Taran), Paul Jenkins (Nan's Father), Eddy Klima (Blind Elder), Suzy Westerby (Old Morna's Voice); Chames-Dine Taha, Mohamed Takourt, Felix Pinto, Djil Hannah, Lesdel Korutos-Chatham (Antelope Soldiers).

Synopsis: In the Iron Age of gods and monsters, the known world was ruled by a dark empire, from their island of Minos. They worshipped the bull, the most powerful of all the gods. The tablets recount that as the empire grew, their hedonism and greed knew no bounds. The people longed for more than stone idols; they demanded a living god. In response, sickened minds indulged in the forbidden arts, and decreed that the queen should offer herself to the bull in order to create the perfect being, a unification of god and man. For 13 months, the creature grew inside her, pure, precious, every care bestowed. To ensure its safe passage into this world, it was cut from the queen's belly and suckled on the blood of its own mother. The newborn was presented to the people; the palace hailed their creation and the power of the empire strengthened. But as the beast grew, so did its hunger. In revenge for the murder of a royal prince, a terrible tax was placed on the village of Thena in the northern territory. Every three years, eight youths, male and female, would be taken to the palace by royal soldiers, lowered into the labyrinth, and sacrificed to the Beast. The power of the bull seemed invincible as the time for the next sacrifice drew near.

As Theo and Danu herd their sheep in the snow-covered mountains, they see the hooded figure of the mysterious Leper, who never appears unless as an omen. His father tells him not to worry about it. Theo is despondent; his love had been taken for the previous sacrifice, but his father tells him he must move on. Theo cannot be taken for sacrifice, as he is next in line as the leader, and the villagers are angry, and not going to take it much longer.

The next day, a wolf kills one of Theo's sheep. When he chases it deep into the woods, he sees a sign carved on a tree that matches the amulet he wears. Then he sees the Leper. The wolf is her familiar. Inside her cave, the Leper tells Theo that although his love has been taken, she has not been sacrificed; she is in the labyrinth of the monster. She tells him that to save his love he must curse a god and kill the Minotaur.

Theo tells his father of his quest, but his father sends him into the mountains. He and Danu are set upon by Tyro and Ziko, two angry young villagers. Their struggle is interrupted by the sight of the ships of the Bull-Soldiers. A thunderstorm breaks as the soldiers gather the eight youths, including their opponents of moments before. Theo distracts one of the soldiers and takes the place of one of the girls.

In a cage, the other youths discover Theo among them, and their reactions are as different as the youths themselves. They are led in a procession to the throne room. The decadent king Deucalion, who continually inhales hallucinogenic gas from a skull, picks two of the girls to show Theo how they prepare virgins for sacrifice. After breathing in the gas, the princess Raphaella forces the girls to breathe in her exhalations. After doing so, they begin to passionately kiss the princess on the lips, and then each other. All are taken back to their cage, and Deucalion tells her never to speak in the chamber again.

In her bedroom, Raphaella tells her handmaiden to bring Theo to her, unnoticed. After being gassed, Theo lies on the bed, where Raphaella slips him the tongue and asks for his help. Deucalion overhears, bursts in, and has Theo removed. He then tells Raphaella that she will be had by every guard and slave in the palace, and then fed to the Minotaur.

Shortly thereafter, Deucalion taunts Theo twice and then has him lowered into the labyrinth. His companions are then lowered in one by one. The Minotaur is awakened, and the girl who gave herself willingly to be sacrificed is the first to go. Meanwhile, Deucalion is speaking to Raphaella; he tells her that he forgives her and prepares to take her to his chambers to love her up. But she breaks away from the procession, telling him she would rather die than bear his child. She throws herself into the pit.

Once there, she is set upon by the group, who were expecting the Minotaur. She tells them she can lead them out, but they do not trust her. As one of the girls loudly voices her hatred for the princess and the others, she is gored from behind, through the mouth, by the Bull-Beast. As Raphaella's handmaiden unlocks the door through which she thinks they can escape, she is discovered by Deucalion and killed. He re-locks the door. To get to the door, though, the group must pass directly through the Minotaur's own grisly stable. Now that they cannot get out through the door, some of the others are convinced it's a trap, and begin to argue, which brings the beast-god down upon them. As they scatter, another is taken.

One-sheet poster design for *Minotaur*.

Deucalion enters through the door through which Raphaella had planned escape. Danu tells Theo he has seen his lost love alive. Danu turns on Theo, who in turn turns on the madman, demanding to know where she is being kept. They are then attacked by the Minotaur, who has been attracted by the screams of Deucalion for Raphaella. The Beast rushes Deucalion and one of his guards; the cowardly Deucalion shoves the guard in front of himself and then locks the door behind him. And then it's the turn of the newly minted lovers, who are trying to climb back up through the opening of the pit. The girl slips from Tyro's desperate grasp and falls onto the horns of the Minotaur.

Theo makes his way through the maze and finds his lost love. They embrace, and she tells him that they have been waiting for him. When he pulls back, he discovers she is actually a skeletal corpse. Morna gives Danu a charm to ward off the beast, and then departs to look for the others. Almost instantly, the Minotaur appears, and Danu's death screams echo through the chambers. Theo, enraged and devastated, throws his amulet, which gives off sparks. Rafaella tells Theo that he was meant to slay the Beast. The Minotaur appears, and Tyro lunges at the monster. As Theo and Rafaella flee, the creature turns its attention to Tyro; soon the walls are red with his blood.

Rafaella and Theo discover a pool of water. Theo calls out the Minotaur, who charges him, but Theo steps aside and the monster crashes into a wall. But the beast is only wounded, and even more insane with rage. Leading the satanic bull through clouds of gas, Theo scrapes his amulet on the walls, causing sparks which ignite the gas. The Minotaur is consumed in a sheet of flame, which Theo and Raphaella escape by jumping into the pool. The flames shoot up through the mouth of the pit, and more explosions are caused by the gas; Deucalion is trapped under a beam, and the statue of the Bull-God topples.

Theo and Rafaella emerge from the pool. But as they make their way through the rubble, the Minotaur, one horn cracked off, crawls from the wreckage. It makes one last lunge at Theo, who gores it with its own broken horn. As the labyrinth continues to crumble, they make their way back to the throne room. The scorched Deucalion proclaims his love for Rafaella, who suffocates him. She tells the people that are hers now to take off their masks. The sacrifices will stop. The reign of the Bull-God has ended.

Review: Although generally panned by both fans and critics alike, the admittedly rather daft *Minotaur* does have some redeeming virtues. Ingrid as the spooky Leper, with a makeup reminiscent of *Countess Dracula*, is effective in her unfortunately limited screen time; and the effects are fairly well-done for a low-budget ($7,000,000) film, which was originally produced for the Sci-Fi Channel and filmed in Luxembourg. But the beast is not the classical Minotaur of legend, a man's body with a bull's head and tail; the monster in *Minotaur* is all bull; gigantic, skeletal, seemingly covered with human skin, and one of the main deviations from the legend on which the film is based. Theo (Tom Hardy from *Blackhawk Down*) is based on Theseus. Also, the king's sister in this film was actually his daughter in the legend, and there were no sexual relations. There is no string to show the way out of the maze. The film also alters the ending of the legend, and ignores the aftermath (Theseus was given the hand of the daughter, who is claimed by a god, who instructs Theseus to abandon her, for which she curses him, which results in his father's suicide). Ingrid's Leper character has no parallel in either the legend or Greek mythology, unless it is very loosely based on the ancient woman, Hecale, whose hut Theseus takes shelter in on his way to kill the Marathonian Bull. But here I am frothing with indignation over the liberties taken by a B-movie that, like most such B-movies, lays absolutely no claim to veracity to the source material! Still, Tony (*Candyman*) Todd as Deucalion gives a deliciously perverse performance, and recalls Dennis Hopper in *Blue Velvet* when he "inhales the sweetness" from his skull-bong, which he does well and often. In some ways, it is a typical "Teenagers Die" movie, but in fairness, at least Bronze Age teens getting gored by zombie bull gods is not yet an overworked genre (and of course, the sacrifices in the legend were youths, so it is accurate in that respect, not simply a sop to modern young audiences). Rutger (*Bladerunner*) Hauer is top-billed, but his part, like Ingrid's, amounts to little more than a cameo. Ingrid insisted that a real wolf be used in her scenes as her familiar, rather than just a dog that resembled a wolf.

Beyond the Rave
2008, Hammer Film Productions

Crew: Producer: Ben Grass: Co-Producer: Alan Raistrick; Executive Producers: Simon Oakes, Marc Shipper; Line Producer: Wendy Bevan-Mogg; Director: Matthias Hoene; Writers: Tom Grass, Jon Wright; Cinematography: Ben Moulden; Editor: Lucas Roche; Production Design: Alex Lowde; Art Director: Melanie Light; Assistant Art Directors: Ryan Haysom, Mia Summerville; Makeup Artist: Beth Roberts-Miller; Special Makeup Effects Artists: Robbie Drake, Tristan Versluis, Jo Wand; Special Effects Hair Technician: Maria Cork; Production Manager: James Harris; First Assistant Director: Richard Newman; Second Assistant Director: James Nunn; Third Assistant Director: Ernest Riera; Storyboard Artist: James Husbands; Prop Maker: Lee Fenton-Wilkinson; Sound Recordist: Ashok Kumar; Additional Sound Recordist: Haresh Patel; Sound Editors: Matt Baird, Scott Laing; Sound Mixer: Kumar; Additional Sound Mixer: Jamie Gambell; Post-Production Sound: Finn Curry; Boom Operator: John Crossland; Additional Boom Operators: Gambell, Simon Bysshe; Foley Editor: Cristina Aragon; Special Effects: Haysom; Special Effects Makeup: Versluis; Pyrotechnician: Neil Jenkins; Visual Effects Supervisor: John D. Bell; Compositor: Robert A. Willis; Stunt Coordinator: Dave Judge; Stunts: Jude Poyer; Stunt Performers: James Nicholas Fuller, Kerry Kisses Dunne, Ian van Temperley; Assistant Camera: Jon Britt; Still Photographer: James Nicholas Fuller; Electricians: Sam Alberg, Arsenio Assin, Michael Franklin, James Leckey, Eren Ozkural; Gaffers: Pawel Polak, Martin Taylor; Grip: Pete Nash; Sparks: James Harverson; Casting: Hanna Birkett, Sue Pocklington; Casting Assistant: James Nunn; Costumer: Lesette Ormond-King; Additional Costume Designer: Rebecca Gore; Assistant Editor: Richard Deeb; Production Coordinator: Kate Glover; Production Assistants: Mark Evans, Benjamin Harris, Peter McLeod, Richard May, Mark Stein; Location Manager: Jacques Groenewald; Unit Publicist: Axelle Carolyn; Script Editor: Nic Ransome; Dialogue Coach: Mel Churcher; Floor Runner: Hugh Kerrigan; Special Thanks: Eddie Dias.

Cast: Nora-Jane Noone (Jen), Jamie Doman (Ed), Tamer Hassan (Rich Crocker), Sebastian Knapp (Melech), Lois Winstone (Lilith), Trevor Byfield (Leopold), Mark Wingett (Ed's Dad), Jody Halse (Big Jim), Steve Sweeney (Tooley), Ingrid Pitt (Tooley's Mum), Sadie Frost (Fallen

Angel), Alexander Newland (Faustino), Leslie Simpson (Belial), Jane Maskall (Strigoi), Matthew Forrest (Necro), Neil Newbon (Nikolai), Lee Long (Danny Crocker), Lee Whitlock (Terry Crocker), Katie Borland (Tina), Oliver Milburn (Sgt.), Lauren Gold (Lucretia), Emma Woollard (Anais), Ruaraidh Murray (Dave), Danny Tennant (Idiot), Tristan Matthie (Adonis), Sophie Holland (Lydia), Jackson Scott (Botz), Vivienne Harvey (Tess), Oliver Gilbert (David), Arron West (Kevin), Elizabeth Elvin (Bea), Colin Dent (Bazarov), Lou Williams (Hotel Girl), Caroline Acosta (DJ), Gethin Anthony (Noddy), Lucy Barker (Psychiatrist), David Doyle (Detective), Paul T. T. Easter, Ryan Haysom, James Nunn, Pete Tong (Ravers), Alexander Ellis (Army Mate), Mark Evans (Ripped Throat Man), Dave Fire Tusk (Vampire Fire Clown Gimp), Norman Gregory (Angry Farmer), James Harris (Soldier), George Hilton (Punter), Irene Lacak (Vampire Sword Girl), Taylor Morgan (Girl One), Luke Nash (Pipsqueak Chav), Beeny Royston (DJ Black Cat), Jeff Rudom (Bouncer), Nicole Verdugo (Iraqi Girl).

Synopsis: A young soldier on night patrol hears sounds in the woods, and comes upon a vampire killing a girl. She gasps his name, and the soldier opens fire on the fiend. The muzzle flashes give way to a scene in a military hospital in Iraq. As the soldier, Ed, is lying on a table, a nurse tells a detective that Ed has been classified as suicidal. He was the last man standing after a savage battle, clutching a Union Jack standard atop a pile of corpses. The detective tells Ed he wants him to answer a few questions, and it is the day before, as Ed's squad receives their orders for deployment, and then given leave until morning. Ed wants to go to one last rave before he leaves. His mate Necro picks him up in his used hearse. He sees that Necro has the initials F.B.P. scratched into his stomach.

Ed asks Necro where his girlfriend Jen is. Necro is forced to tell him about something that had happened at a previous rave: Ed stood Jen up and she was seduced by the mysterious Melech. Melech is seen driving an army truck, with a girl tied up in the back. As the hearse races through the country side, Necro calls a drug dealer. After the conversation, the dealers take a bound man out of their boot, and leave him lying on the ground. That night, a pirate-station DJ is broadcasting from a bunker near a warehouse. Two lads enter and turn him on to coke. Then they reveal their fangs and sink them into him, splattering blood everywhere.

Melech jumps out of the truck, leaving the bloody girl in the back. He picks up Jen and they make their way to the warehouse, where they are told to leave. They bribe the guard to let them rave there. Later, as one of the ravers is walking through the woods, he is attacked by vampires.

Ed and Necro meet the dealers at a strip club, where the dealers think they beat up the vampires who just drained the DJ. The vampires laugh, and then disappear. After getting high with Necro and friends, Ed retrieves a Union Jack standard from his home that he promised his father he would take to war. The vampire duo finds one of the dealers alone, subdues him, and carves the initials F.B.P. into his stomach with a fingernail.

As Ed, Necro and friends do coke, Ed realizes that the initials on Necro's stomach, read backwards, are the numbers of the pirate radio station that can tell them where the rave is. A young punk gives the scratched dealer that information. Another raver wanders off into the woods and is killed by vampires.

Ed and the others arrive at the rave. He finds Jen, and they go outside. He tells her he is shipping out in the morning; they argue and she walks away. Ed goes back in and is shown a pill with a tarantula inside; he is told it contains the blood of the immortals. He takes it and trips hard. He wanders into the woods and shares a spliff with an old man, who tells Ed that he smells death on him.

As one of the ravers relieves himself at a urinal, he is approached by two girls who take him into the woods. Two stoners argue, and then meet the old man, who shares a spliff with them and then tells them he is a vampire. They laugh and walk away, but he chases them down and kills them with a sword. Then he smokes a spliff.

At the rave, Ed attacks Melech, who apologizes for his affair with Jen. Ed and Jen go outside again, where they declare their love for each other. Ed gives her an engagement ring,

Hammer returns, and Ingrid returns to Hammer in this Internet serial from 2008 as pictured on this promotional sticker.

and they succumb to passion. Elsewhere, the girls remove the lucky raver's pants and tie him to a tree. His luck runs out when they bare their fangs and leave him a bloody mess. Inside, a vampire girl on a swing plucks a victim from the crowd. When Ed wanders in on Tooley's mother, she wails and thinks Ed is her son. She is still screaming when he leaves.

In a truck, Necro's girl tells him she is 145 years old, and shows him her fangs. In the warehouse, Jen displays her ring, and Melech declares it is time to begin. The dealers gather up weapons, and gaslines from huge tanks are hooked up to the building. The ravers begin dropping to the floor. Necro bolts from his scene back to the rave, where he sees ravers being slaughtered by vampires. Inside, Ed and Necro's friend Jim lies in a gas-induced stupor and is forced to watch a girl being bound and drained of her blood.

The drug dealers break into the warehouse, and the ravers start to scatter. Ed sees the corpses all around, and picks up a discarded sword. He finds Jen, and is attacked by a vampire, which he kills. The vampires lock the drug dealers in and kill them. A dying dealer gives the vampires the two-fingered salute.

A vampire attacks Jim, but Jim dispatches him. Melech looks for Jen, Ed, and the others. Jim sends Ed and Jen into the bunker to safety while he fends off the bloodsuckers. Jim cuts off a vampire's hand and then kills him before he himself is felled by Melech's crossbow.

Necro finds Ed and Jen, and tells them he has decided to join the vampires. When Ed asks him to think of all the innocent people he will kill, Necro asks him how that is different from what Ed will do in Iraq. He shows them an escape hatch, in which they are attacked by a vampire. Jen decapitates him.

Ed and Jen crawl out of the hatch and onto an ATV. Ed is carrying the Union Jack standard. Melech's crossbow then claims Jen, who proclaims her love for Ed as she dies in his arms. Ed takes off on the ATV, bearing his standard like a lance; he runs it through Melech as Melech hits him with a bolt from the crossbow. It is stopped by a medallion Ed wears. Melech pulls out the standard. As he advances on Ed, the sun comes up. Melech catches fire and then explodes. Ed wanders to the roadside, where he is found by his fellow soldiers. Over his protests, they hustle him into their truck and drive away. A detective surveys the murder scene at the warehouse. Necro, now sporting fangs, turns to his vampire girlfriend and her uncle, the ancient stoner from the woods. They put on their sunglasses and take off in the hearse.

Review: As a sign of the times, *Beyond the Rave* was not released as a complete film, *per se*, but in "webisodes" as an online serial on MySpace (they were later collected on DVD) to "recalibrate the DNA of Hammer Films for a new audience." So in form it harkens all the way back to the Dick Barton serials, and in function, it is basically an updated version of *Dracula A.D. 1972*, where the undead menace are young hipsters. But attempts to modernize the ancient myths like *A.D. 1972* had still contained recognizable elements of classic Hammer gothic: actors like Cushing and Lee, sets, etc. But there's no Cushing or Lee this time around; the only connection to classic Hammer in terms of the actors is Ingrid, but she is on hand for name value only, and her part is very small, though showy (or as showy as one can be in 45 seconds). The horror aspects are as interesting as various questions about moral codes, especially the climactic scene where Ed, who is going to serve in Iraq, questions Necro's killing; in both cases, innocents suffer, so who is "right"? Like the *Urban Gothic* television episode featuring Ingrid, and like *Sea of Dust*, it is an intense and occasionally savage commentary on contemporary decadence and moral corruption, and shows that, even after all these years, absolutely nobody else in the world does female vampires like Hammer.

Tales from the Pitt: This is a platter for today's gourmets. It might be a bit savage and gory for me, but I predict the cognoscenti will love it. [It is] a highly entertaining and remarkable film — even if my part could be missed by an ill-timed sneeze (*Den of Geek*, 3/18/08).

Sea of Dust
2008, 309 Productions

Crew: Producers: Patrick T. Rousseau, Noah Workman; Line Producer: Patrick T. Rousseau; Line Producer of Re-Shoots: Amanda Platner; Executive Producer: Pauline Bunt; Associate Producer: Arlene Wachstein; Director-Writer: Scott Bunt; Music: Jasper Drew; Cinematography: Brian Fass; Film Editor-Sound Editor: Ron Kalish; Costume Designer: Joanne Haas; Key Makeup Artist–Key Hair Stylist: Erica Oddo; First Assistant Directors: Arash Mokhtar, Noah Workman; Set Dresser–Key Production Assistant: R. Zachary Shildwachter; Props: Lora Parker, Rich Parker; Sound Mixer-Boom Operator: Ken Jackson; ADR Mixer–Assistant Sound Re-Recording Engineer: Marc Hayes; Additional ADR Recordist-Sound Re-Recording Mixer: Paul Michael; ADR Mixer in New York: Mark DeSimone; Key Special Effects Makeup Artist: Josh Turi; Visual Effects for On-Line Editor–Colorist: Savvas Paritsis; Stunt Coordinators: Kenneth Robert Marlo, Bill Timoney; Gaffers: Nat Aguilar, Zeynep Oguz Catal, Freddy Cintron, Ahmed Fallat; Key Grips: Christian Miller, George Selden; Grips: Boris Cifuentes, Robert M. Neilsen; Assistant Camera: Peter Yoon; Second Assistant Camera: Pam Dela Pena, Gary Powell; Steadicam Operator: Helge Bernhardt; Digital Imaging Technician: Othmar Dickbauer; Electrical Intern: Miranda Rhyne; On-Set Costumer: Rebecca Edmonston; Wardrobe Assistant: Jennifer Hoddinott; Additional Wardrobe Assistant: Cathy Carrey; Assistant Editor: Andrew Montlack; Production Assistants: Noel Estrada, Scott Friedman, Michele Knotz, Jorge R. Loyola; Production Coordinator: Megan McGowan; Public Relations Director: Edward Ferruggia; Script Supervisor: Stefanie Mitchell; Additional Script Supervisor: Katie Dixon; Special Thanks: Jon Fordham, Daryl Goldberg; Thanks: Rob Roy.

Cast: Tom Savini (Prester John), Ingrid Pitt (Anna), Troy Holland (Stefan Christoph), Bill Timoney (Prof. Sorell), Edward X. Young (Dr. Maitland), Pete Barker (Chalmers), Eve Blangiardo (Harpy), Collen Cohan, Edward Ferruggia (Blood Chamber Torture Victims), Al Contursi (Torture Victim), John Correll (Lord Dunsten), Rosalynd Darling (Harpy Hydrant), Sarah Dauber (Elizabeth), Laura Eff (Black Forest Girl), Suzi Lorraine (Black Forest Woman), Kenneth Robert Marlo (Black Forest Man), Megan McGowan (Meadow Girl), Celina Murk (Siren), Angela Rose Popovic, Maria Rose Popovic (Evil Twins), Dylan Randazzo (Boy), Stuart Rudin (Carla's Father), Darby Lynn Totten (Carla), Amber Wootan (Zombie Villager), Edward A. Young, Elizabeth Young (Dying Couple on Beach).

Synopsis: "For over 800 years, belief existed in a Christian super-king named Prester John, who was said to dwell across a mythical Sea of Dust. Explorers sought him, religions

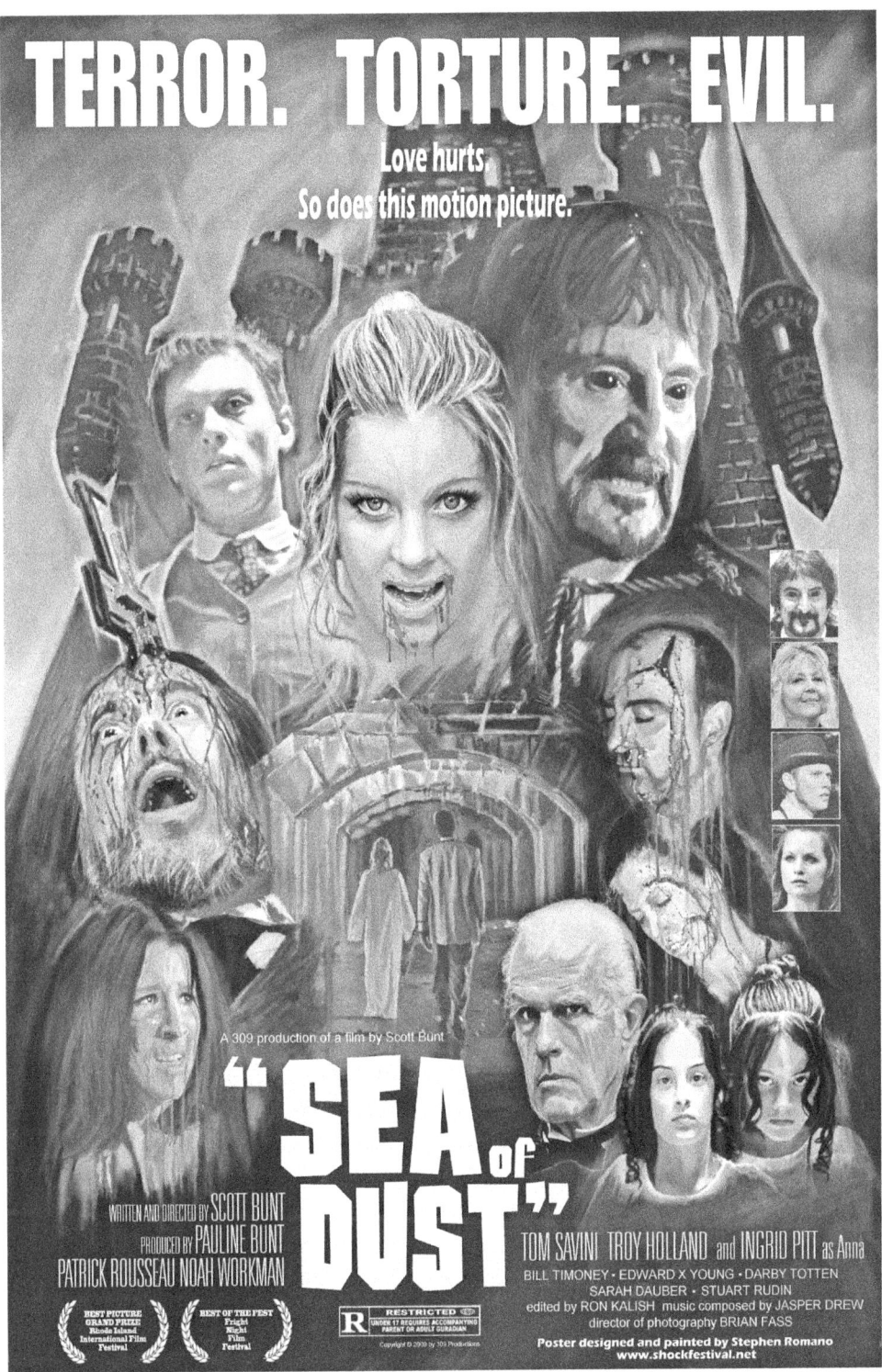

One-sheet poster for *Sea of Dust* (courtesy Scott Bunt).

courted him, and crusaders waged war in his name — until one day, when Prester John began to believe in himself."

A peasant girl frantically makes her way through the rooky wood. She begs a man for help, but to no avail. She runs up the steps of a house, screaming. Her head explodes.

A 19th century medical student, Stefan Christoph, sits in the study of his mentor, Professor Sorel. Stefan can barely bring himself to relate the events that have befallen him since he last saw the professor. Sent to assist an isolated village whose occupants were falling into trances, Stefan admits that he took the opportunity to stop at the home of his would-be fiancée. The following story unfolds in flashback:

Christoph arrives at Elizabeth's palatial estate intending to ask for her hand in marriage. He is given a hateful reception by everyone except the family's maidservant, sweet old Anna. The butler, Chalmers, makes veiled threats. Elizabeth's father, the overbearing Lord Dunsten, tells Christoph never to return. Even Elizabeth seems to reject his overtures.

Christoph dejectedly continues his journey. He is on his way to see Dr. Maitland, the village physician, but his journey is interrupted when he discovers a girl lying in the road. He stops the carriage and takes the disoriented girl, Carla, with him. She seems to have fallen under the same spell as the villagers he is traveling to assist. As he traverses the Black Forest, he has visions. He sees twin girls in white dresses in the woods and the face of a man with vacant black eyes. In her trance, Carla whispers the name Prester John.

Upon arrival, Dr. Maitland is not pleased to see Christoph; he had requested that Professor Sorel come himself. Still, he shows Christoph a body in his lab. It is the headless corpse of the village girl, the latest in a series of mysterious killings. Despite his reservations, Dr. Maitland relates his theories on the matter. He has come to believe that the mythical Christian King, Prester John, has somehow manifest. He's heard Prester John's name whispered by other victims. For some reason yet unknown, Prester

Ingrid gives *Sea of Dust* co-star Edward X. Young a birthday smooch in this behind-the-scenes shot (courtesy Scott Bunt).

John seems to be causing psychologically vulnerable villagers to fall into trances. They awake under his evil influence. And those who attempt to resist, who struggle against his dictates, end up like the corpse that lies before them. Their heads explode from the inside.

Carla awakens with a start and begs Christoph to stay by her side. While he is keeping watch, he falls asleep and has a sexually charged dream about her. She wakes when he does — and promptly stabs him with a knife she has somehow appropriated from a locked cupboard. After she is subdued and securely bound, Maitland insists that Prester John will now try to kill Christoph, since knowledge is the enemy of religion. He urges Christoph to take Carla home in the morning, to witness additional results of the trance. Carla's father was Prester John's first victim.

As Christoph prepares to take Carla home the following day, cleaning up in the nearby lake, he has another vision. This time, he imagines Elizabeth beckoning him from the depths of the lake. A hand reaches up to him from the water, but disappears when he is interrupted by Maitland. Maitland sends the couple on their way, warning Christoph not to untie Carla's hands until she is safely home.

When they get to her house, Carla's father thinks that they have spent the night together and attacks Christoph with an axe. Christoph lands atop a fallen tree, and the old man buries the axe between his legs. The father pulls back hard and leaves the blade buried in the trunk. When Christoph shoves him, Carla's father falls on the blade.

The death of Carla's father seems to unleash something in Christoph. Carla tells him he is "chosen," and asks him if he wants to beat the truth out of her. His brain lights up with the vision of a Siren on a distant beach; he rushes toward her call, and then he is underwater. He ultimately washes up on a faraway shore, across the mythical Sea of Dust, where his body is retrieved by a mariner who tears a hole in his neck with a boathook. Christoph wanders up over the shore and through the surrounding woods to an elegant castle. He enters and is greeted by a bodiless spirit — and then by Prester John, who reveals his dark origins...

Brought into existence by the power of belief and the blood that was shed in his name, he has come to judge mankind by the same standards it has applied to non-believers. The Christian monarch has chosen Christoph to be a general in the army of Christ he is amassing to share the suffering of Christ with an ungrateful world. Prester John has been kidnapping people's souls and transporting them to his domain, where they are tortured until their bodies agree to comply with his wishes on the "other side." He tells Christoph that since men have used him as a symbol for their crusades, he has come to bring the kingdom of Christ to its completion, and woe to those who resist God's will. But is it real, or a nightmare?

Christoph awakes next to Carla's father's corpse. Disoriented, he stumbles back into the Black Forest. Suddenly he is surrounded by bestial sounds and unseen menace. He runs through the forest and right into two women and a man. One of the women, a beautiful blonde, tells him that they have been sent to convert him or kill him; it doesn't matter which to them. He strikes out at them and tumbles, seemingly endlessly, down a hill, and then headfirst into a tree. Then he runs straight into the terrible trio again. The smaller girl kicks him in the shins and the blonde tries to stab him with the same knife

Sea of Dust poster art by Jeff Pittarelli, "Illustrator of the Unreal," with Ingrid at top right (courtesy Scott Bunt).

Carla had previously used. While their male cohort restrains Christoph from behind with a pitchfork, the blonde stabs her partner by mistake. Christoph gains control of the knife and stabs the blonde in her most vulnerable spot — the brain. The man attacks with the pitchfork, but he gets his pitchfork back — squarely in the head.

In Prof. Sorel's study, Christoph finishes his story. Surprisingly, it doesn't seem to have shocked Sorel. It is almost as if he had expected these outcomes. Together they retrace Christoph's steps. First they stop at Elizabeth's and find Chalmers the butler savagely whipping Anna. Sorel asks Chalmers where Lord Dunsten is, and Chalmers replies that he has no master other than Jesus Christ. He says that academics should have their tongues cut out so they cannot profane God's name. Further, he insists that salvation cannot be attained without suffering. Just as he starts to attack Sorel, Christoph knocks him out. They turn their attention to Anna, who realizes that she is in danger of being overtaken by Prester John. She begs them to put her out of her misery and faints.

As Sorel loads her into the carriage, Christoph interrogates Chalmers, giving him the same whipping that Chalmers had just given to Anna. He finds the violence surprisingly exhilarating. Christoph tells Chalmers that he thinks he might be cut out for this type of work after all, and breaks the fingers of one of his hands. Then he breaks the other set. Chalmers tells him that Prester John has sent for Elizabeth, and that he was beating Anna because she was "a non-believer, a danger." It looks like Christoph will beat Chalmers to death until Sorel steps in.

Leaving the butler to his own devices, they travel to Maitland's with Anna in tow. Carla has returned to the doctor's cabin, where Maitland has bound her to a chair. Sorel begins to question her when Maitland calls him to examine Anna. She is hollow inside. Sorel speculates that Prester John has her insides, and that he requires substance on both sides of reality in order to be effective. Maitland asks him if he thinks Carla is hollow, too. Sorel replies "probably," and that Christoph is well on his way. He says their bodies are waiting to be filled — by an ideology. Maitland stitches up Anna and places a cross beside her for protection.

As the group tries to figure out a plan of action, villagers begin to advance on Maitland's. Sorel indicates that the villagers are not there to attack. They are massing because they expect Christoph to order them to action. Like it or not, he is their general, and this suggests another disturbing possibility. Sorel says that perhaps Prester John has already possessed one of them, that the messenger has become the message. As if to reinforce this, Anna rises from the surgery table clutching the cross.

Sorel decides that their only hope lies with Carla. Since Prester John's victims must have substance on both sides of reality, he realizes that Prester John must exist in both spheres too. He hypnotizes Carla in the hope that she will reveal Prester's true identity, enabling them to destroy the evil Christian king. This session is cut short when Maitland thinks he hears villagers breaking into the back of the cabin. On his way to investigate, he notes that Anna's body now seems to have its face covered. He pulls back the sheet, only to find a grinning skull; his anatomical skeleton has been substituted. Before he has time to react, Anna leaps from the shadows and plants the crucifix in his skull. The impaled Maitland drops to the floor, writhing in agony, a sight that brings Anna lucidity.

Sea of Dust Behind-the-scenes shot of Ingrid with director Scott Bunt and his wife Pauline (courtesy Scott Bunt).

She decides to take her own life rather than be a helpless tool of Prester John. Screaming Elizabeth's name, she plunges the cross into her own stomach and falls across Maitland's lifeless body.

The discovery of this bloodbath is too much for Christoph to bear. He concedes defeat. Sorel insists that they press on, instructing Christoph to follow the lead of Christ. Christoph should use his pain to focus on the connection between his pain and the world's. Inspired, Christoph returns to Carla. He now has a plan. "You and Prester may be connected," he tells Carla, "but we're connected too. Stronger." They place her on the operating table and Christoph uses his growing sexual attraction for the girl as a porthole to the other side. Like some messianic figure, he imagines himself reborn for the betterment of mankind.

Suddenly Christoph is back on the beach, surrounded by washed-up souls. Elizabeth's voice calls his name. She tells him that they have all been waiting for him. Since Prester is all-knowing and all-seeing, they have been expecting his arrival. Christoph demands that she take him to Prester.

As they enter Prester's lair, they hear the screams of tortured souls. Christoph is shocked by Elizabeth's pronouncement that this is "the sound of Christ's triumph." He tells Elizabeth that he is not there to lead Prester's armies, but to bury him. Elizabeth vanishes and Christoph must press on alone. He discovers Carla's battered soul, being tormented by the mythological Harpy. Carla begs his forgiveness for the things her body has been forced to do on the other side. She explains that he is the only one who possesses any degree of free will.

As if to reinforce this, Prester reappears. He again tells Christoph that he has been chosen to lead and, dismissing his objections, tells him that the kingdom of God is more important than matters of conscience.

Prester sends Christoph back to the Black Forest, where he finds himself surrounded by the corpses of his previous victims. The blonde and the pitchfork-wielding woodsman rise from the dead to confront him. Even Dr. Maitland appears, belittling Christoph for resisting. Maitland tells Christoph that he doesn't even know what side he's on. The three corpses seize Christoph and torture him with the weapons that have haunted his previous encounters, including the omnipresent knife. Maitland tells Christoph that it is useless to resist. Prester is inside them all.

But the blonde gives Christoph an epiphany: It suddenly occurs to him who the spirit of Prester inhabits. Christoph fantasizes a conversation with Elizabeth's father, in which the evil Lord Dunsten admits his culpability, all the while forcing his daughter to lick her own blood from his fingers. "Sacrifice is the great equalizer," Lord Dunsten tells him. "Allow it to set you free."

Christoph realizes that the only way to defeat Prester/Lord Dunsten is to go back to the beginning. And this is what he does. He is transported back to Elizabeth's house, back to the beginning of the film. But instead of letting her father chase him away, he uses the knife to stab Lord Dunsten and cut him open, while Elizabeth screams in horror. The violent attack also mortally wounds Prester, who appears on a cross and thanks Christoph for the blessing of martyrdom. But does this action really free Elizabeth or is it merely the culmination of Christoph's sexual obsession? Worse, does it represent the fulfillment of Prester's plan? Christoph has no time to contemplate any of this. He ensures the outcome by slitting Lord Dunsten's throat. He has chosen. It will be for his god to decide the morality of his actions.

Review: There are a lot of levels to this film, and it works on every one of them. It is a Hammer "tribute," although it is not merely another imitation of something which can never be imitated. It's a gore film, but it's not non-stop, and that isn't its sole appeal, nor does it degenerate into "torture porn." It's also an art-house film, it's a comedy and, as the icing on the cake, it is one of the strongest anti-intolerance statements made in recent film history (one of the main reasons Ingrid was so excited about working on the film). Ken Russell calls it "substantially mythic."

Ingrid's enthusiasm shows in every line of the role, which, along with *Asylum*, offers up her best latter-day showcase. Actually, the subversive subtext is clearly much more than just icing on the cake; it's the film's reason for existence. So in this sense, while it draws upon the look and pace of films like *Taste the Blood of Dracula*, it also recalls that film's stance on the hypocrisy of those who regulate others' morals and the lengths they will go to, to force their morals on ... well, everyone. The ending somewhat recalls that of another slightly subversive film, *A Clockwork Orange*, when Alex says, "I was cured, all right." But to say that it has the pace of a Hammer classic is to do it somewhat of a disservice, because although it does maintain that overall, the surrealistic heights which it attains are far outside the normal Hammer parameters. The film has been compared to Lynch and Cronenberg as well, although *Sea of Dust* is far more entertaining and far less pretentious than either. In between, there are all sorts of "spot the reference" moments for genre geeks — everything from Fisher and Bava to Raimi, Cocteau, and *Yellow Submarine*! There's a nod to Amicus, who had a character named Maitland in nearly every one of their films. And there is a hilarious scene where Christoph rolls down a simple hill in the woods for what seems like a hundred miles, only to roll right onto a tree! But the influences are woven together so skillfully that it never lapses into mere fourth-order simulation, and is quite able to stand on its own considerable merit.

Tales from the Pitt: My part as Anna is a little ambiguous. I'm sort of *chatelaine de la maison* with matronly duties as well as being the "demonic disciple" of Prester John. As I see everyone around me falling foul of the evil Prester, I have a bit of a change of heart, which doesn't go down well with the Master. I get a good whipping to put me in my place. The whipping peels back my skin to reveal that I am a hollow woman — something very symbolic there, I'm sure. I must admit, blushingly, that I do mad, old, leprous, hollow harridans rather well (*Den of Geek*, 7/28/08).

The Tell-Tale Heart
2009, Redfield Arts

Crew: Producers: Mark Redfield, Stuart Voytilla; Associate Producers: Jessie Lilley, Jennifer Rouse, Wayne Shipley; Director: Mark Redfield; Screenplay: Mark Redfield, Stuart Voytilla; Story Adaptation: M. Christopher New; Based on "The Tell-Tale Heart" by Edgar Allan Poe and the American Civil War stories of Ambrose Bierce; Music: Jennifer Rouse; Cinematography: Jeff Herberger; Editor: Sean Paul Murphy; Costume Designer: Suzanne Devier; Production Manager in Baltimore: Ruth Holmes; Production Manager in Los Angeles: D. J. Summitt; Special Effects: Eric Supensky; Digital Imaging Supervisor for iO Film: Christopher Dusendschon.

Cast: Mark Redfield (Capt. Winter), Ingrid Pitt (Mrs. Clarion), Robert Quarry (Mr. Clarion), Jennifer Rouse (Nora), Kevin G. Shinnick (Charles), Ted Newsom (Occultist), J. R. Lyston (Rev. Bottle), Tony Tsendeas (Capt. Cross), P. J. Foster (Joshua), Ralph J. Lincoln (Abraham Lincoln), Saundra Jordan (Mary Todd Lincoln).

Synopsis: "Set in the final days of the American Civil War and the time of Abraham Lincoln's assassination, *The Tell-Tale Heart* tells the tale of Captain Winter, an army officer obsessed with hunting down and capturing a mad killer who tortured and murdered his comrades during the conflict. The trail to catch the murderer leads to a boarding house on the outskirts of war-torn Richmond, Virginia, run by Mr. and Mrs. Clarion. There, Capt. Winter discovers that the madman is masquerading as the old couple's son and is turning the boarding house into a house of horror" (Redfield Arts website).

Review: This film was never completed, due to the death of Robert Quarry. R.I.P., Count Yorga, we miss you. What a team he and Ingrid would have made!

Tales from the Pitt: We were to play husband and wife.... [O]riginally it was supposed to go in the spring [of]. Then I got a call from the producer, Mark Redfield, to say that shooting had been postponed because his money man had kicked the proverbial bucket. He said he was rescheduling for August-September. Bob rang me a couple of days later. He was still fairly upbeat, but admitted he wasn't too confident about the film. As he explained to me, he felt that if the film didn't shoot before the end of the year, he wouldn't be around to do it. I feel really sad that we didn't have that last chance to work together (*Den of Geek* website column, 3/3/09).

"THE NAUGHTY BITS": HAMMER'S KARNSTEIN TRILOGY

Hammer's "Karnstein Trilogy" (*The Vampire Lovers*, *Lust for a Vampire*, and *Twins of Evil*) all flowed from the wellspring of one story, "Carmilla," by J. Sheridan Le Fanu (August 28, 1814–February 7, 1873). Born in Dublin, Le Fanu worked in many genres, but it is his supernatural and mystery fiction that he will most fondly be remembered for. "Carmilla" is the best-regarded, due to the popularity of the films based on it, but there are other, equally chilling examples, including the classic novel *Uncle Silas*. "Carmilla" was published only a year before Le Fanu's death, as part of *In a Glass Darkly*, a collection of five short stories presented as the posthumous papers of the first fictional occult detective, Dr. Martin Hesselius, who is not himself a character in the story.

The Vampire Lovers (1970, AIP-Hammer)

Crew: Producers: Harry Fine, Michael Style; Associate Producer: Louis M. Heyward; Director: Roy Ward Baker; Screenplay: Tudor Gates; Based on the Story "Carmilla" by J. Sheridan Le Fanu; Adaptation: Harry Fine, Michael Style, Tudor Gates; Music: Harry Robinson; Photography: Moray Grant; Editor: James Needs; Art Director: Scott MacGregor; Costume Design: Brian Cox; Makeup Supervisor: Tom Smith; Hair Stylist: Pearl Tipaldi; Production Manager: Tom Sachs; Assistant Director: Derek Whitehurst; Construction Manager: Bill Greene; Sound Recorder: Claude Hitchcock; Sound Editor: Roy Hyde; Recording Director: Tony Lumkin; Dubbing Mixer: Dennis Whitlock; Camera Operator: Neil Binney; Wardrobe Mistress: Laura Nightingale; Music Supervisor: Philip Martell; Continuity: Betty Harley.

Cast: Ingrid Pitt (Marcilla/Carmilla/Mircalla Karnstein), Peter Cushing (General Spielsdorf), George Cole (Roger Morton), Kate O'Mara (Mme. Perrodon), Ferdy Mayne (Doctor), Douglas Wilmer (Baron Joachim von Hartog), Madeline Smith (Emma Morton), Dawn Addams (The Countess), Jon Finch (Carl Ebhardt), Pippa Steele (Laura), Kirsten [Lindholm] Betts (First Vampire), Janet Key (Gretchen), Harvey Hall (Renton), John Forbes-Robertson (The Man in Black), Charles Farrell (Landlord), Shelagh Wilcocks (Housekeeper), Graham James (First Young Man), Tom Browne (Second Young Man), Joanna Shelley (Woodsman's Daughter), Jill Easter (Woodsman's Wife), Olga James (Village Girl), Lindsay Kemp (Jester), Sion Probert (Young Man in Tavern), Vicki Woolf (Landlord's Daughter).

Synopsis: Via flashback, Baron von Hartog tells his story: His sister has died an unnatural death, and he lies in wait in Karnstein Castle to avenge her. He sees the shrouded vampire leave her unholy tomb, and he knows that the fiend cannot return to the grave without that shroud. After it has shed the ghastly garment to search for victims in the village, von Hartog retrieves it.

Outside the village inn, a drunken young man takes in the night air. He turns and smiles; back inside, they hear screams. When they open the door, the young man is propped in the doorway, blood streaming down his back. Its grisly meal finished, the vampire returns to the grave, only to see von Hartog defiantly waving its shroud from the window of the castle. The vampire advances, and von Hartog waits, sword in hand. When it steps into the torchlight, it is not some loathsome, moldy corpse, but a beautiful young woman. Von Hartog is mesmerized, and the girl embraces him. But as she presses her chest to his, the cross about von Hartog's neck burns her, and she recoils, fangs bared. The baron swiftly recovers his senses, and decapitates her.

Britain's "Z Book" (their equivalent of the American "Player's Directory") features an actor's vital stats, recent roles and contact information for their representatives. This is the portrait attached to Ingrid's entry for 1970.

Back in the present, a birthday ball is being held for General Spielsdorf's daughter Laura. Two new guests arrive; a countess and her daughter, the stunningly beautiful Marcilla. One of the young men immediately asks her to dance; Laura's young man Carl thinks she only has eyes for Laura. Another guest enters: a tall man in black who seeks out the countess and whispers in her ear. She tells Spielsdorf that a dear friend of hers is dying and that she must leave immediately. Spielsdorf offers to have Marcilla as their guest. The countess accepts. Marcilla slips outside, where she sees the man in black on horseback. He smiles, revealing a pair of fangs, before riding away.

The next day, Marcilla and Laura walk in the garden, and Marcilla tells Laura how beautiful she is. That night, Marcilla goes to her window and sees the man in black on the horizon. Laura has a nightmare about a huge cat and a pair of piercing eyes. She awakens with a scream. Marcilla is gone from her room.

Laura's nightmares continue, and she grows weaker by the day. She is grateful for the presence of Marcilla, who tells her that she will never leave her. Marcilla kisses her on the lips and breasts. The next day, General Spielsdorf and Carl discuss their concerns; it seems that Laura will see no one but Marcilla. Spielsdorf sends Carl for the doctor, but by the time they return, she is dead. Upon examination, the doctor discovers two small puncture marks on Laura's breast. Spielsdorf screams Marcilla's name, but Marcilla has

Madeline Smith looks on in horror as Ingrid tries to put the bite on Jon Finch in *The Vampire Lovers*.

disappeared back into the mists surrounding the Karnstein crypt. Laura's friend Emma Morton is overcome with grief. That night, a village girl making her way home through the woods is attacked by a female vampire as the man in black watches.

The next day, when Emma and her father are out for their morning ride, they witness a coach crash. The occupants are unhurt; Mr. Morton helps them from the coach. It is the countess again. She introduces her daughter Carmilla. The countess was hurrying to see her dying brother; Morton offers to have Carmilla as their guest until her mother can return...

Emma's governess, Mademoiselle Perrodon, attempts to teach Emma her lessons, but Emma's mind is on tomorrow's parties. That evening, she goes to Carmilla's room. Carmilla is bathing; exiting the tub, she wraps a towel about her waist and sits topless, combing her hair, at the dressing table. Carmilla encourages Emma to wear one of her dresses, and tells her she must wear it without a bodice. Emma, now nude herself, teases Carmilla. Carmilla chases her around the room, finally catching her on the bed, where they embrace. When they go downstairs for supper, Mr. Morton is surprised to see his daughter looking so grown-up. Carmilla has red wine for supper, looking frustrated.

That night, Emma begins to have the same fearsome nightmares as Laura did. Mme. Perrodon tries to comfort her by telling her it was only a shadow thrown by the cat. But

Rare playing card deck which featured shots from various Hammer films.

the dreams continue, and Emma begins to exhibit signs of anemia. Mr. Morton must leave on business, and he tells Mme. Perrodon to call in the doctor. Carmilla tells him she will take care of Emma as if she were her own sister, and then refuses breakfast. She says she is not hungry...

On the road to his appointment, Mr. Morton has a chance meeting with Carl. He tells Carl of Emma's symptoms, and asks him to call on her. He also tells Carl he'll have two pretty girls to visit, as Emma has a friend staying with her; this of course arouses Carl's suspicions.

That night, as Emma prepares for bed, Carmilla reads to her from one of Emma's romance novels. Emma asks her if she doesn't hope some handsome young man will come into her life. Carmilla says no, and she hopes that Emma doesn't either. Suddenly, she professes her love for Emma, but they are interrupted by Mme. Perrodon. Carmilla bids them both goodnight; Perrodon looks bemused and Emma flustered. Later, a woodsman's daughter is awakened by a female hand reaching out to stroke her face, and the girl smiles. Her mother discovers her bloody corpse, and her screams fill the night. Carmilla again disappears into the mists.

The woodsman's daughter's funeral procession passes by Emma and Carmilla. As the bells peal ever louder, Carmilla loses control. She begs Emma to comfort her. Later,

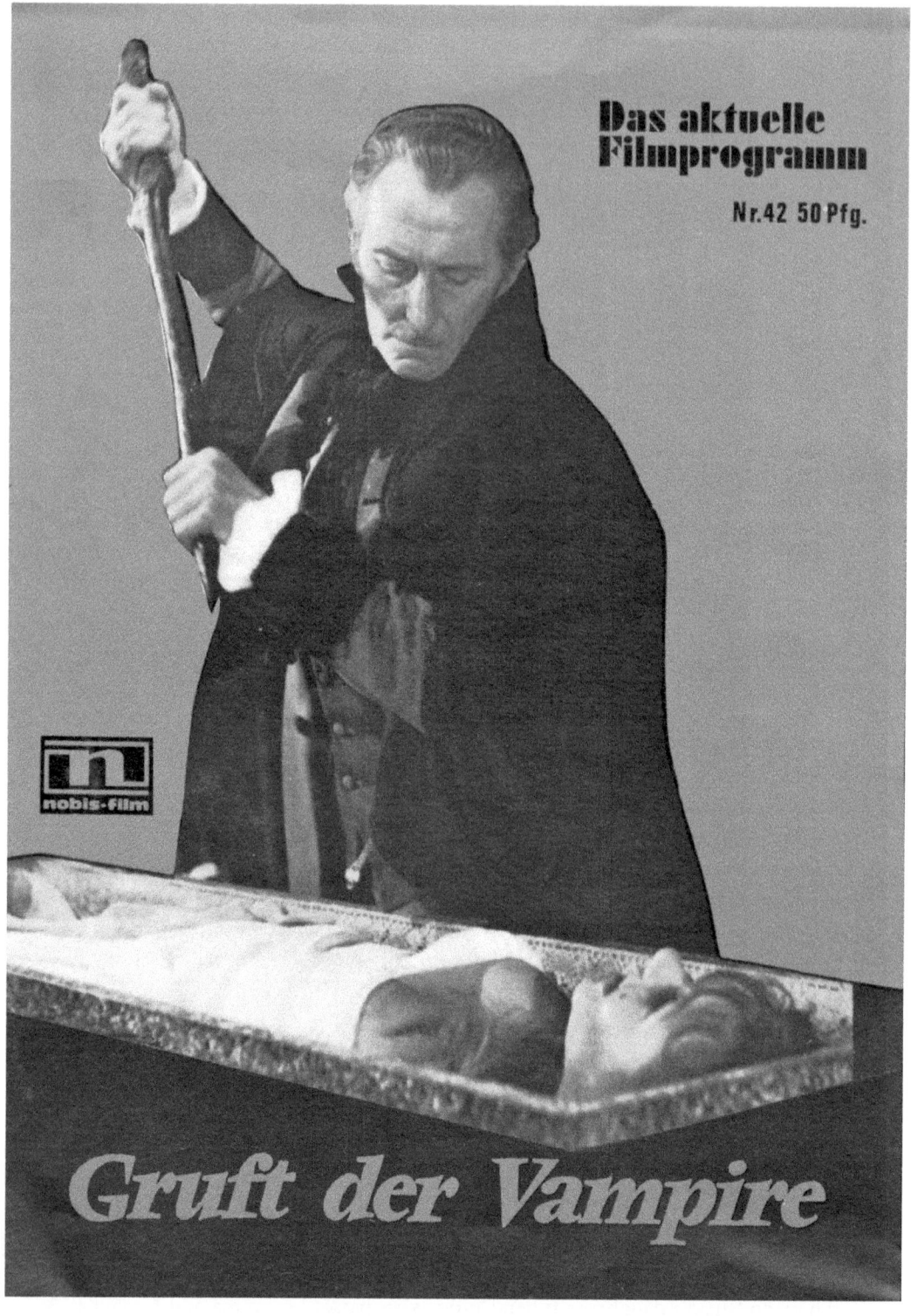

The Vampire Lovers' German program featuring Peter Cushing and Pitt.

as Carmilla again reads to Emma, she tells the girl she must leave. Emma tells her more about her dreams. She tells her that a giant cat crawls over her and lies across her, and then turns into Carmilla. Carmilla tells Emma she will always be safe with her; she undoes the girl's nightgown and begins to kiss her about the neck and breasts. The man in black sits on a distant hill. Mme. Perrodon is writing in her journal. She hears Emma scream, and rushes to her room. Emma tells her she has had another nightmare, and that the cat has bitten her; she shows Mme. Perrodon two small puncture marks on her breast. Carmilla appears and tells Perrodon the holes were caused by a broach. She gives the governess one like it, and after she fastens it to her dress, Carmilla's hands fall slowly, lightly brushing Perrodon's breasts. Mme. Perrodon looks at her knowingly. When they leave the room, Carmilla gives Perrodon a come-hither look, and leaves her bedroom door open. The governess enters and closes the door behind her. Carmilla tells her to turn down the lamp, and slips off her nightgown...

Carl arrives the next morning, but Perrodon tells him to come back next week. The maid discovers Emma's weakened state, and the butler also becomes concerned. Perrodon puts them off as well. That night, the butler gets drunk at the inn and, spurred by the innkeeper's talk, becomes even more suspicious of the truth. On his own, he summons the doctor. The doctor arrives, and Perrodon also tries to send him away, but he will not leave. She runs from the room when the butler brings in garlic flowers. The doctor places a cross around Emma's neck. The man in black waits outside yet again. Carmilla tries to enter Emma's room, but she too recoils from the garlic flowers and cross.

As the doctor rides back to the village, he is thrown from his horse. He is attacked by Carmilla, seen for the first time in her full vampiric fury. The doctor's screams echo into the night. Morton refuses to believe the vampire tales, until the innkeeper tells him of Baron von Hartog and the Karnsteins. As Morton goes to get the doctor again, not knowing he is dead, Carmilla stands at the top of the steps, smiling. On his way to the doctor's, Morton encounters Spielsdorf and Baron von Hartog; their coach also carries the corpse of the doctor. Spielsdorf and von Hartog tell Morton that their destination is Karnstein Castle. The group enters the crypt, where von Hartog begins to relate his tale to Morton.

At Morton's estate, Carmilla begins her seduction of the butler. Von Hartog tells Morton and the others that he did not destroy the whole family; there was one grave he could not find. He shows them a portrait of Mircalla Karnstein, wearing a necklace with a red stone; it is the girl they know as Marcilla and Carmilla. The man in black laughs as Carl races back to the estate. Mircalla completes her seduction of the butler by putting the bite on him. Spielsdorf and the others frantically search for the grave. The butler, now under Mircalla's power, orders the maid to remove the cross and garlic from Emma's room.

Spielsdorf and the others find the grave, as Mircalla enters Emma's room and tells her she is taking her with her. As she leads Emma down the steps, Mme. Perrodon appears and begs Mircalla to take her, too. When Mircalla comes to her, the governess falls into her arms — but she sees Mircalla's fangs too late, and screams. Mircalla sinks her fangs into Mme. Perrodon's flesh. Carl bursts in, sword in hand, and is set upon by Mircalla.

She knocks away the sword, but he uses the hilt of his dagger as a cross to hold her at bay. She disappears into thin air and returns to the crypt, where Spielsdorf and the others lie in wait. She eludes them again, until Morton finds her necklace (the same one as in the painting). They discover her coffin under the floor. Morton prays while Spielsdorf drives a stake into Mircalla. When the hammer strikes, Emma bolts up in bed and screams. Spielsdorf tells the baron there's no other way, and decapitates the corpse. As the man in black watches the men put the coffin in the ground, the portrait of Mircalla decomposes.

Review: With every great actor or actress, regardless of genre, there is the signature role. For the purposes of this book, we can cite Boris Karloff's Frankenstein Monster, Peter Cushing's Dr. Frankenstein, and Bela Lugosi and Christopher Lee's respective Draculas. The list surely also includes Ingrid Pitt as Carmilla Karnstein. *The Vampire Lovers* was not the first adaptation of "Carmilla," nor was Ingrid the first female vampire, nor was the movie the first suggestion of lesbianism in vampire films. Dreyer's *Vampyr* was (very loosely) based on Le Fanu's masterpiece, as was Vadim's (also loosely) *Blood and Roses*; *Dracula's Daughter* and Vadim's film had explored the lesbian subtext to varying degrees. But even though *The Vampire Lovers* certainly exploits the sensationalistic aspects to their fullest, it is still, at its base, a faithful and stylish adaptation of "Carmilla"—the only significant change from Le Fanu is in the character of Mme. Perrodon (in the story, she is middle-aged and rotund, a far cry from stunning Kate O'Mara). And while exploitation in its most crass sense may be the film's *raison d'être*, it transcends those intentions and becomes, at points, truly erotic—particularly in the scene where Carmilla seduces the willing Perrodon.

Ingrid's portrayal of Carmilla represented a new breed of female vampire; Dracula's wives, in the 1931 version, are subservient, and Carroll Borland, although an undeniably striking presence in *Mark of the Vampire*, is still basically ornamental. With Gloria Holden as *Dracula's Daughter*, the female vampire was elevated to the main character, but Countess Zaleska was a most unwilling vampire who wanted nothing more than to be released from her curse, and does what she does simply because she must. Ingrid's Carmilla is more subtly shaded; like Zaleska, her bloodlust is, at times, seemingly a burden, but moreso because of her emotional attach-

The Vampire Lovers stars Madeline Smith (left) and Ingrid (courtesy Ingrid Pitt).

ABC Film Review cover of the most beautiful Hammer Vampire Girls ever in one film (left to right): Madeline Smith, Ingrid Pitt, Kate O'Mara, Pippa Steele, Kirsten Betts (front) of *The Vampire Lovers*.

Every monster knew they'd made it when they appeared on the cover of the legendary *Famous Monsters of Filmland*. *Vampire Lovers* star Ingrid was immortalized via this beautiful Ken Kelly portrait from issue #122.

ment to her victims. But there is no active wish on the part of Carmilla to be released from her curse; it may cause her untold sadness that she must love whom she kills and kills those she loves, but she has accepted her fate, and even enjoys it. Of course, Ingrid's Carmilla is not the first "lusty" screen vampiress; Hammer Films and productions from Mexico had already done a great deal to amp up the aggressive sexuality of the female of the species. But in most cases, the effect was still basically ornamental (more so, actually, in terms of the amount of flesh displayed), even when they were the protagonist; embodiments of pure lust and evil with little or no regard to anything except the satisfaction of their thirst and/or evil schemes. This can even be said of the beautifully mounted, visually stunning *Blood and Roses*, although Annette Vadim as Carmilla is more a representation of pure evil than an embodiment of it. Like Yutte Stensgaard in *Lust for a Vampire*, she is never, in the words of Tim Greaves and Kevin Collins (in *Daughter of the Night*), "convincingly threatening enough as the incarnate with a taste for human blood." Ingrid's performance captures perfectly the balance between pathos and power that has always made for the most effective screen monsters, and in the process opens the door that ensured that female vampires would no longer be content as simple accessories.

Familiar faces are seen in leading and character roles; in both this and *Lust*, Pippa Steele is Carmilla's first victim. Other shared actors between the three films include Harvey Hall, Kirsten Lindholm and Peter Cushing, for true Hammer legitimacy. Cushing would have appeared in the second film as well, but had to bow out at the last minute when his wife Helen fell seriously ill. She died a short time later, and he was never really the same afterwards, although of course he continued to act and give superb performances; the following year he told *The Radio Times*, "Since Helen passed on, I can't find anything; the heart, quite simply, has gone out of everything. Time is interminable, the loneliness is almost unbearable, and the only thing that keeps me going is the knowledge that my dear Helen and I will be united again some day. To join Helen is my only ambition. You have my permission to publish that ... really, you know dear boy, and it's all just killing time. Please say that." They were reunited August 11, 1994.

Young male lead Jon Finch followed up this film with Hammer's *The Horror of Frankenstein*, and also appeared in Hitchcock's *Frenzy*. Ferdy Mayne appeared on the other end of the fangs as Count Von Krolok in *The Dance of the Vampires* (US: *The Fearless Vampire Killers*), and John Forbes-Robertson graduated to the role of Dracula himself in Hammer's *Legend of the 7 Golden Vampires*. And if Ingrid is the Queen of Horror, then one of the greatest ladies-in-waiting was angelically beautiful Maddy Smith; she appeared in this, *Taste the Blood of Dracula* and *Frankenstein and the Monster from Hell* for Hammer, as well as *Theater of Blood*, and was a Bond Girl in *Live and Let Die*.

In *New York* (vol. 4 #7, 2/15/71), Judith Crist amusingly notes that "lesbian-oriented vampires bite their men victims in the neck and their lady victims in the bosom (just above the nipple, accounting for the film's R rating, since those fang marks do, after all, have to be examined)." She also might have noted that vampires now seem to cast a reflection in the mirror, but only if they're gorgeous female vampires. And she was not mocking *Vampire Lovers*, lauding it as a "very well-done film." Joe Baltake of the *Philadelphia Daily News* (3/30/73) concurred, calling it "excellent ... [a] campy, literate, witty and dead-

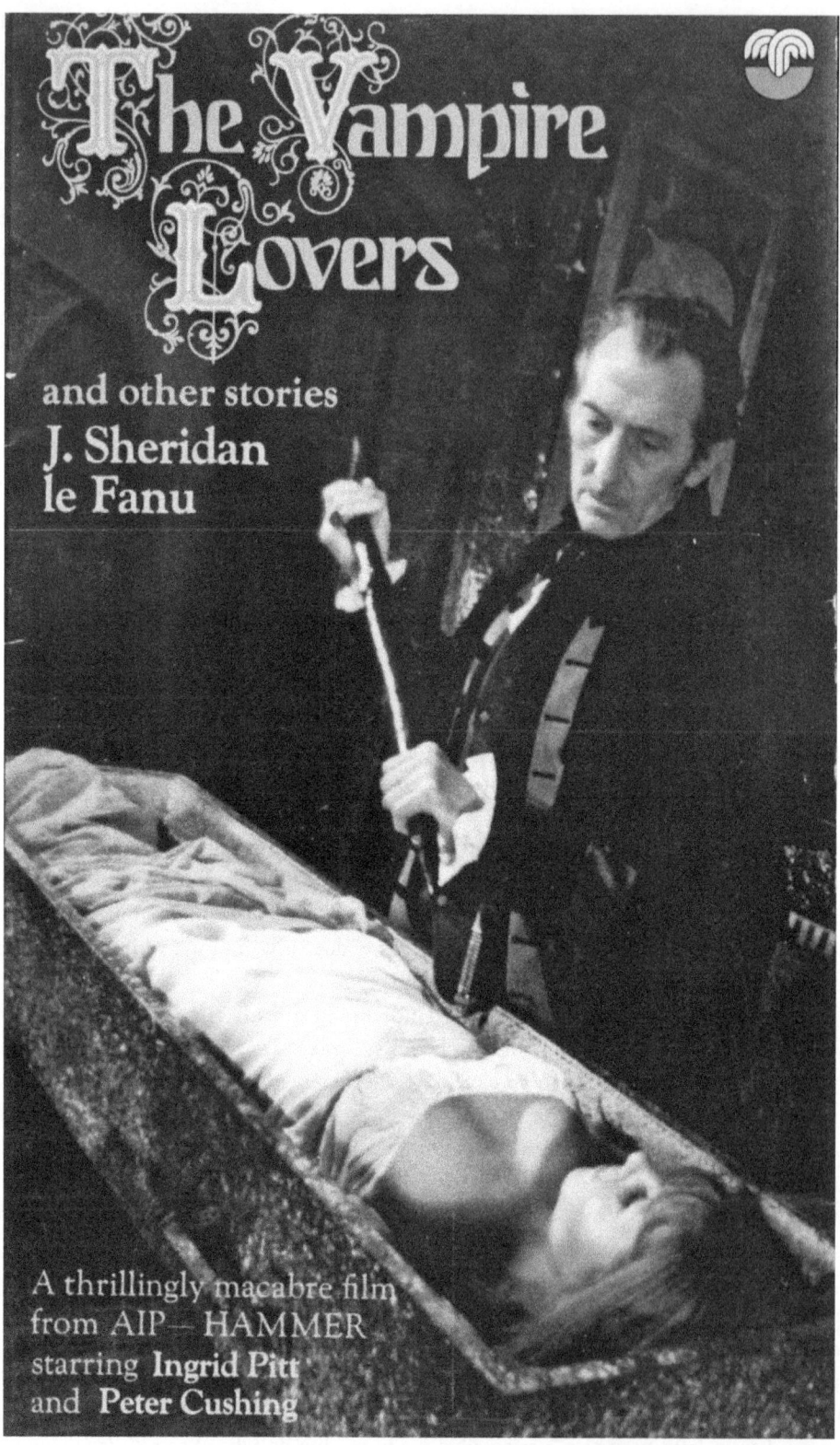

The Vampire Lovers paperback movie edition.

straight vampire movie." The *Los Angeles Times* rated it "an excellent horror film ... a rare and pleasurable experience done with intelligence and taste"; and the *New York Times* said it was "professionally directed, opulently staged, and sexy to boot."

Tales from the Pitt: My first day on the set was quite traumatic. I was dozing in the makeup chair when the makeup man bent down and whispered in my ear that I should see what Peter Cushing was doing to me on the set. I arrived just in time to see Peter swish at something with a sword and come up with what looked like a large turnip in his hand. I looked closer. It was my head! [Director Roy Ward Baker] called "Cut!" and Peter came over and introduced himself: "My dear — what an awful way to meet!" I shook his hand and, I am ashamed to say, said, "I feel a bit cut up about it, too." Yuk! (*Femme Fatales*, vol. 9 #4/5).

I came out of my dressing room wearing a white toweling robe and nothing else, ready for my big scene in the hip-bath. As I walked along the corridor, I saw [producers Harry] Fine and [Michael] Style coming up the other way. They looked so down-at-the-mouth I felt sorry for them. I waited until I was up close, threw open my dressing gown and said "Wheeee!" They walked off up the corridor with a renewed spring in their gait. It's so easy to make the little dears happy; men — I love 'em (*Ibid.*).

Lust for a Vampire (1971)

Crew: Producers: Harry Fine, Michael Style; Director: Jimmy Sangster; Screenplay: Tudor Gates; Characters: J. Sheridan Le Fanu ("Carmilla"); Music: Harry Robinson; Song "Strange Love" Performed by Tracy, Lyrics: Frank Godwin; Photography: David Muir; Editor: Spencer Reeve; Art Director: Don Mingaye; Makeup Supervisor: George Blackler; Production Manager: Tom Sachs; Assistant Director: David Bracknell; Third Assistant Director: Terry Pearce; Construction Manager: Bill Greene; Props: Wally Hockings; Sound Recordist: Ron Barron; Sound Editor: Terry Poulton; Recording Director: Tony Lumkin; Dubbing Mixer: Len Abbott; Dubbing Mixer: Len Shilton; Camera Operator: R. Chic Anstiss; Boom Operator: John Hall; Wardrobe Mistress: Laura Nightingale; Music Supervisor: Philip Martell; Continuity: Betty Harley; Hairdressing Supervisor: Pearl Tipaldi; Choreographer: Babbie McManus; Unit Publicist: Geoff Freeman.

Cast: Yutte Stensgaard (Mircalla/Carmilla Karnstein), Ralph Bates (Giles Barton), Barbara Jefford (Countess Herritzen), Suzanna Leigh (Janet Playfair), Michael Johnson (Richard Lestrange), Helen Christie (Miss Simpson), Pippa Steele (Susan Pelley), David Healy (Raymond Pelley), Harvey Hall (Insp. Heinrich), Mike Raven (Count Karnstein), Michael Brennan (Landlord), Jack Melford (Bishop), Christopher Cunningham (Coachman), Judy Matheson (Amanda), Christopher Neame (Hans), Eric Chitty (Prof. Herz), Caryl Little (Isabel), Jonathan Cecil (Biggs), Kirsten Lindholm (Peasant Girl), Luan Peters (Trudi), Nick Brimble, David Richardson (Villagers), Vivienne Chandler, Erica Beale, Melinda Churcher, Melita Clarke, Jackie Leapman, Sue Longhurst, Patricia Warner, Christine Smith (Schoolgirls); Valentine Dyall (Voice of Count Karnstein).

Synopsis: A peasant girl parts company with her boyfriend, coyly telling him she may or may not see him that night. As she walks home through a meadow, she is observed by

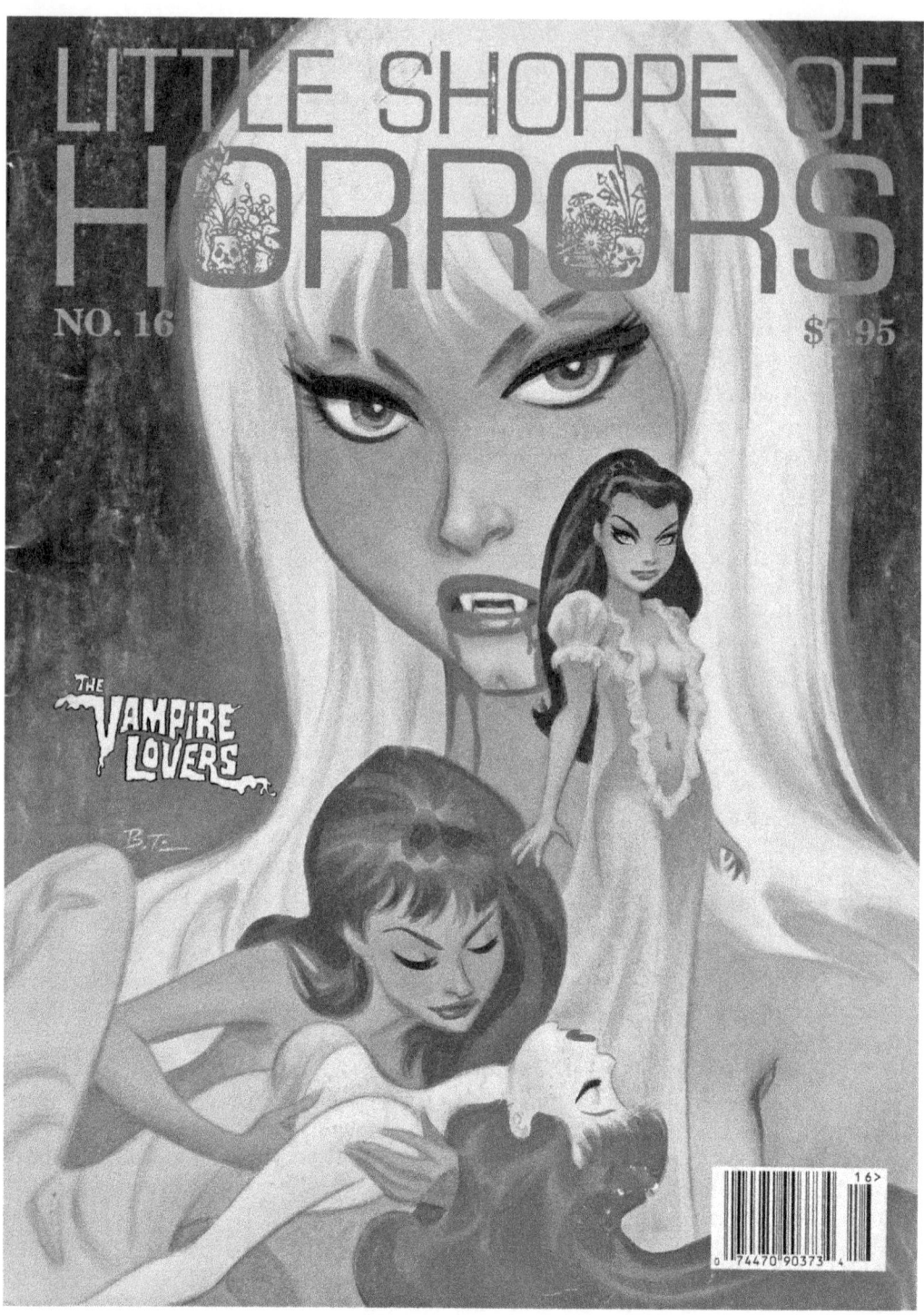

Little Shoppe of Horrors—Issue #16 of the all-time greatest Hammer fanzine was devoted to the Karnstein Trilogy and featured this montage from all three films, painted by Bruce Timm (courtesy Richard Klemensen and Bruce Timm).

a figure in a hooded black cloak. The figure motions for a waiting coach. The carriage stops beside the girl, who smiles sweetly at the occupant and gets in. Her smile soon turns into a scream.

Arriving at a castle, the driver carries the unconscious girl inside and places her on an altar. A tall black-cloaked man with a knife appears, and is joined by the hooded figure. The coach driver pulls the lid from a coffin, revealing a skeletal figure in a dress. The man in black hands the knife to the hooded figure, who receives it with a female hand. She slits the girl's throat and drains her blood into a chalice while the man in black prays to the lord of darkness. The blood is poured on the remains, which begin to gradually reassemble. As the man in black completes the invocation, the lightning flashes, and a beautiful young girl rises from the coffin.

At the village inn, the innkeeper tells Lestrange a young fop, tales of the Karnsteins, whose castle overlooks the village. Lestrange, a novelist, laughs off the vampire tales. The innkeeper tells him that the Karnsteins reappear every 40 years, and the anniversary is nigh. And one of their village girls is missing. Lestrange says he will go to the castle after lunch.

Lestrange arrives at the castle and surveys the empty courtyard. Then he discovers blood on the altar. He is approached by a hooded figure; then another, and another, and soon he is surrounded. A voice rings out ("Girls, girls!") and informs Lestrange that the girls are members of a nearby finishing school. The voice is that of their teacher, Giles Barton, who has brought them to the castle to help him research the Karnsteins.

The group leaves the castle and returns to the school. Introductions are made as the girls practice Greco–Roman dancing. Lestrange is introduced to the owner of the school, Miss Simpson. As they speak, a coach arrives bearing a countess and her niece, the school's newest pupil — Mircalla.

That night, Mircalla says she is tired from the dancing lessons, and a pupil named Susan offers to rub her shoulders. Mircalla lets her gown slide down over her breasts. Susan suggests they go for a moonlight swim, and kisses Mircalla's neck, but the headmistress, Miss Playfair, walks in on them.

Back at the inn, Lestrange regales the patrons with stories of the beautiful "vampires." As the crowd roars with laughter, one of the barmaids goes outside to feed her dog. She turns and smiles sweetly, and offers up her lips to ... death. Her screams shatter the mirth, and her corpse is found with two bloody holes in the neck. Susan and Mircalla meet at the lake; Susan is already nude in the water when Mircalla arrives. Mircalla sheds her own gown and dives in, swimming out and embracing Susan. They kiss passionately and joke about Giles spying on them. The man in black watches them.

At the inn that night, Lestrange meets a fan even more foppish than he, who tells him that he is a writer as well — but as yet unpublished. As it turns out, he is also on his way to the finishing school to teach English. Since Lestrange has yet to find a way to insinuate himself into school matters, he tells the man that he would like to collaborate, and convinces him to go to Vienna to do research.

Lestrange takes over the English class, and immediately offers Mircalla "personal" tutoring. The girls' next class is with Barton, whose lecture on the Karnsteins makes Mircalla uncomfortable. Lestrange now shares living quarters with Barton, whom he jokingly accuses of trying to become a vampire. Giles promptly disappears. When Richard goes outside to look for him, he hears a scream. He then sees Mircalla coming across the lawn, and blurts out that he loves her. Mircalla rebuffs him strongly at first, but then strokes his cheek and walks away. Susan's corpse is dragged away from the spot where she was killed, and dumped down a well by Barton.

Miss Simpson and the headmistress, Miss Playfair, argue over what to do about Susan's disappearance while Barton takes the girls on another field trip to Karnstein Castle. He shows them the coffin of Carmilla Karnstein. As the girls file into the castle, Barton pulls Mircalla aside and tells her that she must meet him there that night. When she does, he tells her that he knows she is Carmilla. He falls at her feet and tells her he will do whatever she demands. She sinks her fangs into his willing neck, and leaves him crawling after her as she disappears into the mist.

The countess pays a visit to the school. Barton's corpse is discovered by the girls, and the countess' doctor says that Barton has died of a heart attack. The doctor is the man in black. That night, Miss Playfair discusses her suspicions with Lestrange. She asks him to go to the police with her the next day, and he says he will consider it. When she leaves, he goes through Barton's sketches and books on the occult. In one tome he finds a portrait of Carmilla Karnstein. It is the same face as Mircalla's.

Looking at Barton's body lying in state, Lestrange sees the puncture marks on the neck. During class, he arranges to meet Mircalla at the castle that night. There, she tells him that she is indeed a Karnstein. She asks him if he thinks she is a vampire. He tells her to make love to him to prove she's not.

When he returns home, he finds Miss Playfair waiting for him. He tells her that she should not go to the police. She berates him and leaves in tears. He sleeps and not only dreams of her, but of Mircalla and the dead as well. The next day, a policeman grills Miss Simpson while Lestrange and Mircalla meet in a gazebo. They embrace passionately, and she makes him swear he will not reveal their love to the countess. Meanwhile the copper has discovered Susan's body in the well. As he is climbing out, someone cuts the rope and he is killed in the fall.

That night, Miss Playfair declares her love for Lestrange but, seeing that he is besotted with Mircalla, leaves in a huff. She is watched by the man in black. When she gets home, Mircalla is waiting for her. Miss Playfair falls under her spell as Mircalla beckons her to the bedroom. She undoes Janet's blouse, but is driven away by the cross nestled in her cleavage.

Susan's father arrives and demands that she be exhumed. The pathologist he employs sees the holes in the dead girl's neck, but says nothing. The countess tells Mr. Pelley that Susan committed suicide. Later, at the inn, the pathologist finally reveals his findings, but cannot believe the conclusion they lead him to. As they are joined by a bishop, the villagers prepare to storm the castle.

Meanwhile, Mircalla has claimed another victim. Lestrange runs for the school but instead runs into the angry villagers, imploring them not to attack. The man in black, Count Karnstein, is joined by the countess and Mircalla. They lock themselves in the

American *Lust for a Vampire* one-sheet poster.

castle while their vampiric coachman plunges his rig into the midst of the villagers. But he is stopped, pulled down, and staked by the innkeeper.

The villagers set fire to the castle. Lestrange runs into the flaming edifice calling for Mircalla. She tells him to leave, but with a wave of the count's hand, she smiles and embraces him. She bares her fangs. Lestrange tosses her down on a staircase, and a burning beam falls from the ceiling to impale her. The Count and Countess Karnstein merely stand and watch as they are enveloped by the flames. Lestrange is rescued by Mr. Pelley. The bishop prays as the castle burns.

Review: Lust for a Vampire was not as critically well-received as its predecessor. *Cue*, which had been effusive with praise for *The Vampire Lovers*, called it an "only moderately successful effort"; *Variety* was not quite so diplomatic, carping that it was "tepid" and "more humorous than frightening." Leading man Ralph Bates, in *Little Shoppe of Horrors*, levied the unkindest cut of all: "I consider it to be one of the worst films ever made." True, it isn't nearly on the same level as *Vampire Lovers*, and it really is the weakest of the three films, but it is not as bad as Bates made it out to be. In fact, it's Bates' utterly delicious performance as Barton that helps to make it memorable. Bates was a '70s Hammer fixture, appearing in this, *Horror of Frankenstein*, *Taste the Blood of Dracula*, *Doctor Jekyll and Sister Hyde*, and *Fear in the Night*, and passed away at 51 in 1991. *Lust for a Vampire* really only suffers by comparison with the previous film in the series and the subsequent one; the direction is not as stylish as Baker, but some sequences are quite well-mounted in what is more or less a remake of *The Brides of Dracula*. The main problem, as it were, is the casting of Carmilla; Yutte Stensgaard is beautiful, and does an adequate job, and taken by itself, it's a perfectly adequate performance, but she lacks Ingrid's depth and acting abilities.

Tales from the Pitt: I remember why I didn't do *Lust for a Vampire*—because I did *The House That Dripped Blood*. I did *The Vampire Lovers*, and then I did *Countess Dracula* immediately after that. Then *Jason King*, which was a big TV series in England at the time, and after that I immediately did *The House That Dripped Blood*—and that's when they were doing *Lust for a Vampire*; I couldn't possibly do it (*Ingrid Pitt: Queen of Horror*).

Twins of Evil (1971)

Crew: Producers: Harry Fine, Michael Style; Director: John Hough; Screenplay: Tudor Gates; Characters: J. Sheridan Le Fanu ("Carmilla"); Music: Harry Robinson; Photography: Dick Bush; Editor: Spencer Reeve; Art Director: Roy Stannard; Makeup: George Blackler, John Webber; Production Manager: Tom Sachs; Production Supervisor: Roy Skeggs; Assistant Director: Patrick Clayton; Second Assistant Director: David Munro; Third Assistant Director: Chris Carreras; Construction Manager: Arthur Banks; Sound Recordist: Ron Barron; Sound Editor: William Trent; Dubbing Mixer: Ken Barker; Sound Re-Recording Mixers: Graham V. Hartstone, Otto Snel; Camera Operator: Dudley Lovell; Wardrobe Mistress: Rosemary Burrows; Music Supervisor: Philip Martell; Continuity: Gladys Goldsmith; Hairdressing: Pearl Tipaldi; Casting:

James Liggat; Special Effects: Bert Luxford; Special Effects Photography–Second Unit Photographer: Jack Mills; Stunt Coordinator: Joe Dunne; Dialogue Coach: Ruth Lodge

Cast: Peter Cushing (Gustav Weil), Madeleine Collinson (Frieda Gellhorn), Mary Collinson (Maria Gellhorn), Inigo Jackson (Woodsman), Judy Matheson (Woodsman's Daughter), Harvey Hall (Franz), Alex Scott (Hermann), Sheela Wilcox [Shelagh Wilcocks] (Lady in Coach), Kathleen Byron (Katy Weil), Roy Stewart (Joachim), Luan Peters (Gerta), Damien Thomas (Count Karnstein), Dennis Price (Dietrich), Maggie Wright (Alexa), Katya Wyeth (Countess Mircalla), David Warbeck (Anton Hoffer), Isobel Black (Ingrid Hoffer), Kristen Lindholm (Staked Girl), Peter Thompson (Jailer), Roy Boyd (Dying Man); Maxine Casson, Vivienne Chandler, Doreen Chanter, Irene Chanter, Jackie Leapman, Janet Lynn, Annette Roberts (Schoolgirls); George Claydon (Midget); John Fahey, Harry Fielder, Kenneth Gilbert, Derek Glynne-Percy, Jason James, Sebastian Graham-Jones, Bill Sawyer (Puritans); Cathy Howard (Tomb Girl), Peter Stephens (Brotherhood Member), Garth Watson (Chief Priest).

Synopsis: Men on horseback thunder through the woods. They are a group of fanatical puritans called the Brotherhood, led by the gaunt Gustav Weil. Inside a tiny cabin, a woodsman hears the hoofbeats, and goes outside with his axe. He disappears, and is replaced in the doorway by Weil. The woodsman's young, beautiful wife begs for mercy, telling Weil she is not a witch. The Brotherhood members burn her at the stake.

A carriage bearing lovely twin girls, Maria and Frieda Gellhorn, and an older couple, heads for the village. The girls see a castle, and ask the old woman whose castle it is. With a look of disdain, she replies, "Karnstein Castle." The girls' parents have died, and they have been put under the guardianship of their aunt and uncle. When they arrive, dressed in the latest fashions from the continent, their Aunt Katy tells them that they must change in order not to offend their uncle — Gustav Weil.

Weil enters and is immediately offended by their clothing. He sends them to their room and then leaves for a meeting of the Brotherhood. Franz tells the assembled group of a woman that he suspects is a witch, and off they ride. Back at his home, Maria and Frieda are in their beds. Although the girls are twins, their personalities could not be more different. Frieda, the "bad girl," says that she knows what men of God are like — that Gustav would like to catch them staying up past their bedtime just so he could punish them. When Maria argues that they must do as he says because he is their guardian, Frieda tells her that he will not be *her* guardian long.

The Brotherhood bursts into the woman's cabin, but she is not alone. Count Karnstein berates, and then taunts Weil, asking him if he's looking for more innocent girls to burn. He goads Weil to the point that Gustav is ready to shoot him, but since Karnstein is close to the emperor, all Weil can do is stalk away in impotent rage. As the Brotherhood rides past a cemetery, they hear moans. Investigation yields the body of a young man, bearing the mark of the vampire. They see a pretty young girl walking down the road, so they chase her down and burn her at the stake.

Weil returns home and rails to Katy about the decadent Karnstein, which greatly excites Frieda, who is eavesdropping. At the castle, the bored, jaded Karnstein holds a black mass. After a nude girl is placed on the altar, Karnstein chases out the priests. He prays to Satan and then stabs the girl; her blood flows down through the crevices and drips onto a figure interred below. Smoke swirls, and the shrouded figure approaches

Twins of Evil—American one-sheet poster for the original double-feature release.

Karnstein. A hand reaches out — the hand of a beautiful woman. It is the long-dead Countess Mircalla Karnstein. They make love. Mircalla tells him to look in the mirror, where he cannot see her reflection. Then she fully initiates him into the ranks of the undead.

On the twins' first day at school, Karnstein just happens to stop by. Frieda rushes out to meet him, but Weil sees this and tells Karnstein to stay away from his nieces. Karnstein agrees, smiling. That night, Frieda argues with Maria and sneaks out of their room. She is on her way to the castle through the woods, when she is grabbed and shoved into a carriage and taken there. After a dinner at which Karnstein argues with his procurer and mistress, he chains up his mistress, and shows Frieda that he is a vampire. As he makes Frieda one as well, Maria feels a pain in her neck. The newly vampirized Frieda then kills the mistress as Karnstein laughs.

The Brotherhood burns yet another young and pretty girl. As the headmaster and headmistress of the school, Anton and his sister Ingrid, discuss what can be done about it, Anton reveals that he is infatuated with Frieda. Frieda, meanwhile, continues to leave the house at night, while Maria, who covers for her, is beaten by Gustav. Maria does not notice that Frieda now casts no reflection in their mirror.

The next day, Weil goes to the girls' school and accuses Anton of being in league with the Devil, for Anton has had the temerity to complain about Weil and his methods. Not only is there no trial for the accused, but he tells him that he cannot kill a vampire with fire anyway; a vampire must be staked or decapitated. Weil warns him not to interfere again, and leaves. Anton tells Ingrid that she should go away for a few days. That night, Maria pleads with Frieda not to go out, but to no avail. Frieda kills again.

The following morning, Anton is conducting class when the Brotherhood bursts in, bearing Ingrid's vampirized corpse. Later, Frieda is again on the hunt when she spies a member of the Brotherhood. She sinks her fangs into him, and his screams are heard by the Brotherhood. They surround Frieda, who tries to lie to Weil, but when he flashes a cross, she flashes her fangs and recoils. Weil cries out that the Devil has sent him twins of evil.

He goes home to beat Maria, but Katy will not let him. She tells Weil the girl is asleep, cross around her neck. She asks what will happen to Frieda, and he says that is for the Brotherhood to decide, for now they are required to have trials. As Maria talks of Karnstein in her sleep, he appears at her bedside, but is kept at bay by the cross. The Brotherhood declares Frieda guilty and decides to burn her. The cross falls from Maria's hand and she is kidnapped by Karnstein. She is taken to the jail and put in Frieda's place.

Anton rushes to the Weil home, where he finds Frieda, who he thinks is Maria. While she is seducing him, Maria is led to the stake. But as they embrace, Anton notices that Frieda casts no reflection. The truth revealed, she attacks him, but he throws a cross which burns her hand. Anton then rushes to tell the Brotherhood that they have the wrong twin, but Weil will not believe him. Weil begins to light the fire, and Anton screams to him to hold up a cross to Maria. He does, and she thanks God. Weil is overcome at the thought of what he might have done.

Anton shames The Brotherhood for what they have done to innocents. The Brotherhood wants to burn Karnstein Castle, but Anton tells them again that flames will not kill a vampire. This time they listen, and sharpen their stakes and axes. Karnstein sees them advancing on the castle, but he still believes that they will only burn him. When his mute servant Joachim signals otherwise, Karnstein flies into a rage and panics. He and Frieda flee to the crypt, leaving the servant to hold off the Brotherhood. After Joachim gorily dispatches two of them, he himself is staked. Karnstein sends Frieda out of the crypt first, and she is beheaded by Weil. Maria knows something has happened, and she goes to look for Frieda; instead she is grabbed by Karnstein. The Brotherhood finally breaches the castle, but Karnstein keeps most of them at bay using Maria as a hostage. Weil advances on him with an axe but, rattled by Karnstein, he misses and plants the axe in the door behind the count. Karnstein grabs his axe and plants it firmly in Weil's back, and then throws him over the railing. He turns his attention back to Maria, but before he can realize any evil intentions, he is impaled by Anton's spear. Anton holds Maria in his arms, and the Brotherhood gathers around the corpse of Weil as Karnstein decomposes.

Review: By the time of the third film of the trilogy, the character of Carmilla has been reduced to that of virtually a cameo; she is no longer the central character, merely the reason for Count Karnstein's vampirism, and fails to make an impression. That is not to say the film doesn't, though; in fact, it's a marked improvement over *Lust*.

Its connection to the trilogy is somewhat tenuous. The vampires could have been named anything as much as Karnstein, and whereas the first two films concentrated on exploiting the nudity and lesbian aspects, those qualities are in short and no supply, respectively, in this film. (Luscious female vampires have returned to casting no reflection in mirrors.) The Collinson twins were *Playboy*'s first twin sisters centerfold, but they showed perhaps more flesh in the layout than they do in this film; and the majority of the vampire victims in the movie are male. More girls die by the hand of Gustav Weil than by the hand of Karnstein, and that's the most interesting aspect of the film; like *Taste the Blood of Dracula*, it's not so much concerned with vampirism as it is showing the hypocrisy and intolerance of those appointed or considered to be guardians of morals. Of course, the title is supposed to refer to the Collinson girls, supported in the film by one of Peter Cushing's lines, but it could just as easily refer to Weil and Karnstein. Even at his most brutal as Dr. Frankenstein, Cushing could always be counted on to engender at least a modicum of sympathy from the audience, but there is naught but a brief glance in this, his most rigid and ideologically inflexible role ever, somewhat like Vincent Price's similar turn in *Witchfinder General* (US: *Conqueror Worm*).

Twins of Evil is not so much a fitting end to the Karnstein Trilogy as it is simply one of Hammer's best late-period vampire films. The reviews were generally better than for *Lust for a Vampire*; Kevin Thomas in *The Los Angeles Times*, who had not liked *Lust* as much as *Lovers*, was effusive: "*Twins of Evil* and *Hands of the Ripper* are among the most sophisticated horror pictures ever produced by England's Hammer Films. Not only are these two films distinguished by exceptionally well-wrought scripts, but are also strong in richly detailed period atmosphere ... *Twins of Evil* attacks the interlocked evils of ignorance, superstition, and bigotry while maintain a most contemporary respect for the occult powers."

There are changes to the character of Carmilla over the course of the three films. As noted in the beginning of the chapter, the films started out to exploit female nudity and the voyeuristic aspects of lesbianism, and much has been made in some quarters of this sensationalism. And while it is correct that these characteristics of Le Fanu's original story are bosomed up to the more permissive standards of Hammer in general and the '70s in particular, there really isn't anything in *The Vampire Lovers* that is drastically different. If anything, the lesbian subtext is just as emotionally explicit, if not as physically, in the original:

> She kissed me silently. "I have been in love with no-one, and never shall," she whispered, "unless it should be you." How beautiful she looked in the moonlight.

And although that aspect was certainly exploited again in *Lust for a Vampire*, Carmilla by this time seems much more decidedly bisexual. In the first film, the only relations that Carmilla has with men (other than the seeming influence of the Man in Black) are attacking them, and the one that she does seduce is merely a pawn in her game, not an object of actual interest. By the second film, she has no problem either helping Giles Barton realize *his* fantasy (again, Bates' character's sense of submissive orgiastic release is perversely palpable), or actually falling in love with the dashing young male hero. In *Twins of Evil*, the main Karnstein is a decadently heterosexual male, and Carmilla, as noted, in practically a cameo, only makes love to a man (and her descendant, at that). So in the course of the three films, the character of Carmilla could not be said to evolve as much as devolve. In the first, as in the story, despite being a bloodsucking vampire, she has a certain purity of intention and nobility of character. In the second, she is much more ruthless in intention and practice, and by the third, she's making love to her grandson or nephew or whatever; a portrait rendered in very broad strokes which reduced Carmilla into possibly a more elemental force of pure evil, but also one that is fairly faceless and again, could have been called Smithers-Jones as much as Karnstein.

As previously noted, *The Vampire Lovers* was not the first screen adaptation of Le Fanu's story, but it and *Countess Dracula* opened the floodgates for further explorations of the story itself, and for increasingly bloody and permissive variations on the theme. Nineteen seventy-two brought *La Novia Ensangrentada*, a.k.a. *The Blood-Spattered Bride*, from Spain; Alexandra Bastedo played Carmila/Mircala (sic). It was much more bloody than permissive, the opposite of the '70s film *Blood Lust*, a "blue" version of the story directed by *Knave Magazine* publisher Russell Gay. Some subtlety was restored by Meg Tilly in "Carmilla" (1989), part of TV's *Nightmare Classics* series and a fairly faithful adaptation which, for some reason, moves the setting of the story to the Deep South of the United States. All that was thrown to the winds with 1998's *Carmilla*, which featured Maria Pechukas in the title role; it was the bloodiest and most sexual version to that point. The following year saw Carmilla on screen twice: first as a supporting character in *Shadow Tracker: Vampire Hunter*, and then back to her rightful place in *Carmilla*, a.k.a. *J. Sheridan Le Fanu's "Carmilla."* Our increasingly self- and cross-referential pop culture gave us *Barely Legal Lesbian Vampires: The Curse of Ed Wood* in 2003 and *Vampires vs. Zombies*, a.k.a. *Carmilla the Lesbian Vampire*, the following year. Scream queen Debbie Rochon continued the further adventures of Carmilla in 2007's *A Feast of Flesh*; and as of 2010, a new film based on the original story was made with Simone Kaye as Carmilla; the lovely young Ms. Kaye also co-wrote and co-produced the project. The character of Carmilla has survived for over 130 years; and while all of the other versions of the story have their varying degrees of entertainment value, the only one that can make the same claim to timelessness is still *The Vampire Lovers*.

"The Boob Tube": Television

This chapter covers Ingrid's television appearances in character roles, both in series episodes and made-for-TV films.

Aqui España (1966)

Tales from the Pitt: "Manolo [Escobar] introduced me to a man from the main Spanish television station. He was putting on a variety-chat show and was looking for a presenter. I convinced him that I would be perfect. The show was called *Aqui España* and although the format wasn't too original, it worked. On each show, I would present a piece about Spain and in the entertainment industry, introduce a guest, usually a singer or a visual entertainer — no writers — and then sit back while the guest entertained the audience. One of the guests was Julio Iglesias."

When Iglesias seemed more hopeful of a soccer career than a singer's, Ingrid told him to learn to sing in English, go to America, and conquer the world. "I must have inspired him because he went to England and spent two years singing in a pub in Kent learning English, and just look at him now" (*Life's a Scream*).

Dundee and the Culhane
(1967; 13 episodes) Filmways Television
"The 1000 Feet Deep Brief" (Episode # 7)

Episode Cast: John Mills (Dundee), Ingrid Pitt (Tallie Montreaux), Jim Boles (Murtaugh), Ralph Meeker (Maximus Tobin), Michael Pataki (Charlie Hughes), William Phipps (Turpin), John Pickard (Watchman), Bing Russell (H.P. Graham), Irene Tedrow (Widow Hughes).

Tales from the Pitt: I played the "perk" for a traveling judge in the Old West with a gunslinger as bodyguard. Ralph Meeker was the local star. It was great working with two old pros like [John Mills and Meeker]. I love Westerns and this one was tremendous fun (*Life's a Scream*).

Ingrid in *Dundee and the Culhane* (courtesy Ingrid Pitt).

Ironside
(1967–1975; 197 episodes)
Harbour Productions Limited
"The Fourteenth Runner" (Episode # 15)

Episode Crew: Producer: Cy Chermak; Executive Producer: Frank Price; Associate Producer: Jeannot Szwarc; Director: Don Weis; Teleplay: Donn Mullally; Story: Leon Tokatyan; Creator: Collier Young; Music: Quincy Jones; Photography: Lionel Lindon; Editor: Edward Haire; Art Director: Lloyd S. Papez; Set Decorators: John McCarthy Jr., Joseph Reith; Makeup Artist: Bud Westmore; Hair Stylist: Larry Germain; Assistant Director: Joe Boston; Sound: David H. Moriarty; Costumes: Grady Hunt; Editorial Supervisor: Richard Belding; Color Coordinator: Robert Brower; Music Supervisor: Stanley Wilson; Production Executive for Harbour Productions: Leonard H. White; Stunts: Bob Herron, Kim Kahana, Hubie Kerns, Dean Smith.

Episode Cast: Raymond Burr (Robert T. Ironside), Don Galloway (Detective Sgt. Ed Brown), Barbara Anderson (Officer Eve Whitfield), Don Mitchell (Mark Sanger), Ingrid Pitt (Irene Novas), Steve Ihnat (Zarkov), Edward Asner (Marlon Davis), John Van Dreelen (Varinyi), Gene Lyons (Commissioner), Philip Chapin (Yuri Alexeyovich Azneyeff), Ollie O'Toole (Undertaker), Lee Miller (Bartender).

Synopsis: In this first-season episode, Ironside and his squad are hot on the heels of a Russian long-distance runner who has disappeared. Has he defected, or is there a more sinister reason? Ingrid is the guest star, playing a beautiful fellow Russian athlete who has already defected. She is used by both Ironside (overtly) and KGB officials (sneakily, of course) to uncover the missing marathon man's whereabouts.

Review: San Francisco Chief of Detectives Robert Ironside was cut down by a sniper's bullet, which left him wheelchair-bound. He is assigned a crack task force to help him solve cases that other detectives can't. *Ironside* was the long-running follow-up to Burr's evergreen *Perry Mason*. Genre fans will always remember him as reporter Steve Martin from *Godzilla, King of the Monsters!*

As is often the case, Ingrid's *Ironside* part is small but integral to the plot, and she brings a real "big screen" presence to her appearance, the only really notable point in an otherwise routine episode of the show.

Jason King
(1971–72; 26 episodes)
Incorporated Television Co. (ITC)

"Nadine" (Episode #15)

Episode Crew: Creators: Monty Berman, Dennis Spooner; Producer: Monty Berman; Director: Cyril Frankel; Screenplay: Philip Broadley; Executive Story Consultant: Dennis Spooner; Cinematography: Frank Watts; Editor: Lee Doig; Assistant Director: Ken Baker; Music: Laurie Johnson; Production Supervisor: Ronald Liles; Art Director: Charles Bishop; Creative Consultant: Cyril Frankel; Continuity: Doreen Soan; Camera Operator: Jack Lowin; Music Coordinator: Paul Clay; Sound Recordists: Dave Bowen, Bill Rowe; Sound Editor: Roy Baker; Set Dresser: Roger Christian; Scenic Artist: A. J. Van Montagu; Casting: Anne Donne; Production Buyer: Peter Dunlop; Makeup: Eddie Knight; Hairdresser: Alice Holmes; Costume Supervisor: Laura Nightingale; Stunt Coordinator: John Sullivan; Supervising Electrician: Ted Hallows; Post-Pro-

Ingrid Pitt, Peter Wyngarde in *Jason King* (courtesy Ingrid Pitt).

duction Supervisor: Philip Aizlewood; Post-Production Sound: Cinesound/Magna-Tech; Titles: Chambers & Partners.

Episode Cast: Peter Wyngarde (Jason King), Ingrid Pitt (Nadine), Harry Brooks Jr. (Gerhard Roder), Clive Cazes (Kyriacou), Al Garcia (Tony Mussoni), Stacey Gregg (Kim), John Hamill (Chuck), Al Mancini (Placide), Alfred Marks (Renzo), Patrick Mower (Achille), Walter Randall (Male Secretary), Anne Sharp (Nicola Harvester).

Synopsis: Jason's editor sends him to Athens for inspiration for his next "Mark Cain" novel, but as usual, Jason's "research" lands him squarely in the middle of trouble — and in the arms of the beautiful-but-deadly Nadine. Ingrid essayed the title role of the episode, a woman who is hired by criminal masterminds to terminate Jason and his frilly cuffs without prejudice (well, at least towards Jason, anyway), but finds herself falling for him instead.

Review: Two years prior, producers Berman and Spooner had created ITC's *Department S*, a 28-episode series built around the adventures of a group of special Interpol agents; Jason King was a member. King was the archetypal '70s macho man, with a daft Fu Manchu mustache and appalling sideburns; this hedonistic womanizer had left the department in order to write trashy detective novels. He more or less gets caught up in cases while doing research for his novels, or occasionally is employed by British Intelligence under threat of arrest for unpaid back taxes. But despite a slightly dotty lead character, the stories were fun and sometimes downright bizarre, certainly easier to digest than Austin Powers.

Ingrid gets quite a bit of screen time as the femme fatale and makes the most of it, alternately vulnerable, saucy and sly. She very much recalls Rita Hayworth in *The Lady from Shanghai* with the line "One always comes back to one's own self." Patrick Mower, who plays Achille, reunited with Ingrid in 2000 for *The Asylum*.

The Adventurer
(1972–73; 26 episodes)
Incorporated Television Co. (ITC)
"Double Exposure" (Episode # 20)

Episode Crew: Producer: Monty Berman; Associate Producer: Barry Delmaine; Creative Consultant–Director: Cyril Frankel; Executive Story Consultants: Dennis Spooner, Marty Roth; Screenplay: Marty Roth; Theme Music: John Barry; Music Supervisor: Don Kirshner; Music: Paul B. Clay; Cinematography: Frank Watts; Editor: Derek Hyde-Chambers; Casting: Anne Donne; Art Director: Albert Witherick; Makeup Artist: Colin Garde; Hair Stylist: Michael Jones; Post-Production Supervisor: Philip Aizlewood; Assistant Director: Ken Baker; Scenic Artist: Bill Beavis; Production Buyer: Peter Dunlop; Set Dresser: Michael Ford; Construction Manager: Jock Lyall; Sound Recordists: David Bowen, Dennis Whitlock; Sound Editor: Wilfred Thompson; Stunt Coordinator: Alf Joint; Camera Operator: Jack Lowin; Supervising Electrician: Ted Hallows; Wardrobe Supervisor: Laura Nightingale; Continuity: Sally Bell; Executive Story Consultants: Marty Roth, Dennis Spooner; Post-Production Sound: Cinesound/Magna-Tech; Titles: Coppin/Meluta Graphimation.

Regular Cast: Gene Barry (Gene Bradley), Barry Morse (Mr. Parminter), Catherine Schell (Diane Marsh), Garrick Hagon (Gavin Jones), Ingrid Pitt (Elayna), Carl Duering (Col. Kazan), Donald Houston (Jan de Groote).

Synopsis: The Adventurer— While aboard his private plane, Gene Bradley receives an urgent summons diverting him to Amsterdam. He is met by Mr. Parminter, who tells him that his old friend, industrialist Jan de Groote, has married a woman named Elayna (Ingrid), unaware that she is a Russian agent. She arranged for both of them to be taken into custody, so Jan still trusts her. The Russians substitute a double for Jan. Bradley calls in his own double, plus his associates Diane and Gavin, to get to de Groote of the problem.

Review: Yet another creation of the Berman-Spooner team, *The Adventurer* featured Gene (*The War of the Worlds*) Barry as a millionaire businessman-film star who also happens to be a secret agent, much like his Amos Burke on TV's *Burke's Law*. A bit too old and paunchy for both the character and the awful '70s fashions he was fitted with, Barry nonetheless approaches his sub–Bond role with something approaching gusto, and is lent able support by the reliable Barry Morse and the lovely Catherine Schell, who went on to join Morse in *Space: 1999*. Schell had been a Bond Girl in *On Her Majesty's Secret Service*. Garrick Hagon later appeared in *The Spy Who Loved Me* as well as the first *Star Wars*. A familiar genre face, Donald Houston had appeared in *Where Eagles Dare* with Ingrid five years previous, and had played Dr. Watson in *A Study in Terror* three years before that. Ingrid plays the beautiful-but-deadly Russian agent Hummingbird, a role that strongly suggests that, given a form-fitting black spandex outfit (yes, I know, the mind boggles), Ingrid would have made the perfect embodiment of Marvel Comics' Black Widow.

New Faces
(1973; 8 episodes)
Associated Television (ATV)

Series Crew: Producer: Les Cocks; Director: John Pullen; Writer: Philip Parsons; Production Design: Martin Davey; Musical Director: Johnny Patrick; Theme Composer: Carl Wayne

Series Cast: Derek Hobson (Host), Marti Caine (Hostess), Lynsey De Paul, Nina Myskow, Mickie Most, Clifford Davis, John Smith, George Elrick, Martin Jackson, Jimmy Henney, Ted Ray, Jack Parnell (Panelists), Ingrid Pitt, Arthur Askey, Tony Hatch (Judges).

Notes: Besides Ingrid, there's also some big British pop music names involved in this series: Mickie Most had produced The Yardbirds, Jeff Beck, The Animals, Herman's Hermits, Lulu and Donovan; theme song (*You're a Star*) composer Carl Wayne had been a member of the seminal The Move, and Tony Hatch, of course, composed the themes for *Crossroads* and *Neighbours*, as well as classic hits like *Downtown*, *Sign of the Times*, and *Don't Sleep in the Subway* for Petula Clark and many others.

New Faces was a showcase for new talent in the form of a competitive show. Ingrid

Pitt served as one of the judges on the show, working with a virtual who's-who of pop music from the period.

Ski Boy (1973)

Tales from the Pitt: I was offered a job in Switzerland. It was a children's television show called *Ski Boy*. It went like a dream, and Steffanie loved Switzerland and the snow. I played a journalist and had great fun both with the part and working with a pro like [longtime British actor] Michael Culver (*Life's a Scream*).

Thriller
(1973–76; 43 episodes)
Associated Television (ATV)
"Where the Action Is" (Season 4, Episode # 6)
a.k.a. "The Killing Game" (ITC below)

Episode Crew: Producer: John Cooper; Director: Don Leaver; Creator-Writer: Brian Clemens; Music: Laurie Johnson; Gaming Advisor: Ray Marioni; Art Director: Henry Graveney; Lighting: Alistair Morrison; Makeup: Shirley Muslin; Costume Designer: Ann Hollowood; Sound: Bob Woodhouse; Editor: Stanley Staffe; Camera Operators: Bill Brown, Tony Mander, John Willment, Carole Legg; Music Coordinator: Paul Clay; Senior Floor Manager: Sen O'Farrell; Stage Manager: Mari Markus; Administrator: Ron Brown; Main Title Sequence ("The Killing Game"): Film-Rite, Inc., Creative Productions.

Episode Cast: Edd Byrnes (Eddie Vallance), Ingrid Pitt (Ilse), James Berwick (Wallace "Daddy" Burns), Trevor Baxter (Mr. Winters), George Innes (Zac), Oliver MacGreevy (Henry), Larry Cross (Tommy Vaughn), Ray Marioni (Croupier), Suzanna Williams (Maid), Frank Coda (Pursell).

Synopsis: After Eddie Vallance loses big at the roulette table, the beautiful-but-mysterious Ilse (Ingrid) invites him back to her room. He wakes up in the heavily-guarded house of gambler-supreme "Daddy" Burns, who hates to lose—and will go to any length to make sure that he doesn't. It turns out that Ilse is Daddy's mistress, and while she is more than willing to use her wiles in "Daddy's" service, she also has her own moral code, that she adheres to with deadly results.

Review: After Boris Karloff and before Jacko, *Thriller* was a British television anthology series created and written by Brian Clemens, whose horror and mystery genre credits are impeccable—*The Avengers* and *The New Avengers* (producer, writer, story editor, presenter), the Hammer films *Captain Kronos Vampire Hunter* (producer, director, writer) and *Dr. Jekyll and Sister Hyde* (producer, writer), *The Golden Voyage of Sinbad* (screenplay and story), the 1960 *The Tell-Tale Heart* (writer), *Curse of the Voodoo* (writer); and writer of episodes for *H.G. Wells' Invisible Man, The New Adventures of Martin Kane, Danger Man* (a.k.a. *Secret Agent*), *Hammer House of Mystery & Suspense,* the new *Alfred Hitchcock Presents,* the new *Perry Mason,* and *The Father Dowling Mysteries.*

Again, Ingrid is cast as a mistress, but she makes her part believable. She tells Vallance that it's not a man's looks that excite her so much (entirely acceptable, given "Daddy" Burns' looks), but that he is a good gambler, and so her shock at discovering that Burns is a cheat shows that she has some sort of moral code. Vallance is played by former teen idol Edd Byrnes, who performed in many television shows, and is best known for playing "Kookie" Kookson III on *77 Sunset Strip* and *Hawaiian Eye.*

The episode was re-broadcast by ITC as a stand-alone mystery under the title of *The Killing Game* sans the *Thriller* imprint, and with new title and end credits sequences.

Ingrid returns from a dip in *Thriller*'s "Where the Action Is" (courtesy Ingrid Pitt).

The Zoo Gang
(1974; 6 episodes)
Incorporated Television Co. (ITC)
"Mindless Murder" (Episode # 2)

Episode Crew: Producer: Herbert Hirschman; Assistant Producer: John Pellatt; Associate Producer–Director: John Hough; Title Theme: Paul & Linda McCartney; Music Composer & Conductor: Ken Thorne; Music Editor: Norman Cole; Based on the Book by Paul Gallico; Script Consultant: Howard Dimsdale; Developer: Reginald Rose; Cinematography: Robert Paynter; Editor: Lee Doig; Art Director: Roy Stannard; Production Manager: Geoffrey Helman; Assistant Director: Bert Batt; Assistant Art Director: Alan Cassie; Set Dresser: Tessa Davies; Sound Recordist: David Bowen; Dubbing Mixer: Ted Kamon; Dubbing Editor: Peter Lennard; Camera Operator: Douglas F. O'Neons; Continuity: Phyllis Townshend; Casting Director: Weston Drury Jr.; Makeup: Phil Leakey; Hairdresser: Barbara Ritchie; Wardrobe Supervisor: Jackie Cummins.

Episode Cast: Barry Morse (Alec "The Tiger" Marlowe), Brian Keith (Steven "The Fox" Halliday), John Mills (Thomas "The Elephant" Devon), Lilli Palmer (Manouche "The Leopard" Roget), Seretta Wilson (Jill Burton), Michael Petrovich (Lt. Georges Roget), Roy Boyd (Michel), Clinton Greyn (Anthony Martin), Ingrid Pitt (Lyn Martin), Aharon Ipale (Paul), Morris Perry (Herbault), Lois Negin (Claude), Alex Scott (Jean).

Synopsis: The Gang investigates a series of elaborate jewel heists staged by a band of extortionists. The extortionists' next target is the volatile movie actress Lyn Martin (Ingrid), and The Gang can't decide which is more difficult — trying to trap murderous extortionists or trying to safeguard a diva with the personality of Mount Vesuvius.

Review: Zoo Gang stars Keith, Mills, Palmer and Morse were all seasoned pros; they have good chemistry, and the series was intelligent and fun, a sort of *Mission: Impossible* for and of the senior set (they're called the Zoo Gang because each of them used the code name of an animal during World War II as members of the Resistance). Ingrid, playing movie star Lyn Martin, is absolutely venomous, and a damned sight more evil and scarier than a vampire (her character was allegedly based on Elizabeth Taylor). It's a clichéd role, true, but Ingrid plays it to the hilt. She had already done a show with John Mills, *Dundee and the Culhane*. Barry Morse is best-remembered as the inspector from TV's *The Fugitive*, and was also featured, among others, in *Space 1999* and *Asylum*. There are no fantastic elements in this series or show, but plenty of the other actors in the cast had strong genre classic credits: Seretta Wilson (*Tower of Evil*, *Psychomania*), Alex Scott (*Fahrenheit 451*, *The Abominable Dr. Phibes*, *Twins of Evil*), and Roy Boyd (*Twins of Evil*, plus *The Wicker Man*, *The Omen*, and *Biggles* with Steffanie). Phil Leakey had been the makeup man for the original brace of Hammer classics: the first two Quatermass films, *The Abominable Snowman*, *The Curse of Frankenstein*, *Horror of Dracula*, and *The Revenge of Frankenstein*. Another neat feature is the catchy theme song by Paul & Linda McCartney, fresh off of *Band on the Run*.

Tales from the Pitt: The atmosphere during the shooting was rather strange. Barry was friendly, but distant. Brian was very butch and American — reminded me a little bit of John Wayne in the way he was overly polite and condescending to everyone. I got on quite well with Lilli, but she was always very busy and insisted on going to bed early, and Clinton was keen to exercise his rights as my screen lover off set. It was most peculiar. I think it was the first time I was ever anxious to finish a shoot and get home to do some wallpapering (*Den of Geek*, 2/10/09).

BBC2 Playhouse
(1974–83; 107 episodes)
British Broadcasting Corporation (BBC)

"Unity" (Season 7, Episode # 18)

Episode Crew: Producer: Louis Marks; Director: James C. Jones; Script: John Mortimer; Author: David Pryce-Jones; Production Designer: Oliver Bayldon; Costume Designer: Dinah Collin; Script Editor: Stuart Griffiths; Series Creator: Sarah Pia Anderson.

Episode Cast: Lesley-Anne Down (Unity Mitford), Jeremy Kemp (Putzi Hanfstaengl), Ernest Jacoby (Adolph Hitler), Sheila Allen (Lady Redesdale), Ingrid Pitt (Fraulein Baum), Nigel Havers (Philip Colindale), James Villiers (Hilary Martin), Hans Meyer, Emma Relph.

Synopsis and Notes: Based on history, *Unity* tells the story of Unity Mitford, a British woman born in 1914 who became infamous as a Nazi and a member of Hitler's inner circle. As a young girl, she involved herself with right-wing politics as a means to shock her family, but soon became deadly serious and committed to the cause. Her sister Diana abandoned her husband for an affair with Oswald Mosley, the head of the British Union of Fascists, and Unity attended the Nuremberg Rally, where she first saw Hitler. She made it her life's mission to meet him, which she finally did after much persistence. She developed a close relationship to Hitler, who played her against Eva Braun's affections until Braun attempted suicide. When Britain declared war on Germany, Mitford attempted suicide, but succeeded only in seriously wounding herself. She was eventually returned to England, where she died of meningitis caused by cerebral swelling around the bullet. Unity is played by Lesley-Anne Down, who had previously appeared with Ingrid in *Countess Dracula*, and the film was directed by James C. Jones, who later directed Ingrid in *The Comedy of Errors* (see below). There are other players from notable horrors: James Villiers had appeared in *Blood from the Mummy's Tomb* for Hammer and *Asylum* for Amicus, and Jeremy Kemp had also done time with Amicus, in *Dr. Terror's House of Horrors*.

Artemis 81 (1981)
British Broadcasting Corporation (BBC)
(Made-for-TV movie)

Crew: Producer: David Rose; Associate Producer: Dawn Robertson; Director: Alistair Reid; Writer: David Rudkin; Photography: David Jackson; Music: Dave Greenslade; Gordon Crosse; Organ: Peter Dickinson; Production Assistant: Jenny Brewer; Assistant Designer: Rob Hinds; Camera Operator: Ian Churchill; Graphic Designer: Ann Jenkins; Visual Effects Designer: Tony Harding; Scenic Artist: Brian Bishop; Property Buyer: John Broome; Costume Designer: Al Barnett; Makeup: Carol Ganniclifft; Dubbing Mixer: David Baumber; Editor: Mike Hall; Production Designer: Gavin Davies; Recordist: Dennis Cartwright; Script Editor: Roger Gregory; Assistant Floor Manager: Michael Murphy; Production Managers: Bob Jacobs, William Hartley.

Cast: Hywel Bennett (Gideon Harlax), Dinah Stabb (Gwen Meredith), Dan O'Herlihy (Dr. Albrecht Von Drachenfels), Siv Borg (Pastor's Wife), Sylvia Coleridge (Library Scholar), Roland Curram (Asrael), Daniel Day-Lewis (Library Student), Sevilla Delofski (Magog), Cornelius Garrett (Pastor), Ingrid Pitt (Hitchcock Blonde), Mary Ellen Ray (Sonia), Ian Redford (Jed Thaxter), Anthony Steel (Tristam Guise), Gordon "Sting" Sumner (Helith), Frode Berg (Pastor's Son), Ysanne Churchman (BBC Radio Announcer), Eleanor Forsythe (Mother), Patricia Gallimore (Nurse), Rigmor Moller (Old Danish Woman), Phil Parry (Subaltern), W. Claydon Smith (Cyclist), Michael Tracy (Whitecoat), Margaret Whiting (Laura Guise), Alan Towers (Television Reporter).

Synopsis: Paranormal author Gideon Harlax sits at his typewriter and begins to work. Under two suns, there is a tree by a shore. Beside the tree is a large rock in the shape of a woman. Two brothers, Helith and Asrael, good and bad, converge on the rock. Asrael implores their "mother," Magog, to awaken, while Helith begs her to stay asleep. Her eyelids crack open. An old man, Dr. Von Drachenfels, looks at a replica of the stone figure in a museum case.

Dr. Von Drachenfels stands on the deck of a ferry from Denmark to England, gazing out to sea. On other parts of the ship, a black family talks amongst themselves while a minister and his wife entertain their child. A film director and his mistress sit in deck chairs. The ferry arrives and the passengers all set out for their respective destinations by car, except for Von Drachenfels, who leaves on foot. The film director drives to a lake; the black family pulls into their garage. A truck driver sits frozen to death in his truck.

Gideon is working and watching television, refusing to answer the phone. He sees the black family being taken from their house on stretchers; they have all committed suicide. The director's wife leaves a message on his phone that her husband has committed suicide. There is also a message from Gideon's friend Jed, who teaches a film class and invites Gideon to sit in on it. Gwen calls, and they make arrangements to go to Von Drachenfels, after Gideon inspects a tower he's having renovated.

After they arrive at the organist's to talk about a piece of music, Gideon leaves Gwen and Von Drachenfels to their discussion while he wanders around the churchyard. Gideon is standing by an open grave when Von Drachenfels emerges and begins to talk about death. Gwen comes out looking dejected, and she and Gideon leave. Asrael tells Von Drachenfels he has done well. Gideon and Gwen get separate rooms at the inn, and Von Drachenfels goes to an underground chamber where his wife is on life support. While Gwen and Harlax have dinner, she makes it obvious that she loves him, but he won't respond in kind. Later he has a surreal dream in which he is back at the church.

While Gideon is on the phone with Gwen, the television shows footage of the minister from the ferry, who has also committed suicide. Harlax goes to Von Drachenfel's and takes Gwen's music. He wakes up on the side of the road and finds a small stone head but pays it no mind. Harlax goes to a library, where he asks a student to help him translate what he thinks are Greek letters that Von Drachenfels has annotated the score with. As he is speaking, a note offering him aid is slipped over his shoulder, and he sees a woman's legs in seamed stockings disappearing up the staircase.

On the upper level, the woman, a silent, mysterious blonde, begins to undress him. He protests that he is the wrong sex, and an old woman yells at him to keep his fantasies to himself. His shirt and pants are unbuttoned; then the blonde is gone, taking the score with her. Gideon runs outside to catch her, but she has been struck dead by a car. He retrieves the bloody score and goes to look through clippings of the recent suicides. When he visits the director's wife, she too says that Tristram was already dead before he died. When Harlax leaves, she takes a black stone leg out of a box.

Back at his apartment, Gideon discovers that the symbols on the score are not Greek, but a type font that uses symbols for letters. The symbols translate to "Magog." Gideon goes to his other home in Wales and calls Gwen, telling her that Von Drachenfels is under the influence of the dark angel Asrael. As usual, their conversation ends in argument; Gwen looks out the window and sees Asrael watching her from across the street.

Gideon makes a chart of the pattern of suicides, and realizes that the stone head he found in Gwen's van is the head of Magog. The angel Helith appears outside Harlax's window, but Gideon doesn't see him. Harlax runs outside to call Gwen, and while he's on the phone, his vehicle blows up, and he is caught in the blast.

A rescue copter picks up the mangled Harlax. Helith is aboard, telling Gideon Harlax will be out of action for quite some time. When Harlax awakes, his face is healed but his leg is game. Helith tells Harlax that he is not of this earth. By the tree on the shore, Gideon tells Helith that he loves him, and wants them to stay there always. They spend the night together, and then Helith says it is time for them to go back across the sea. As they prepare to leave, Harlax sees that Helith casts no reflection in the mirror.

They get on a bus where everyone is coughing; one woman falls over as she coughs up blood. Gideon is forced off the bus and separated from Helith, who merely stares out the window as the bus disappears into the mist. Harlax finds himself in a bizarre, grimy, overpopulated dream world. A woman asks him for his autograph and then whispers into his ear that she will meet him at the cathedral the next day. Gideon spends the night cold, alone and hungry.

Harlax goes to the cathedral and finds a high heel on the stairs leading to the belltower. He finds the woman hanging by the neck, although she's not dead yet. He cuts her loose and she falls to a ledge, but then falls to her death. As Gideon runs from the cathedral, he sees blood on the steps and the woman's face on every TV screen in a store. Helith tells him he is afraid he is becoming part of this world, and Gideon tells him how much he loves him and begs him not to leave. For the first time, Helith feels the cold, and so Gideon gives him his coat. Helith sees himself in the mirror, so when Harlax has put the coat around his shoulders, he leaves.

Harlax wanders about the bleak landscape, and then discovers an underground hospital where all of the people who have a piece of the Magog are being tested. Harlax strangles the doctor and finds Gwen. Above, Asrael makes a phone call and gives orders to seal the project. Gideon, disguised in the dead doctor's coat, finds Jed in one of the rooms. Jed tells him that he is one of the chosen. Gideon kisses Jed, and Jed screams and dies. Gwen kills her nurse and dons her bloody smock. Gideon and Gwen escape in a truck, driving into a blinding white light. They come out above ground, where Gwen tells him that his books contribute to the evil in the world by always relying on a higher power for intervention; and then in real life, when that power doesn't save people, they despair and don't think for themselves.

In Gwen's car, they hear a program on which Von Drachenfels is to be featured. As they rush to the spot, they have a flat. When they stop to fix it, a huge flock of birds flies past. As Von Drachendels begins to play, Gideon sees a headless horseman, and then hears a crowd of children, but Gwen urges him on. By the time they arrive at the abbey where Von Drachenfels is performing, the concert is over, but the master organist has begun to improvise. On a ledge above Gwen and Gideon, the reassembled Magog starts to open. Gideon grabs it; Gwen tells him to let go, while Asrael tells him to hold on. Harlax releases it and falls, but it is Asrael who completes the fall and is impaled. Von Drachenfels, ears bleeding, drives towards the light; it is his domain afire; he joins his wife and they die together.

Gwen stands across a road from a grave marked *Magog*. She joins Harlax on a shore and asks him what happened to his coat. He says he gave it to a poorer man. Under two suns, Helith holds the coat, and then it disappears.

Review: If you think the synopsis is confusing, just wait until you see the movie. Advertised as "The Cult BBC Science Fiction Film," but perhaps more accurately described as Weird Science-Fantasy, it is self-consciously disjointed and surreal; to quote William Everson again, "almost a sure-fire way to create a cult film!"

Ingrid plays the mysterious "Hitchcock Blonde," and her lack of dialogue makes her presence even more striking; but for the most part, the numerous Hitchcock references are fairly obvious and heavy-handed. And if there's anything worse than a lame Hammer tribute, it's a lame Hitchcock tribute. At some points, one gets the sense that the reason the rest of the scenes make little sense is that they were merely some sort of attempt to link the various Hitch references together. That's not to say there aren't some good bits; Ingrid is the very image of the Hitchcock femme fatale and Dan O'Herlihy (*RoboCop*, *Twin Peaks*) gives a spooky performance despite some dreadful dialogue (but that hampers the whole cast). Daniel Day-Lewis is very good as the student in a role that, like Ingrid's, amounts to no more than a cameo. That can't be said for Gordon "Sting" Sumner, better known as bass player for the bleached-blond New Wave band The Police. Sting started out in a bit part in (appropriately enough) *The Great Rock'n' Roll Swindle*, and went on to play parts in the awful *Dune* (1984) and the *really* awful *The Bride* (1985); he is to acting what the Police were to Reggae.

Smiley's People
(1982; 6 episodes)
British Broadcasting Corporation (BBC)
"Episode #1.1"
"Episode #1.2"

Episode Crew: Producer: Jonathan Powell; Director: Simon Langton; Teleplay: John Le Carre, John Hopkins; Based on the Novel *Smiley's People* by John Le Carre; Music Composed & Conducted by Patrick Gowers; Photography: Kenneth Macmillan; Editor: Clare Douglas (Episode #1.1), Chris Wimble (Episode #1.2); Production Designer: Austen Spriggs; Costume Designer: Sheila Beers; Makeup Artist: Elizabeth Rowell; Production Managers: Richard Cox, Marion McDougall, Jeremy Silberston; Graphic Designer: Stewart Austen; Properties Buyer: David Privett; Dubbing Mixer: Ken Hains; Dubbing Editor: Michael Parker (Episode #1.1), John Strickland (Episode #1.2); Field Recordist: Malcolm Webberley; Stunt Arranger: Remy Julienne; Chief Grip: Roy Russell; Dog Trainer: Joan Woodgate; Production Assistant: Diana Brookes; Production Associate: Marcia Wheeler; Location Managers: Antoine Gannage, Olivier Peray; Assistant Floor Managers: Lynn Richards, Gordon Ronald.

Episode #1.1 Cast: Sir Alec Guinness (George Smiley), Curt Jurgens (The General), Eileen Atkins (Madame Maria Ostrakova), Dudley Sutton (Oleg Kirov), Vladek Sheybal (Otto Leipzig), Bill Paterson (Lauder Strickland), Anthony Bate (Oliver Lacon), Michael Elphick (Detective

Chief Superintendent), Ingrid Pitt (Elvira), Paul Herzberg (Villem Craven), Stephen Riddle (Nigel Mostyn), Harry Walker (Murgotroyd), Trevor Cooper (Sgt. Pike), Renny Krupinski (Attaché Kuznetsov), Germaine Delbat (Madame La Pierre), Jacques Maury (Sergei), Alex Jennings (P.C. Hall), Vincent Grass (Taxi Driver), Yves Peneau (Dmitri), Catherine Ohotnikoff (Warehouse Woman), Francois Clavier (Warehouse Man), Andre Penyem (Waiter), Okon Jones (Mr. Lamb), Gita Denise (Russian Embassy Official), Louba Guertchikoff (Metro Woman), Margit Rauthe (Leipzig's Girlfriend).

Episode #1.2 Cast: Sir Alec Guinness (George Smiley), Curt Jurgens (The General), Eileen Atkins (Madame Ostrakova), Maureen Lipman (Stella Craven), Vladek Sheybal (Otto Leipzig), Michael Gough (Mikhel), Anthony Bate (Oliver Lacon), Ingrid Pitt (Elvira), Paul Herzberg (Villem Craven), Okon Jones (Mr. Lamb), Andrew Bradford (Ferguson), Alan Rickman (Mr. Brownlow), Jan Carey (Paris Hospital Sister), Anna Wing (Westbourne Terrace Woman), Ken Sicklen (Taxi Driver), Peter Guinness (Hare Krishna Monk), Tanya Rees (Becky Craven).

Synopsis: Maria Ostrakova has had her identity stolen by the KGB for unknown reasons. Her old friend Vladimir surmises that she has been used to provide a front for someone in the service of master spy Karla. Vladimir is called "The General," because he is a former Soviet general turned British agent. He tries to contact his old friend George Smiley through "The Circus" not realizing Smiley has retired. Vladimir is not taken seriously until he turns up dead (shot in the face). Smiley is called out of retirement to investigate the brutal murder and the reasons behind it — reasons that the Circus would just as soon not know. Following a trail of murder, torture, and deception by friend and foe alike, Smiley finds that Karla is diverting official funds to the care of his mistress's daughter, who has been committed to a mental institution using the Ostrakova identity. If the Circus can prove this, they can force Karla to defect or face disgrace and execution. Smiley proves it, and Karla defects. But it is a hollow victory for Smiley, whose methods of obtaining the necessary information are just as ruthless as the ones that Karla employs in the service of his own ideology. When a colleague congratulates him on having "won," Smiley merely replies, "Yes, I suppose I did."

Review: The novel *Smiley's People* was published in 1979, the third part of the Karla trilogy which began with *Tinker, Tailor, Soldier, Spy* and *The Honourable Schoolboy.* The mini-series, although a bit more linear than the novel, is still thrillingly complex and quite faithful to the novel. James Bond alumni Curt Jurgens (*The*

Ingrid and Curt Jurgens in *Smiley's People* (courtesy Ingrid Pitt).

Spy Who Loved Me) and Vladek Sheybal (*From Russia with Love*) are on hand; and Sir Alec Guinness is, as always, a rock. Ingrid Pitt fans will be disappointed at the brevity of her role. She plays a secretary, a small part that occurs in two of the episodes. She is also the ex-lover of the "General" at the beginning of the series.

Smiley's People was enthusiastically received by both the public and the critics, winning four awards from the British Academy of Film and Television Arts: Best Actor, Best Actress, Best Film Cameraman, and Best Original Television Music. It was nominated for six more BAFTA awards (Best Design, Best Drama Series, Best Film Editor, Best Film Sound, Best Graphics, and Best Makeup) as well as three Emmys (Outstanding Direction in a Dramatic Series, Outstanding Lead Actor in a Dramatic Series, and Outstanding Limited Series).

The Comedy of Errors (1983)
British Broadcasting Corporation (BBC)
(Made-for-TV movie)

Producer: Shaun Sutton; Director: James C. Jones; Based on the Play "The Comedy of Errors" by William Shakespeare; Music Composed & Conducted by Richard Holmes; Editor: Peter Reason; Production Designer: Don Homfray; Costume Designer: Jane Hudson; Makeup Artists: Cecile Hay-Arthur, Monica Linford; Production Manager: Peter Hider; Second Assistant Director: Christopher Landry; Sound: Chick Anthony; Camera Supervisor: Geoff Feld; Lighting Technician: Dave Sydenham; Vision Mixer: Julie Mann; Production Assistant: Raquel Ebbutt; Technical Coordinator: John Bird; Assistant Floor Manager: Kate Bradley; Production Associate: Fraser Lowden; Literary Consultant: John Wilders.

Cast: Michael Kitchen (The Antipholi), Roger Daltrey (The Dromios), Suzanne Bertish (Adriana), Joanne Pearce (Luciana), Sam Dastor (Angelo), Cyril Cusack (Aegeon), Charles Gray (Solinus, Duke of Ephesus), Ingrid Pitt (Courtesan), Nicolas Chagrin (Mime Master); Nick Burnell, Graham Christopher, Ross Davidson, Howard Lee, Daniel Rovai, Paul Springer, Jenny Weston (Mime Troupe Members); Bunny Reed (Jailer), Noel Johnson (First Merchant), Alfred Hoffman (Second Merchant), Marsha Fitzalan (Luce), David Kelly (Balthazar), Frank Williams (Officer), Geoffrey Rose (Pinch), Wendy Hiller (Amelia), Peter Mackriel (Messenger).

Synopsis: Solinus, the duke of Ephesus, tells aged Aegeon that unless he pays his death, he will be put to debt. But thereby hangs the tale of Aegeon. He was once a prosperous merchant, with a wife and two ships. Identical twin sons are born to his wife, and the thoughtful father aids a poor woman by buying her own twin sons to serve as slaves to his own. A storm at sea separates the boat and the family, and Aegeon hasn't seen his wife or sons since; his grief has kept him from finding gainful employment. This arouses the duke's pity, although not his pardon. In a magnificent display of benevolence, the duke gives Aegeon 24 hours to beg or borrow the money.

To Ephesus comes Antipholis and his slave Dromio. Antipholis gives Dromio money

Ingrid Pitt and Michael Kitchen on the set of the BBC's 1983 production of *A Comedy of Errors* (courtesy Ingrid Pitt).

to secure lodgings, and Dromio sallies forth. No sooner has Dromio left than he reappears, telling Antipholis he is late for dinner. Antipholis asks him where the money he gave him is. Dromio tells Antipholis that he is late for dinner. Antipholis asks him where the money is. Dromio tells him he is late for dinner. Antipholis beats Dromio.

Adriana, the husband of Antipholis, frets while her sister Luciana knits. She believes that her husband is unfaithful, and thinks of the germs that could infect the family jewels. Dromio returns to the house and tells her that Antipholis is mad. Adriana tells Dromio to fetch her husband, or she will beat him.

Dromio encounters Antipholis and tells him the lodgings are secure; Antipholis asks him if he is done with his jest. When Dromio tells Antipholis that he hasn't seen him since he sent him with the money to find lodgings, Antipholis beats him.

Adriana and Luciana approach Antipholis and Dromio. Antipholis tells Adriana that he has never seen her before, and does not know how she knows their names, but he agrees to go home with them for dinner. She tells Dromio to guard the door, and under no circumstances let anyone enter — or she will beat him.

Antipholis parts company with Angelo the jeweler and another friend. When Dromio finds him and tells him how he has beaten him, Antipholis beats him. Antipholis demands entrance to his house and demands to know who denies it, and when Dromio, inside, says Dromio, Antipholis turns to Dromio outside and beats him. Antipholis decides not to cause a scene; he beseeches Angelo to bring him the gold chain he has ordered for Adriana, while he goes to find solace with a courtesan.

When they have finished dinner, Luciana tells Antipholis that even if he doesn't love her sister, at least he should put up a good front. He says that he is not Adriana's husband, and that he loves Luciana. Luciana is shocked and stunned. Antipholis tells Dromio to arrange passage from Syracuse. He sees Angelo from the window, and Angelo throws him the gold chain, telling him he will be back at five for the money. Antipholis puts on the chain and leaves. From a distance he is seen by Antipholis, who thinks he is groggy from too much grog.

A creditor demands money from Angelo, who tells him he will pay him as soon as he collects from Antipholis. On their way to his home, they see Antipholis. Antipholis tells Dromio to go and buy a rope, and beats him. Angelo asks him for the money or the chain. Antipholis tells him he has neither. Angelo has Antipholis arrested. Dromio enters and tells Antipholis that the ship is ready to go. After considering beating Dromio, Antipholis tells him to go home and get the money for his bail.

Dromio tells Adriana that Antipholis has been arrested. She gives him the bail money, telling him to bring Antipholis home. Antipholios wanders the streets, still confused as to how everybody seems to know his name. Dromio tells him he has the bail money. Before he can beat him, the courtesan asks him for the chain that he promised her in return for a ring. Antipholis calls her a witch and makes a hasty exit. The courtesan decides she will go to his home and tell Adriana that he is mad and that he stole her ring.

Dromio brings the rope to Antipholis. Antipholis asks him where the bail money is. Dromio tells him he sent him for rope. Antipholis beats him. Adriana appears with the courtesan and a conjurer, who accuses Antipholis of being possessed. Adriana tells him that he had dinner with her. She tells him that she sent the bail money with Dromio, but Dromio denies it. Antipholis flies into a rage. He and Dromio are bound and taken to the house. The arresting officer tells Adriana that Antipholis was arrested because he owed money for a gold chain which he denied having received, and the courtesan says that she saw him with the chain. Adriana demands to see Angelo. Instead, she sees Antipholis and Dromio, which causes her to flee.

As Angelo converses with his debtor, they see Antipholis wearing the gold chain. Antipholis denies having denied having it. Just as swords are drawn, Adriana rushes in and orders Antipholis and Dromio bound, but they take sanctuary in the abbey. The abbess declares that none shall pass. Adriana pleads her case with Solinus, who has arrived to execute Aegeon.

Adriana relates her version of the day's events to Solinus. Solinus bids the abbess appear. Another of Adriana's servants rushes in to tell her that Antipholis has broken his bonds, but she says that he and Dromio are inside the abbey. Then she sees Antipholis beating the conjurer in the window. After he has finished, he enters the scene, and tells Solinus his version of the day's events, after which he beats Dromio. Aegeon tells Antipholis that he is his father, but Antipholis claims never to have seen him before. As Aegeon expresses his disbelief and sorrow, the abbess appears with Antipholis and Dromio. Antipholis calls Aegeon his father and Aegeon calls him his son, and the abbess calls Aegeon her long-lost husband. Antipholis and Dromio were taken from her after they were saved. Antipholis and Antipholis and Dromio and Dromio are the long-separated twins. The abbess gets her husband back, Antipholis gets his brother just as Dromio gets his, Antipholis gets his wife back, Antipholis gets Luciana, Antipholis gives the money back, Antipholis offers to pay Aegeon's debt, the duke waves the penalty, Antipholis gives the ring back to the courtesan, the abbess invites everyone into the abbey, Solinus takes the courtesan's arm, there is much rejoicing, and all's well that ends well.

Review: In this filmed performance of the play, seasoned and likable actors give sincere performances. Charles Gray (*You Only Live Twice, Diamonds are Forever, The Devil Rides Out*) reminds all and sundry what a fine actor he could be, given the right material, and Ingrid as the sexy, scheming courtesan again demonstrates how deft a comedienne she is, given the right material. Star Michael Kitchen had done his bit at Hammer in *Dracula A.D. 1972*, and went on to become part of the James Bond filmic legacy in *The World Is Not Enough* in 1999. The show is somewhat stolen by Roger Daltrey, lead singer of The Who, who gives an engaging comic performance as the Dromios.

Although the movie was made from Shakespeare's play, Shakespeare had his own influences: Key plot elements are borrowed from two comedies by the Roman Plautus. The main premise of the mistaken identity of identical twins with the same name is taken from *Menaechmi*, while from *Amphitruo* he borrows the like-named twin servants, as well as the scene where the wife locks out her husband while dining with a lookalike.

Dr. Who
(1963–89; 696 episodes)
British Broadcasting Corporation (BBC)

"The Time Monster" Part 5 (Season 9, Episode 25, 1972)
"The Time Monster" Part 6 (Season 9, Episode 26, 1972)
"Warriors of the Deep" Part 1 (Season 21, Episode 1, 1984)
"Warriors of the Deep" Part 2 (Season 21, Episode 2, 1984)
"Warriors of the Deep" Part 3 (Season 21, Episode 3, 1984)

"The Time Monster" Parts 5 and 6 Crew: Producer: Barry Letts; Director: Paul Bernard; Writers: Robert Sloman, Barry Letts; Music: Dudley Simpson; Title Theme Composer: Ron Grainer; Production Designer: Tim Gleason; Special Sound: Brian Hodgson; Visual Effects Designer: Michael John Harris; Script Editor: Terrance Dicks. Editor: Martyn Day; Costume Design: Barbara Lane; Makeup Artist: Joan Barrett; Sound (Studio): Tony Millier; Film Sound: Derek Medus; Film Camera: Peter Hamilton; Studio Lighting: Derek Hobday; Production Assistant: Marion McDougall; Assistant Floor Manager: Rosemary Hester.

"The Time Monster" Part 5 Cast: Jon Pertwee (The Doctor), Roger Delgado (The Master),

George Cormack (King Dalios), Ingrid Pitt (Queen Galleia), Donald Eccles (Krasis), Melville Jones (Guard), Katy Manning (Jo Grant), Derek Murcott (Crito), Aidan Murphy (Hippias), Susan Penhaligon (Lakis), Dave Prowse (Minotaur), Michael Walker (Miseus), Nick Hobbs (Guard).

"The Time Monster" Part 6 Cast: Jon Pertwee (The Doctor), Roger Delgado (The Master), Ingrid Bower (Face of Kronos), Mark Boyle (Kronos), Ian Collier (Stuart Hyde), George Cormack (King Dalios), Ingrid Pitt (Queen Galleia), Donald Eccles (Krasis), Melville Jones (Guard), Katy Manning (Jo Grant), Derek Murcott (Crito), Aidan Murphy (Hippias), Susan Penhaligon (Lakis), Dave Prowse (Minotaur), Michael Walker (Miseus), Nick Hobbs (Guard), Nicholas Courtney (Brigadier Lethbridge-Stuart), John Levene (Sgt. Benton), Wanda Moore (Dr. Ruth Ingram).

Synopsis: "The Time Monster"— In this six-episode story arc, the Doctor and Jo Grant travel to ancient Atlantis when they, Col. Lethbridge-Stuart and UNIT battle the Doctor's old nemesis, the Master. The Master has discovered the means to summon Kronos, the "Time Monster," with whose aid he can both defeat the Doctor and (dare I say it), rule the world. He is aided in his mad quest by the beautiful, scheming Queen Galliea (Ingrid Pitt) and by the legendary Minotaur, but the only result of their machinations is a sinking feeling.

Review: Doctor Who was introduced by the BBC in 1963, and has since become the longest-running science fiction television series in history. Often, when an actor associated with a series leaves that series, it means that the audience's interest leaves with them, leading to its eventual demise. This contingency is actually taken into consideration in the overall plot to the series, and so when a new Doctor is introduced, it is known as "regeneration" and each actor brings his own interpretation of the Doctor to the role. Undoubtedly the most popular regeneration was Tom Baker, who played the role from 1974 until 1981, and got the role based on his performance in *The Golden Voyage of Sinbad*. He was the Fourth Doctor and the immediate successor to the Doctor of "The Time Monster," Jon Pertwee, who played the role from 1970 to 1974, and was second only to Baker in popularity and number of years in the role.

Ingrid as Queen Galleia from *Doctor Who*'s "The Time Monster."

Pertwee and Ingrid were no strangers; they appeared in *A Funny Thing Happened on the Way to the Forum* and *The House That Dripped Blood*; she would also see Donald Eccles again soon in *The Wicker Man*. The only fault that can be found with Ingrid's slick portrayal of the beautiful,

Another beautiful shot of Ingrid as the queen in *Doctor Who*'s "The Time Monster" (courtesy Ingrid Pitt).

scheming Queen Galleia is that there's not enough of it; one wishes a way could have been found to work her into the storyline earlier. This cast was a virtual Amicus and Hammer horror haven; besides Pertwee and Ingrid, the man playing the Doctor's old foe the Master was Roger Delgado, who had appeared in *The Terror of the Tongs* with Christopher Lee and *The Mummy's Shroud* for Hammer; Susan Penhaligon went on to play Lisa Clayton in *The Land That Time Forgot*; and David Prowse was in *Horror of Frankenstein*, *Frankenstein and the Monster from Hell*, *Vampire Circus* and *The People that Time Forgot*, as well as the classic *A Clockwork Orange* and the first three films of the *Star Wars* series (as Darth Vader). Delgado and Pertwee were close friends in real life; they opposed each other in 37 episodes of *Doctor Who* between 1971 and 1973. Delgado, like Ingrid, also appeared in episodes of *Jason King* and *The Zoo Gang* (although not the same ones). He died in 1973.

"Warriors of the Deep" Parts 1–3 Crew: Producer: John Nathan-Turner; Director: Pennant Roberts; Writer: Johnny Byrne; Production Designer: Tony Burrough; Special Sound: Dick Mills/BBC Radiophonic Workshop; Visual Effects Designer: Mat Irvine; Script Editor: Eric Saward; Incidental Music: Jonathan Gibbs; Production Manager: Michael Darbon; Production Associate: June Collins; Production Assistant: Norma Flint; Assistant Floor Manager: Adrian Hayward; Engineering Manager: Alan Woolford O. B. Camera Supervisor: Alastair Mitchell; O. B. Sound: Chris Holcombe; Video Effects: John Mitchell (Part 3 only), Dave Chapman; Vision Mixer: Nigel Finnis; Technical Manager: Alan Arbithnott; Camera Supervisors: Bob Baxter, Alex Wheal; Videotape Editor: Hugh Parson; Lighting : Peter Smee; Sound: Martin Ridout; Costume Designer: Judy Pepperdine; Makeup Artist: Jennifer Hughes; Title Sequence: Sid Sutton; Stunt Double/Peter Davison: Gareth Milne.

"Warriors of the Deep" Part 1 Cast: Peter Davison (The Doctor), Janet Fielding (Tegan Jovanka), Mark Strickson (Vislor Turlough), Tom Adams (Commander Vorshak), Ingrid Pitt (Dr. Solow), Ian McCulloch (Nilson), Nigel Humphreys (Bulic), Martin Neil (Maddox), Tara Ward (Preston), Norman Comer (Icthar), Nitza Saul (Karina), Stuart Blake (Scibus), Vincent Brimble (Tarpok), Christopher Farries (Sauvix), James Coombes (Paroli/Voice of Sentinel Six); Mike Brayburn, Steve Kelly, Dave Ould, Jules Walters, Chris Wolfe (Sea Devils Warriors); Russell Brook, Joanna Garcia, Joycea Gobern, Arnold Lee, Ling Tai (Seabase Crew Members); Peter Caton, Ridgewell Hawkes, Julian Hudson, Julian Larousse, Barney Lawrence, Dana Miche, Dorothy Ottey, Rose Pridmore, Trevor Steedman (Seabase Guards).

"Warriors of the Deep" Part 2 Cast: Peter Davison (The Doctor), Janet Fielding (Tegan Jovanka), Mark Strickson (Vislor Turlough), Tom Adams (Commander Vorshak), Ingrid Pitt (Dr. Solow), Ian McCulloch (Nilson), Nigel Humphreys (Bulic), Martin Neil (Maddox), Tara Ward (Preston), Norman Comer (Icthar), Nitza Saul (Karina), Stuart Blake (Scibus), Vincent Brimble (Tarpok), Christopher Farries (Sauvix), James Coombes (Paroli/Voice of Sentinel Six); John Asquith (The Myrka); Mike Brayburn, Steve Kelly, Dave Ould, Jules Walters, Chris Wolfe (Sea Devils Warriors); Russell Brook, Joanna Garcia, Joycea Gobern, Arnold Lee, Ling Tai (Seabase Crew Members); Peter Caton, Ridgewell Hawkes, Julian Hudson, Julian Larousse, Barney Lawrence, Dana Miche, Dorothy Ottey, Rose Pridmore, Trevor Steedman (Seabase Guards); William Perrie (Myrka Stunt Double).

"Warriors of the Deep" Part 3 Cast: Peter Davison (The Doctor), Janet Fielding (Tegan Jovanka), Mark Strickson (Vislor Turlough), Tom Adams (Commander Vorshak), Ingrid Pitt (Dr. Solow), Ian McCulloch (Nilson), Nigel Humphreys (Bulic), Martin Neil (Maddox), Tara Ward (Preston), Norman Comer (Icthar), Nitza Saul (Karina), Stuart Blake (Scibus), Vincent Brimble (Tarpok), Christopher Farries (Sauvix), James Coombes (Paroli/Voice of Sentinel Six); John Asquith (The Myrka); Mike Brayburn, Steve Kelly, Dave Ould, Jules Walters, Chris Wolfe (Sea Devils Warriors); Russell Brook, Joanna Garcia, Joycea Gobern, Arnold Lee, Ling Tai (Seabase Crew Members); Peter Caton, Ridgewell Hawkes, Julian Hudson, Julian Larousse, Barney Lawrence, Dana Miche, Dorothy Ottey, Rose Pridmore, Trevor Steedman (Seabase Guards); William Perrie (Myrka Stunt Double).

Ingrid and Peter Davison from *Doctor Who*'s "Warriors of the Deep" (courtesy Ingrid Pitt).

Synopsis: Dr. Who—"Warriors of the Deep"—At Seabase, an underwater military complex, radar picks up an unidentified craft, but then it disappears. The craft belongs to the Silurians, a race of reptilian beings. The Silurians' mission is to revive the Sea Devils, a warrior race that has lain entombed for hundreds of years. They are aided in their mad quest by enemy agents aboard Seabase, one of whom is the beautiful, scheming Dr. Solow (Ingrid Pitt).

Review: Ingrid returns to the series for three episodes, not as royalty, but as a doctor—and an enemy agent at that. She is suitably menacing, and even gets to show off her karate skills (she is a black belt, and has shared a few falls with the King himself, Elvis), but her performance is somewhat eclipsed by the series' penchant for odd costuming, set design and particularly the surreal low-budget special effects. For instance, Ingrid and the rest of the Seabase females are not only subjected to a bizarre heavy eye makeup but, even worse, are forced (along with the rest of the crew) to wear uniforms which bear a horrifying resemblance to the clothes worn by the Jacksons on their "Victory" tour, right down to a big V stitched onto the back. The Myrka is an undersea-monster variation on the two-men-in-a-horse-suit routine. The Silurians have a great look, sort of a cross between the Creature from the Black Lagoon, Godzilla, and the Kraken from *Clash of the Titans*, but their mouths do not move, their bodies are obviously suits, and in one scene, the edges of their facial masks flap about outside their vests. The "Manipulator" that they use to bypass Seabase's guidance systems looks like a cotton candy machine, the Sea Devils look like walking snapping turtles in samurai outfits, and the bed covers in the crew members' quarters are large rectangles of the bubble wrap that is used in mailing packages. But all of this only adds to the charm in one of the most memorable story arcs in the Peter Davison regeneration. Ingrid has made one other contribution to the Dr. Who series; for that contribution, see the chapter on her books, p. 216.

The House (1984)
Channel Four Television Corporation
(Made-for-TV movie)

Crew: Producer: Nigel Stafford-Clark; Associate Producer: Peter Jacques; Director-Writer-Music: Mike Figgis; Cinematography: Roger Deakins; Production Designer: Andrew McAlpine; Art Director: Caroline Hanania; Gaffer: John Higgins; Transportation Captain: Richard Booz; Production Coordinator: Laura Julian.

Cast: Stephen Rea (The Soldier), Jonathan Cecil (Bishop Wooler), Nigel Hawthorne (Gen. Flagg), Dudley Sutton (Mr. Janek), Alun Armstrong (Mr. Smeth), Caroline Embling (Miss Von Eisen/Village Girl), Diana Hardcastle (Mrs. Janek), Ingrid Pitt (Countess Von Eisen), Roderic Leigh (Lairdlaw), Richard Marner (Count Von Eisen), Lizza Aiken (Sarah), Pam Ferris (Mrs. Smeth), Philomena McDonagh (Maid), Stefan Kalipha (Butler), Chris Bowler (Kitchen Girl), Ronan Wilmot (Communardist), Emil Wolk (Russian Officer), Louis Figgis (Child), Peter Jacques (Priest).

Notes: This was the first directorial effort of Mike Figgis, who would gain fame with such

Ingrid in *The House* (courtesy Ingrid Pitt).

later theatrical releases as *The Crying Game* and *Internal Affairs*. The film was an adaptation of Figgis's performance piece, *Slow Fade*, and was commissioned by Channel 4. Pitt plays Countess von Eisen in the wartime period.

Bulman
(1985–87; 20 episodes) Granada Television
"Chicken of the Baskervilles" (Season 2, Episode 4)

Episode Cast: Don Henderson (George Bulman), Siobhan Redmond (Lucy McGinty), Peter Armitage (Jake), Luke Hanson (Hoffman), Tony Matthews (Lord Kilmartin), Ingrid Pitt (Laura), John McGlynn (Art Mason), Rosalind Knight.

Ingrid and Don Henderson in *Bulman* (courtesy Ingrid Pitt).

Notes: This series was spun out of two previous shows, *The XYY Man* and *Strangers,* in which Bulman was a detective sergeant. In this 20-episode series, Bulman, a man with issues (to say the least), has quit the police force and is operating as a private detective, which irritates both the underworld and the law. Star Don Henderson had teamed with Peter Cushing in *The Ghoul* (1975) and did so again two years later in *Star Wars*. Ingrid Pitt plays "Laura" in "Chicken of the Baskervilles," an episode that has Bulman and company investigating the disappearance of the butler of a country estate, as well as other nefarious goings-on in the area.

Urban Gothic
(2000–01; 22 episodes)
Blackjack Productions
"Vampirology" (Season 1, Episode 2)

Episode Cast: Keith-Lee Castle (Rex), Julienne Davis (Emmanuelle), Charles De'Ath (Giles), Danny Edwards (Ricardo), Emily Hamilton (Tyler), James Maclear (Soundman), Saskia Mulder (French Girl), Kate Stevenson-Payne (Irmina), Ingrid Pitt (Ingrid Pitt).

Synopsis-Review: *Urban Gothic* was a short-lived, low-budget British television horror series, made by and for people who take their horror very seriously — the very people that this episode seems to mock. The episode is filmed as a *faux* documentary, chronicling a night's worth of exploits of a chap who claims to be a real vampire. And if ever there were a more compulsive argument against joining the ranks of the undead, it surely has yet to be filmed, as Rex and all of his friends are so self-involved, narcissistic and amoral that, by the end, becoming a real vampire is the last thing anyone would want to do. As such, it is an intense and occasionally savage commentary on contemporary decadence and moral corruption.

Although Ingrid appears as "herself," it is still within the context of a fictional story, so for all intents and purposes Ingrid Pitt plays "Ingrid Pitt," a role for which she is eminently suited. After Rex says that the person he'd most like to be is Ingrid, she just "happens" to enter a restaurant where Rex is drinking and smoking. Being rude and interrupting her at her table, he tells her what a big fan he is — and then he tells her he's a real vampire. Ingrid chuckles and asks him if he has fangs. He leaves in a huff, complaining how actors don't respect people like him. The interviewer asks Ingrid how often this happens to her, and she answers, "One or two times a week, darling; I don't know why they just can't ask me for my autograph." The series, at first glance, is an anthology of unconnected stories, but the last episode of the first season revealed that all of the initial stories had taken place within the same shared continuity, and the second series gradually revealed an ongoing storyline involving the paranormal branch of British Intelligence, C-TEC and "The Heart," an ancient and powerful supernatural entity that serves as the lifeforce of London, feeding on the pain, fear and misery of its inhabitants — usurping the traditional role of the monarchy.

Tales from the Pitt: The big laugh was that I was playing me. It was about a vampire who thinks I'm a real vampire and tries to come onto me as a possible soul mate. He's seen all the films and tells me that I have become a bit of an icon for the vampire clan. Bit flattering, I thought (*Darkness Before Dawn*).

"Being Ingrid Pitt": Documentary and Guest Appearances, Archive Footage, Website and Fan Club, Magazines

This chapter contains information about television shows, films, documentaries and promotional films which feature Ingrid Pitt as herself. Information about archival footage is also provided. The second part of the chapter features information on Ingrid's website, the Pitt of Horror, as well as a listing of notable genre magazines featuring Ingrid.

Documentaries

On Location: Where Eagles Dare
1968, Kaleidoscope Ltd.
Documentary-Promotional-Short

Cast: Richard Burton, Clint Eastwood, Ingrid Pitt, Mary Ure, Brian Hutton, Elizabeth Taylor (Themselves), Richard Carlson (Narrator).

An entertaining and picturesque 13-minute promotional piece shot to accompany the film, detailing the trials and tribulations of the enormous operation the making of the film required. It doesn't shy away from the fact that the filming rekindled uncomfortable memories for the townspeople, and so every effort was made to involve them in the production. The characteristics of the region are applied to Ingrid, who is shown on a break from the action: "Beauty and danger ... personified by German actress Ingrid Pitt, who made her own daring escape from East

A mid–70s shot of Ingrid and publicity relations agent Theo Cowan (courtesy Ingrid Pitt).

Photograph from the *London Daily Express* of Ingrid at the Royal premiere of *Where Eagles Dare* (courtesy Kim Holston).

Berlin." She says, "You know, to be out here in Austria at this time, it's like living through the entire war again ... er, not that I'm that old, that I would remember the entire last war ... but there's shooting going on, and explosions and tanks and battalions, and I mean, it really seems to be the war going on. So I take this sled and go out into the fields for quiet...." She actually gets more footage than the female lead, Mary Ure, which again points out how disproportionate her exploitation was to her actual billing. Elizabeth Taylor plays no role in the proceedings; she is seen for a brief moment visiting the set.

Hammer: The Studio That Dripped Blood!
1987, Documentary

Cast (in new footage and/or archive footage): James Bernard, Sir James Carreras, Michael Carreras, Peter Cushing, Bette Davis, Terence Fisher, Len Harris, Paul Henreid, Anthony Hinds, Christopher Lee, James Needs, Ingrid Pitt, Jimmy Sangster, Martin Scorsese, Don Sharp, Aida Young; narrated by Charles Gray.

Ingrid in the lobby of London's A.B.C. Theatre at the premiere of *Little Big Man* (photography by *London Daily Express*; courtesy Kim Holston).

Editor: Paul Willey; Thank You: Len Harris, Christopher Wicking.

Synopsis-Review: Bravo! Produced seven years before *Flesh and Blood* (see below), this is an equally fine Hammer documentary, whose only fault is its length (an hour that ends much too soon). Well, perhaps that and the title, which curiously references to a famous movie from that *other* British horror company, Amicus; confusion or careless cynicism?

It's still a cracking show, with rare graphic treats and a good deal of behind-the-scenes footage — Hammer Home Movies, if you will. Whereas *Flesh and Blood* would take a more genre-by-genre, or monster-by-monster treatment of the company's history, *Hammer: The Studio That Dripped Blood* employs a chronological approach. Peter Cushing and Christopher Lee get some nice moments, with Lee in particular getting the royal treatment in terms of atmosphere; he tells his sometimes quite forcefully voiced anecdotes surrounded by candles and velvet drapery. Ingrid, looking radiant, only has one segment, but it is a lengthy (within the time frame) one where she gets to relate her best *Vampire Lovers* stories. There are other good ones, like how *The Curse of the Werewolf* had originally been planned as a film about the Spanish Inquisition, but nobody expected the Spanish Inquisition, so it became a werewolf movie instead.

Flesh and Blood: The Hammer Heritage of Horror
1994, Bosustow Media Group; Documentary

Crew: Producers: Tee Bosustow, Ted Newsom; Associate Producers: Joe Dante, Bill Kelley, Richard Nathan, Roy Skeggs; Associate Producer–Stills: Michael Baron; Director-Writer: Ted Newsom; Composer of Archive Music: James Bernard; Editors: Tee Bosustow, Alexander Gittinger, Noriko Miyakawa, Sean Okin; Assistant Director in Los Angeles: Kevin M. Glover; Assistant Director in New York: Bruce G. Hallenbeck; Assistant Director in Canterbury: Jane [Hughes] Herd; Assistant Director in Manchester: Stephen Laws; Assistant Director in London: John Stoker; Assistant Directors: Donald F. Glut, Chrissie Hines, Harry Nadler; Sound Recordists: Harvey Edwards, Matthew Harrison, David Lakin, Robert Meeker; Lighting Technicians: Tee Bosustow, Janis Erwin; Camera Operators: Ron Hamill, Robert Lloyd, Anthony Penatta, Andy Watt; Main Title Animation: Gary Heilman; Off-Line Editorial Assistants: Michael Costanza, Tom Reichlin; Title Music Conductor & Musician: Phillip Kimbrough; Conductors of Archive Music: Philip Martell, Neil Richardson; Music Producer of Archive Music: Eric Tomlinson; Film Clips: Ray Atherton of Wavelength Video, Ken Cramer of The Clip Joint, Bernard Gordon of Motion Picture Holdings, Bill Longen of Trailers on Tape, Greg Luce of Sinister Cinema, Woody Wise of Discount Video, George Stover; Filmclips Courtesy of Joe Dante, Ernest Farino; On-Screen Talent: Daniel Berwick, J'Aime Cohen, Sterling Powers, Mike Sizemore; Acknowledgments: Lance Alspaugh, David Booth, Lori Broda, Joyce Broughton, Colin Cowie, Sue Cowie, David Del Valle, James Fitzpatrick, Sophie James, Russ Lister, William Lustig, Mark Miller, John Robins, Max Rosenberg, Roy Skeggs, Steve Swires, Bob Tinnell, Mark Verheiden, Richelle Wilder, Ron Wilson.

Cast: Peter Cushing, Christopher Lee, Roy Ward Baker, James Bernard, Martine Beswicke, Veronica Carlson, Michael Carreras, Hazel Court, Joe Dante, Freddie Francis, Val Guest, Ray Harryhausen, Anthony Hinds, Andrew Keir, Francis Matthews, Ferdy Mayne, Caroline Munro,

Christopher Neame, Ingrid Pitt, Jimmy Sangster, Raquel Welch.

Synopsis-Review: A documentary that is affectionate, honest, well-researched and well-presented. There are neat little revelations (Val Guest says that the monster in *The Quatermass Xperiment* was literally a piece of tripe) and rare behind-the-scenes footage. The most coverage is devoted to the Frankenstein and Dracula series, although everything is pretty well covered, with the rather glaring exceptions of the "Cornwall Classics," *The Reptile* and *The Plague of the Zombies.* Ingrid doesn't get as much screen time as some others, but she does get to tell the story of how her fangs kept falling out of her mouth and into Kate O'Mara's cleavage shooting the climactic scene of *The Vampire Lovers.* A couple of unnecessary potshots are taken at Universal; Hammer's decline is noted as well. (Ironically, Hammer became famous for its use of color, breasts and blood, but as these elements became commonplace, Hammer became more imitator than imitated, and the company could not compete without losing its identity.) Christopher and Peter Cushing also provide the narration; they fittingly have the last word. The frailty in Cushing's voice, recorded not long before he passed away, is poignant and heartbreaking.

EX-S
1994, 6 episodes;
British Broadcasting Corporation (BBC);
Documentary
"The Wicker Man"

Episode Cast: John Walters (Narrator), Edward Woodward, Christopher Lee, Ingrid Pitt, Barbara Rafferty, Tony Roper, Douglas T. Stewart, Jake Wright.

Bride of Monster Mania
2000, American Movie Classics (AMC)
Made-for-TV Documentary

Crew: Producer: Dawn Ostlund; Executive Producer: Kevin Burns; Writers: Brian Anthony, Jerry Decker, Ed Singer; Editor: Bryan Richert; Production Assistant: Karen G. Hernandez; Special Thanks: Cassandra Peterson [Elvira], Mark Pierson.

Guests: Elvira, Martine Beswick, Ingrid Pitt, Mary Jo Cysewski, Bill Warren, Dr. Jo-An Anderson, Dr. Mark Goulston.

Synopsis-Review: Part of a trilogy produced by the American Movie Classics channel, *Bride of Monster Mania* is not simply punningly titled, but actually concentrates on the changing role of women in horror films. (The series' *Monster Mania* had covered the classic male creatures, while *Attack of the 50-Foot Monster Mania* covered all of the classic giant creatures.) The DVD packaging for each individual title is beautiful; designed to resemble a vintage *Famous Monsters* cover, and even featuring art from two of those covers: *Monster Mania* showcases James Bama's Frankenstein portrait from the 1965 *FM Yearbook*, while *Bride* features the *Bride of Frankenstein* portrait of Elsa Lanchester by Basil Gogos, which originally appeared on *FM* #18.

This installment does a fairly good job of charting the course from women as victims or helpless heroines to monsters themselves and strong female characters. Footage from as far back as *Haxan* (1922) is included, and the scope and range is impressive, although it seems to hold the curious attitude that all sequels improve on the original films of any series. For instance, they cite *Twins of Evil* as the best of the Karnstein Trilogy, and claim that the message of the *Alien* series became even more powerful with each film. The only other fault is that they devote more time to doctors or authorities telling us why the films affect us the way they do than to the women who have actually appeared in them. Ingrid and Martine Beswick save the day with witty and insightful comments. Ingrid: "I think in some ways, the female predator is more powerful than the male, because you don't expect it from them. You *know* it's there, but I don't think one is too eager to see it."

Once Upon a Time in Europe
2001, Documentary

Crew: Producer: S. Gibbings; Directors: Manel Mayol, Carles Prats; Writer: Joan Ferrer; Music: Salvador Rey; Cinematographers: Pere Ballesteros, Angel Puig; Editor: Lolo Munoz; Art Director: Frank Plant; Costume Designer: Maria Domingo; Makeup Artist: Silvia Parra; Sound: Josep Perales; Production Coordinator: Patricia Lora; Production Assistant: Frankie Colome; Auto-Cue Operator: Fatima Casas; Researcher: Rafael Dalmau.

Cast: Carlos Aguilar, Alessandro Alessandroni, Dario Argento, John Barry, Martine Beswick, Erika Blanc, Barbara Bouchet, Artur Brauner, Mario Caiano, John Cater, Damiano Damiani, Tonino Delli Colli, Amando de Ossorio, Jacques Deray, Fernando Di Leo, Sergio Donati, Eduardo Fajardo, Jess Franco, Christopher Frayling, Ricardo Freda, Caron Gardner, Gianni Garko, Guiliano Gemma, Jose Giavonni, Uschi Glas, Jorge Grau, Antonio Isasi-Isasmendi, Marianne Koch, Michael Latimer, Carlo Leva, Antonio Margheriti, Eugenio Martin, Sergio Martino, Ennio Morricone, Patrick Mower, Caroline Munro, Paul Naschy, Rosalba Neri, Franco Nero, Ingrid Pitt, Wolfgang Preiss, Lina Romay, Carlo Rustichelli, Aldo Sambrell, Conrado St. Martin, Janette Scott, Julio Sempere, Sergio Sollima, Bud Spencer, Jack Taylor, Tonino Valerii, Florestano Vancini, Horst Wendlandt, Virginia Wetherall.

Host: Christopher Lee

The Wicker Man Enigma
2001, Blue Underground; Documentary

Crew: Producer-Director: David Gregory; Executive Producers: Jay Douglas, William Lustig; Associate Producers: Carl Daft, Lizette Pena; Line Producer: Jake Shaw; Editor: Mike Murphy;

Production Manager: Jonathan Mardukas; Sound Recordist: Nicolino Giammetta; Additional Sound: Tom Echlin; Camera Operator: Glen Warrillow; Additional Camera Operators: Nathan Sheppard, Ira Speir; Production Coordinators: David Flint, Louis Achille; Interview Transcript: Louis Achille; Program Consultant: Allan Brown; Special Thanks: Miranda J. Green.

Cast: Anthony Shaffer, Peter Snell, Robin Hardy, Christopher Lee, Ingrid Pitt, Jonathan Sothcott, Jake Wright, Edward Woodward, Seamus Flannery, Roger Corman, Eric Boyd-Perkins, John Alan Simon, Gail Ashurst, Peter Cross, John Punter.

Synopsis-Review: This is an informative, entertaining documentary on a textbook example of a "troubled production." Ingrid comments: "It was like a nightmare all through its making, through its post-production, through its travails to get distribution. Ever since the film got started in script form, there was a nightmare over it, like a black cloud." Anthony Shaffer, famous for such brainy thrillers as *Sleuth* and *Frenzy*, also brought a detective element to this film, a script designed to be different; Ingrid: "I think I was enormously impressed by the script, actually, because usually I used to read the horror scripts, and this was not a horror script; this had so much depth."

Apparently even the casting of Sgt. Howie was troubled: Director Robin Hardy originally wanted Michael York, who was unavailable. David Hemmings was also considered before Shaffer and Peter Snell recommended Woodward, whom Snell had apparently wanted from the outset. In this documentary, it is stated that Christopher Lee had pressed for Peter Cushing to play the part, but that Cushing had to decline because of other commitments. Ingrid's part was hers from the beginning: "[My] part isn't very much, actually, I mean, what can a nymphomaniac librarian do? You know, not very much, but I thought it'd be interesting to be involved in this kind of film, because I thought at the time it was going to be important." Christopher Lee agreed; so much so that "I got paid nothing, and I keep repeating that to people, and they don't believe it, but it's true, I've got the contract to prove it.... Sometimes you do things for love." This dedication on the part of the cast was exhibited by the actors in rather adverse conditions; for although the film was supposed to be set in May, Ingrid revealed: "It was just freezing all the time, because this is a springtime film, and we're shooting in October and November, and in Scotland, that's not fun; I mean, it's like Poland, it's like … eeeccchhh … I'm one of those Polacks who can't stand the cold." As for star Woodward, she says, "He just had this shift on, and he was barefoot. And he kept coming to me because I was sitting on the ground, pretending to be warm; and he kept coming and putting his freezing plates [feet] under my frock, and I said, 'Edward! Stop that! They're going to take you and burn you — your feet won't be cold then!'" Assistant Director Jake Wright thought that one incident clearly delineated the character of the three leading ladies. During a break in filming, coats were brought out to each of the three leading ladies: "Britt Ekland just grabbed hers and put it on; Diane Cilento said thank you, and then accepted hers and put it on, and Ingrid Pitt said, 'If the extras don't have time to put coats on, then I don't have time.'" During his time inside the Wicker Man, Woodward was reportedly repeatedly urinated on by frightened goats, but as real animals were allegedly killed in the shooting of this scene, they certainly had a reason to be frightened; for Shaffer to make light of it (and people who would be concerned about such things) reveals a stunning lack of sensitivity. And even after all that had already happened, then came the final indignity: The original negative was used as filler for British highway M 3. Ingrid: "The trucks came to take away all the rubbish and all the (film) trimmings, and some idiot put it in the wrong can." Christopher Lee expresses the opinion that it still exists somewhere; the restored scenes in the director's cut were taken from a print of the film that had been sent to Roger Corman in hopes of securing a distribution deal. Lee thinks it's the best film he's ever done, and he may very well be right. Ingrid stated: "I didn't think it was *Citizen Kane* or *The Battle of Britain*, but it was quite a nice film. This vehemence in slogging to get distribution, and paying money, and all the people deceiving each other in the process of just getting it made, yes, I am quite amazed that *The Wicker Man* is still around."

Burnt Offering: The Cult of the Wicker Man
2001, Nobles Gate; Documentary

Crew: Producer: Russell Leven; Directors: Russell Leven, Andrew Abbott; Writer: Mark Kermode; Editor: Gillian Simpson; Sound: Paul Buscemi, Duncan Moore, Ruth Wedgwood; Dubbing Mixer: Chris Phinikas; Camera Operators: Andrew Begg, Danny Dimitroff, Nigel Dupont, Ira Speir; Production Assistants: Rachel Davison, Cherise Saywell; Production Associates: Giles Clark, Carl Daft; Titles: Gavin Evans; Acknowledgment for Still Photographs: Eric Boyd-Perkins, Sean Flannery; Thank You: Gail Ashurst, Ali Catterall, Dave Lally, Simon Wells.

Guests: Christopher Lee, Edward Woodward, Britt Ekland, Ingrid Pitt, Roger Corman, Seamus Flannery, Robin Hardy, Mark Kermode, Anthony Shaffer, Peter Snell.

Sex at 24 Frames Per Second
2003, Prometheus Entertainment; Documentary;
a.k.a. *Sex at 24 Frames Per Second:*
The Ultimate Journey Through Sex in Cinema

Crew: Producer-Writer: Steven Smith; Co-Producers: Rick Davis, Brent Zacky; Executive Producer: Kevin Burns; Executive Producer for American Movie Classics: Jessica Falcon; Field Producers: Tracy Allan, Gloria Jean Sykes; Coordinating Producer: Gloria Jean Sykes; Editors: Ben Bulatao, Sam Fricke, Scott B. Morgan; Makeup Artists: Julea Araujo, Jude Calder, Deborah Green, Patri Lucy-Romolo, T. C. Thecla Luisi; Production Managers: Michelle Pritchard, Chrissy Richards; Executive in Charge of Production for American Movie Classics: Nancy McKenna; Sound: Steve Epstein, Sandy Fellerman, Alan Halcon, Kevin L'Heureux, Sheila O'Neil, John Stedwell, Austin Storms, Robin Waas, Frank Zambetti; Sound Re-Recording Engineer: Brian Gerstner; Assistant Sound Re-Recording Engineer: Joe Kalish; Camera Operators: Steve Bernstein, Wally Hawkins, Patrick Higgins, John Lawrence, Lyle Morgan, Dan Walworth; Assistant Editors: Carey Devore, Alyssa Dressman, Ken Mittleider, Ben Wishrain, Jason Tam; Additional

Editors: Greg Byers, Jeffrey Frey, Bryan Richert; On-Line Editor: Mark W. Jacobs; Post-Production Coordinator: Jose Valencia; Music Supervisors: Tim Aarons, Lloyd Hardy; Assistant Production Coordinator: Chris Beal; Clearance Coordinators: Susan Brownstein, Claudia Ellis; Researchers: Bonnie Daly, Bo Palinic, Mara Sommer; Production Counsel for Foxstar Productions: Erin Feldmar; Production Intern for Prometheus Entertainment: Rebecca Gullion; Vice-President, Development & Production for Prometheus Entertainment: Scott Hartford; Assistant Accountant: Dennis Jelovic; Media Manager: Calvin Lee Jones III; Clearance Director: Jerianne Keaney; Vice-President of Production for Alta Loma Entertainment: Jill Liberman; Vice-President of Production for Foxstar Productions: Shelley Lyons; Media Assistants: Jeff McIlwain, Jessie Lee Stout; Additional Clearances: Jennifer McNeil; Unit Publicist: Michelle Parker; Production Coordinator for Prometheus Entertainment: Wendy Radwan; Media Technician: Tyrone Richardson; Production Accountant: Vicki Rocco; Chairman, Alta Loma Entertainment: Richard Rosenzweig; Production Assistants: John Russo, Bryan Tyler, Lauren Yurfest; Copyright Researcher: Elias Savada; Assistant Accountant: Patrick Smith; Key Accountant: Amy (Smoley) Fitzer; Acknowledgments: Todd Boyd, Roger Ebert, Teri Garr, Brad Geagley, Don Glut, Leonard Maltin, Ingrid Pitt, Tim Rothman, Raquel Welch; Still Photographs Courtesy of Donna Deitch, Erica Gavin, Siouxan Perry; Special Thanks: Richard Bann, Thomas C. Grane; Very Special Thanks: Hugh M. Hefner.

Cast: Brandy Snow (Narrator); *Interviewees:* Shannon Tweed, Richard Roeper, Paul Verhoeven, Virginia Campbell, Jerry Offsay, James Peterson, Mark A. Vieira, Raquel Welch, Hugh M. Hefner, Rex Reed, Gerald Gardner, Gloria Steinem, Michael Medved, Jami Bernard, Camille Paglia, Anthony Quinn, Stanley Donen, Henry T. Weinstein, Martine Beswick, Leonard Maltin, Patty Duke, Robert Culp, Burt Reynolds, Roger Ebert, Todd Boyd, Don Glut, Ingrid Pitt, Paul Schrader, Richard O'Brien, Donna Deitch, Hilary Swank, Ang Lee, Tom Rothman, Steve Hirsch.

Synopsis-Review: This *Playboy* documentary could be called the moving picture version of their yearly "Sex in the Cinema" feature, which recounts the sexiest scenes seen on screen the previous year. Like all *Playboy* product, it is slick and glossy and fairly sexy, but like some other documentaries, a bit too short (101 minutes) to really do justice to its subject. It's very gratifying to see Ingrid included with other heavyweights like Marilyn and Raquel.

The Last of the Gentleman Producers
2004, Funnyman Films; Documentary

Crew: Producer: Jonathan Sothcott; Associate Producer: Zoe Brown; Director: Simon Sprackling; Music; Alan Barnes; Cinematography: Sam Moon; Thank You: Tony Earnshaw, David Wickes.

Cast: Linda Hayden (Narrator), Euan Lloyd, Roger Moore, Ingrid Pitt, John Glen, Kenneth Griffith, Rosalind Lloyd, Sir Sidney Samuelson, Norman Spencer, Joan Armatrading.

Notes: This is a 37-minute documentary spotlighting the life and career of Euan Lloyd, who produced *Who Dares Wins* and the *Wild Geese* movies. The short film featured actors, actresses and technicians who had worked with Lloyd, and was narrated by Linda Hayden (*Taste the Blood of Dracula*).

The Perfect Scary Movie
2005, Visual Voodoo; Documentary

Crew: Producer: Toby Dye; Executive Producer: Tony Moss; Associate Producer: Lissa Blomley; Makeup Artist: Kelly Napoli; Production Manager: Caroline Daly; Graphics: Barney Jordan; Sound: Paul Smith; Colorist: Sonny Sheridan; Camera Operators: John Halliday, Steve Robson, Pete Rowe; Assistant Camera: Ben Lidell; Camera Operator — Rostrum: Ken Morse; On-Line Editors: Clyde Kellett, Tamer Osman; Insert Editor: James Collett; Archive Researchers: Cassie Bennett, Beatrice Read; Researcher: Rebecca Mills; Junior Researcher: Taniya Holland-Parkin; Program Consultant: Kim Newman; Location Fixer in Los Angeles: Lisa Marie Tobin.

Cast: Alexander Armstrong (Narrator), Richard O'Brien, Darrell Wilkins (The Apparition), Jenny Agutter, Paul Anderson, Rick Baker, Linda Blair, Joe Bob Briggs, Liz Bonnin, Emily Booth, Prof. Joanna Bourke, Ed Byrne, Bruce Campbell, John Carpenter, Veronica Cartwright, Alice Cooper, Roger Corman, Sean S. Cunningham, Joe Dante, Prof. Graham Davey, Roger Dicken, Robert Englund, Gunnar Hansen, Ralph Harvey, James Herbert, Tobe Hooper, Robert Kerman, Carla Laemmle, John Landis, Heather Langenkamp, Josh Leonard, David McGillivray, Judith O'Dea, Simon Pegg, Ingrid Pitt, Eli Roth, Ellen Sandweiss, David J. Skal, Abigail Stone, Marcel Vercoutere, Edgar Wright.

Notes: A cheeky documentary that looks at both the good and bad ingredients of the "recipe" with which to create "the perfect scary movie." The subjects range from *Nosferatu* to Hammer and *The Wicker Man* through *The Blair Witch Project*.

Crumpet! A Very British Sex Symbol
2005, Scarlet Television; Documentary

Crew: Producer-Director: John Moulson; Executive Producer: Paula Trafford; Executive Producer for BBC Scotland: Alan Tyler; Idea: Julie Burchill, Jane Garcia; Camera: Den Pollitt; Sound: Steve Earle; Editor: Mark Wharton; Dubbing Mixer: Hanna Fairclough; Colorist: Ray King; Researcher: Caron Miles; Production Coordinator: Erinn Campbell; Production Manager: Karen Bonnici; Development Consultant: Katie Lander.

Cast: Tony Livesey (Host), Robin Askwith, Alexandra Bastedo, Jonathan Benton-Hughes, Honor Blackman, Carol Cleveland, Lynsey De Paul, Diana Dors, Shirley Eaton, Julie Ege, Dr. Germaine Greer, Dylan Jones, Valerie Leon, Austin Little, Jeremy Lloyd, Barbara Lord, Linda Lusardi, Caroline Munro, Leslie Philips, Ingrid Pitt, Wendy Richard MBE, Ned Sherrin, Madeline Smith, Sally Thomsett, Sue Upton, Dee Dee Wilde, Barbara Windsor, Shirley English, Charles Hawtrey, Sid James, Joan Sims, Kenneth Williams.

Synopsis-Review: Charming, funny, wistful and, above everything else, unashamedly sexy, this documentary explores the heyday, the evolution and appeal of British "crumpets" (outdated British slang for a "tasty," beautiful woman). Typical Hollywood glamour was not the crumpets' appeal; they were the girl next door who, as host Tony Livesey notes, never seemed to live next door; an obtainable unobtainable beauty. From the *Carry On* ... films through Bond Girls, Hammer glamour, Monty Python, Page Three Girls, and of course, Benny Hill, not a stone is left unturned, nor a skirt unlifted. Ingrid gives a wonderful performance — and indeed, performance is the correct word. While most of the other interviewees are content to give their opinions, Ingrid turns her spot into a delightfully funny and sexy romp. One of the few males interviewed is one of Ingrid's co-stars from *The Asylum*, Robin Askwith, who had appeared in the successful British sex comedy *Confessions of a Window Cleaner.*

Joe D'Amato at Eurofest
2007, Severin Films; Documentary short film

Eurofest Organizer–Footage Courtesy of Trevor Barley [Roman Nowicki].

Guest Appearances

The Eamonn Andrews Show
1964–69, 4 episodes;
Associated British Corporation Weekend Television
Episode # 3, March 3, 1968

Guests: Edith Evans, Ingrid Pitt, Gloria Swanson, A.J.P. Taylor, Dee Wells.

Notes: Eamonn Andrews was an Irish television host born on the same street as George Bernard Shaw. In 1950, he began presenting programs for the BBC, becoming famous for his boxing commentaries; in 1965 he left the Beeb to join the Associated British Corporation, where he pioneered the talk show format in Britain. He is most fondly remembered as the host of the British version of *This Is Your Life.*

Movie Memories
1981–85, 35 episodes; Anglia Television
Episode # 1.4

Notes: Series host Roy Hudd interviewed one guest per week and discussed their career; other notables featured on his show included Richard Greene (*The Hound of the Baskervilles*, 1939), Lionel Jeffries (*First Men in the Moon*), George Colouris (*Citizen Kane*), Guy Rolfe (*Mr. Sardonicus*), Eunice Gayson, Diana Dors, and Googie Withers.

The Mind of David Berglas
1986, 6 episodes; Tyne Tees Television (UK)
Episode #1.1

Guests: Christopher Lee, Ingrid Pitt.
Notes: David Berglas, "The International Man of Mystery," is one of the world's leading illusionists and mentalists, and was one of the first magicians to appear on British television with *Meet David Berglas* in 1954. He did a number of series after that, all of which garnered great praise across Europe, including this one. He was also a creative consultant for a number of famous films, beginning with the Bond spoof *Casino Royale* (1967) and for five other "real" Bond films, including *Octopussy*. Guests on other *Berglas* episodes with ties to Ingrid included Omar Sharif (*Doctor Zhivago*) and Britt Eklund (*The Wicker Man*).

Mondo Rosso
1995, 1 episode;
British Broadcasting Corporation (BBC)
"Freaks"

Crew: Producer-Director: Asif Zubairy; Executive Producer: Elaine Bedell; Music: Mykael S. Riley; Editor: Guy Yorke-Wilkinson.
Guests: Ingrid Pitt, Jarvis Cocker.
Synopsis-Review: Jonathan Ross is best remembered by genre fans for his hugely informative and entertaining *Incredibly Strange Films Show* and the follow-up, *Son of Incredibly Strange Films*. Whether this was planned as a one-off or just failed to make an impression isn't clear, but what is clear is that host Ross brought the same love of pop culture and cheeky attitude to this show, which featured Ingrid in a laugh-filled interview. The other guest, Jarvis Cocker from the Britpop group Pulp, was best known for their hit "Common People."

Light Lunch
1997–98, 150 episodes;
Channel Four Television
Season 1, Episode 58: "A Quite Frightening Lunch"

Episode Crew: Executive Producer: Henrietta Conrad; Series Producer: Eve Tomlinson; Producer: Tania Fallon; Assistant Producers: Emma Hardy, Rachel Tatton-Brown; Director: Ian

Guest: *Light Lunch* (1997–98)

Ingrid takes a break from filming on *Where the Action Is* to make a personal appearance at her friends' circus. Ingrid's shorter co-stars often commented on how much they enjoyed "working under the big top" (courtesy Ingrid Pitt).

Lorimer; Editorial Consultant: Sebastian Scott; Production Designers: Patricia Boulter, Toby Kalitkowski; Titles: Tamsin McGee, Hugo Moss; Props Master: Jake Hamilton Davies; Floor Manager: Katie Thompstone; Sound Supervisor: Charles Braithwaite; Camera Supervisor: Phil Piotrowsky; Lighting Director: Alex Gurdon; Vision Mixer: Simon Sanders; Production Team: Tara Marcangelo, Sasha Olswang, Jo Pratt; Production Coordinators: Clare Burgess, Bettina Lyster; Script Supervisor: Hayley Boyd; Production Manager: Tracy Garrett; Researcher: Ilya Colak-Antic; Food Producer: Melanie Jappy; Additional Material: Ivor Baddiel; Cooking: Susan Weaver.

Episode Cast: Mel Giedroyc, Sue Perkins (Hosts), the Peach Boys, the Non-Stick Pans People, Ingrid Pitt, James Herbert, Ken Russell.

Synopsis-Review: This was not Ingrid's first appearance on a cooking show; she had also done an episode of *Who's Cooking Dinner* for the Food Network the previous year.

Light Lunch was a bizarre combination of cooking and talk show, with its own band and even a dance troupe, The Non-Stick Pans People (whose name was a take-off on the popular dancers from *Top of the Pops*, Pan's People). Ingrid makes chocolate pudding, which looks absolutely delicious and surely added five pounds to anyone watching. The talk session is quite entertaining; Ingrid is her usual effervescent self. Ken Russell provides a big, blustery presence; he would later write the foreword to Ingrid's *Bedside Companion for Vampire Lovers* and famed horror author James Herbert gets to display a textbook-like knowledge of monster movies.

Cast & Crew
2002–05, 7 episodes; IWC Media
"The Wicker Man," Episode 7

Episode Crew: Producer: Elspeth O'Hare; Executive Producer: Alan Clements; Director: Don Coutts.

Episode Cast: Kirsty Wark (Presenter), Christopher Lee, Edward Woodward, Ingrid Pitt, Gary Carpenter, Seamus Flannery, Robin Hardy.

Notes: Each of the seven episodes featured members of the cast and crew of a specific film, sharing their memories and re-visiting old locations. Other films that got this treatment included *If...*, *Saturday Night and Sunday Morning* and *Quadrophenia*.

British Film Forever 2007, 7 episodes; British Broadcasting Corporation (BBC)
"Magic, Murder and Monsters: The Story of British Horror and Fantasy" (Season 1, Episode 5)

Episode Crew: Producer: Garry John Hughes; Executive Producer: Ricky Kelehar; Archive Producer: Caroline Julyan; Talent Producer: Rob Katschmaryk; Music: Simon Lacey; Cinematography: Joe Dyer; Editor: John Edwards; Production Manager: David Potter; Sound Recordists: David Harcombe, Mat Jackson, Ian Sands; Dubbing Mixers: Lindsey Green, Richard Lee; Camera Operators: Jamie Cairney, Conall Freeley, John Halliday; Gaffer: Mark Johnson; Animators: Gareth Harrison, Alan Smith, James Torry; Production Coordinators: Tessa Blakeley, Allison Smith; Series Consultant: Sir Christopher Frayling; Production Executive: Mark Hannell; Production Team: Asha Ali-Ismail, Anna Amico, Richard Binks, Jo Clark, Sophie Collins, Andy Cooke, Ben Cooke, Rob Darlington, Lindsey Hammond, Stephanie Page, Zoe Russell-Stretton, Nuria Valado-Gamallo; Specialist Researcher: Roger White; Archive Researcher: Cy Young.

Episode Cast: Jessica [Hynes] Stevenson (Narrator), Simon Pegg, Danny Boyle, Anne Bilson, Mark Gatiss, John Landis, Sumit Bose, Jenny Agutter, Rufus Sewell, Jonathan Rigby, Jimmy Sangster, Kim Newman, Christopher Frayling, Phil Jupitus, Martin Scorsese, David McGillivray, Martin Stephens, Barbara Shelley, John Hamilton, Ken Russell, Anna Massey, Michael Powell,

Stanley A. Long, Michael Winner, Roman Polanski, Ian Ogilvy, Steve Coogan, Danny Baker, Roy Ward Baker, Richard Todd, Sylvia Sims, Christopher Lee, James Carreras, Ingrid Pitt, Tudor Gates, Shauna MacDonald, Madeline Smith, Yutte Stensgaard, Pete Walker, Terry Gilliam, John Boorman, Rupert Grint, Timothy Spall, Mischa Barton, Neil Marshall, Jimi Mistry, John Hurt, David Lynch, Freddie Francis, Anthony Hopkins.

Synopsis-Review: A seven-episode British TV series that used each of the 90-minute shows to showcase a different genre and England's contributions to it; besides this installment, there were six other alliterative overviews: "Guns, Gangsters and Getaways" (thriller), "Longing, Loving, and Leg-Overs" (romance), "Hardship, Humour and Heroes" (realism), "Corsets, Cleavage, and Country Houses" (costume drama), "Bullets, Bombs and Bridges" (war), and "Sauce, Satire and Silliness" (comedy). This episode, like the others, is nicely done, including many Hammers as well as *The Wicker Man*, *28 Days Later*, *Brazil*, *Doctor Who and the Daleks*, *The Elephant Man*, the *Harry Potter* series, *Shaun of the Dead* and *Witchfinder General*.

Martina Cole's Lady Killers
2008, 6 episodes; Free at Last TV

"Elizabeth Bathory" (Episode 6)

Episode Crew: Producer: Janette Clucas; Series Producer: Katie Kinnaird; Reconstruction Director: Sean Crotty; Cinematographers: Geraint Evans, Lawrence Jones; Editors: Brian P. Campbell, John McMullin; Second Unit Director: Mike Le Han.

Episode Cast: Martina Cole (Presenter), Susanna Fiore (Elizabeth Bathory), Ingrid Pitt, Karen Krizanovich.

Synopsis-Review: In this interesting six-episode mini-series, British mystery writer Martina Cole (*The Ladykiller*, *Hard Girls*, and *Dangerous Lady*) examines the lives and times of six of the most notorious female killers in history, asking: Why do women kill, and why does it shock so? Naturally, Ingrid is called in for the episode on Bathory. Other female fiends featured included Myra Hindley, Amelia Dyer, Beverly Allitt, Rose West and Mary Ann Cotton.

The Return of Count Yorga
1971, Peppertree Productions; AIP

Crew: Producer: Michael Macready; Director: Bob Kelljan; Writers: Bob Kelljan, Yvonne Wilder; Music Composed & Conducted by Bill Marx; Cinematography: Bill Butler; Editors: Laurette Odney, Fabien D. Tordjmann; Production Designer: Vincent M. Cresciman; Makeup Artist: Mark Busson; Production Manager: Carl Olsen; Assistant Director: Jack Oliver; Property Master: Erik L. Nelson; Sound: Rod Sutton; Special Effects: Roger George; Stunt Coordinator: Gary Kent; Chief Electrician: Dennis Bishop; Key Grip: Tom Dezin; Wardrobe Supervisor:

Ingrid puts in a radiant personal appearance at the 1994 FANEX convention (photograph by and courtesy of Kim Holston).

Jeannie Anderson; Music Editor: Milton Lustig; Animal Trainer: Vee Kasegan; Script Supervisor: Joyce King.

Cast: Robert Quarry (Count Yorga), Mariette Hartley (Cynthia Nelson), Roger Perry (Dr. David Baldwin), Yvonne Wilder (Jennifer Nelson), Tom Toner (Rev. Thomas), Rudy De Luca (Lt. Madden), Philip Frame (Tommy), George Macready (Prof. Rightstat), Walter Brooke (Bill Nelson), Edward Walsh (Brudda), Craig T. Nelson (Sgt. O'Connor), David Lampson (Jason), Karen [Ericson] Huston (Ellen Nelson), Helen Baron (Mrs. Nelson), Jesse Wells (Mitzi Carthay), Michael Pataki (Joe), Corinne Conley (Witch), Allen Joseph (Michael Farmer), Peg Shirley (Claret Farmer), Liz Rogers (Laurie Greggs), Paul Hansen (Jonathan Greggs), Marilyn Lovell (Voice), Ingrid Pitt and Ferdy Mayne (Filmclip from *The Vampire Lovers*).

Notes: There's a wonderful in-joke included in this second of the two classic Count Yorga films: Robert Quarry, in the title role, sits watching *The Vampire Lovers* on television.

Tales from the Pitt: People kept writing to me and asking me if I'd seen the film ... because there was a scene from *The Vampire Lovers* ... and they wanted to make sure that I saw it, but I never did. When I first met Bob, it was one of the first things he asked me. When I told him I hadn't seen it, he promised to send me a copy. I never got it (*Den of Geek* website column, 3/3/09).

Archive Footage

World of Hammer 1990, 13 episodes; Best of British Films Productions

Episode # 4 — "Vamp"

Crew: Executive Producer: John Thompson; Producer-Director: Robert Sidaway; Creators-Writers: Robert Sidaway, Ashley Sidaway; Composer of Main Title: Brian Bennett; Editor: Ashley Sidaway; Production Manager: Evan M. Jones; Sound: Paul Hamilton; Production Secretary: Joanne Atkins; Production Assistant: Caroline Beecham; Film Archivists: Mike Dragesic, John Herron, Steve Rickerby, Steve Leroux; Online Editing: Mike Peatfield; Assistant Editors: Amanda Jenks, Alyssa Osment; For Hammer: Graham Skeggs, Karen Woods, Wendy Smith.

Narrator: Oliver Reed

Synopsis-Review: Produced in 25-minute installments, this was less a documentary than a "Best of Hammer" compilation show, featuring lengthy clips from the films and the welcome, velvety tones of Oliver Reed to pull them all together. As advertised by the title, this episode spotlights the incomparable female vampires of Hammer, with clips from *The Brides of Dracula, Dracula Has Risen from the Grave, The Kiss of the Vampire*, and the Karnstein trilogy. There are no interviews, and there is no revelatory information, but it is a nicely produced clips show that, for once, doesn't leave the viewer feeling clipped.

Cinema Mil 2005, 11 episodes; Televisio de Catalunya (TV3)
Episode #1.8

Crew: Producer: Alfons Morist; Line Producer: Oriol Sala-Patau; Director: Jaume Figueras; Writer: Begona Garcia Pla.

Host: Jaume Figueras

Synopsis: Ingrid is one of scores of players seen in archive footage.

Festival of Fright
2006, TheMonsterClub.com

Crew: Producers: Philip E. Hopkins, Ralph E. Stevens; Mastering-Authoring: John Keegan of Madhouse Productions; Music Producer: Barry Fasman; Artist: Kerry Gammill.

Synopsis-Review: A theme-free but hugely entertaining DVD compilation of classic horror movie trailers, from Hammer (*The Vampire Lovers, The Mummy, The Revenge of Frankenstein*) to psychotronica (*Monstrosity, Daughter of Horror, Carnival of Souls*). There's really something for everyone here, as a mere sampling of the titles shows: *The Cyclops, She Demons, The Fiendish Ghouls, Dementia 13, Black Sabbath, Caltiki the Immortal Monster, Black Sunday, Frankenstein 1970, Black Pit of Dr. M, A Bucket of Blood*, and *Dr. Terror's House of Horrors*. There's no narration, but there is an alternative audio track with a party music score, so perhaps there is a theme after all — fun! It features a very attractive package design, with Ingrid prominent among the excellent portraits by Kerry Gammill.

Celebrity Nude Revue: The Saucy '70s, Volume 2
2010, Citrus Cinema

The Pitt of Horror: The Website and Official Fan Club

Many celebrities have excellent and informative websites, and Ingrid Pitt is no exception; she established the inimitable Pitt of Horror.com in the mid-nineties, and it is still going strong with the help of the hardest-working personal assistant in show business, Barbro Ryan. It's more than just the usual vehicle for merchandise, although there's everything a fan could want and more, including items that are available to fan club members only ... and just the fan club package in itself is wonderful, with all sorts of unique items, all hand-signed and personalized by Ingrid. "Ingrid Says" is a column devoted to Ingrid's thoughts about — well, basically, whatever's on her mind, from the rise and fall of the British Empire to world peace, in which she is a fervent believer. Forums allow fans to swap ideas and information, and there's a lively message board, on which Ingrid often appears in person. There are even links to dating sites!

As with all these networks, sometimes it's abused and used to bitch at and smear other fans, one of the most unfortunate aspects of Internet culture, but overall it demonstrates that Ingrid still has a devoted, articulate fan base. What separates it from most of the other sites is the personal touch which serves to cement the bond between Ingrid and her fans, which had been strong from the start.

Magazines

ABC Film Review

Ingrid made the cover of this long-running British film magazine a record three times in one year:

January 1970 (Vol. 20 # 1) — A photograph featuring Ingrid as Heidi, with Richard Burton, in the tavern scene from *Where Eagles Dare*; the issue also includes a four-page article on the film.

February 1970 (Vol. 20 # 2) — Solo publicity shot as Heidi from *Where Eagles Dare*.

October 1970 (Vol. 20 # 10) — Publicity still from *The Vampire Lovers* featuring Ingrid, Madeline Smith, Kate O'Mara, Pippa Steele, and Kirsten Lindholm.

Castle of Frankenstein

1972 Vol. 5 # 2 (# 18) — Although neither Ingrid nor art from the film appeared on the cover, *The House That Dripped Blood* gets top billing for the featured articles, as well as a two-page spread inside the magazine. Ingrid and "The Cloak" merit the top praise of the review, which calls the segment, a "highly amusing, bright, neat spoof ... and oh, that Ingrid Pitt — Va Va Voom!"

A certain famous monster menaces a certain famous horror actress's daughter on this promotional flyer for one of Ingrid's yearly Pitt of Horror Fan Club reunions (courtesy Ingrid Pitt).

The Pitt of Horror Fan Club newsletter regularly informs fans of the latest comings and goings of the Queen of Horror.

The Pitt Tapes, a DVD example of the unique merchandise available from the Pitt of Horror.

Continental

May 1970 — A British "Film Review for the Aware Audience," which meant that they covered films in which people were uncovered. A photo of Ingrid from *The Vampire Lovers* graces the cover, accompanied by a shot of her in the bath from the same film; there's also a two-page spread entitled "Pleasurable Shudders."

Daughter of the Night

(1994) — Another one-shot publication from Tim Greaves, this time in tandem with Kevin Collins. This edition features coverage of the Karnstein Trilogy and other cinematic adaptations of "Carmilla." As always, it is copiously illustrated; Greaves did similar wonderful chapbooks on a number of other Hammer beauties, including Maddy Smith, Valerie Leon, and Yutte Stensgaard. See also *Femme Fatales*.

Famous Monsters of Filmland

The greatest monster movie magazine of all time always had time for Ingrid, both in its pages and at its conventions; significant issues include:

86 (September 1971) — Poster art from *The House That Dripped Blood* is featured on the cover; inside is a six-page preview of the Amicus classic, and of course it includes *that* shot of Ingrid!

90 (May 1972) — Although the cover spot was claimed by poster art from Amicus' *Scream and Scream Again*, *The Vampire Lovers* staked out the inside front cover. There was also a fang-tastic five-page foto feature with synopsis.

122 — Ingrid finally takes her rightful place in the *FM* cover legacy with a beautiful Ken Kelly portrait of her as Carmilla, which doubled as an ad for the 1975 FM Convention, at which she was guest of honor. The issue also featured a four-page article, "Meet Ingrid Pitt," which fans could do at the convention.

1975 Famous Monsters of Filmland Convention Book — Guest of honor Ingrid was spotlighted in two articles in the souvenir magazine produced for the Hammer-themed convention (the other guests of honor were Peter Cushing and Michael Carreras), "The Pitt ... and the Pendulum" and a preview of *The Vampire Lovers*.

Femme Fatales

This sexy sister publication of *Cinefantastique* (which itself published a *Wickerman* issue) has featured Ingrid prominently on the covers and inside articles of two issues (she was also featured in an article in issue # 3):

Ingrid and *The Vampire Lovers* made the cover of this men's magazine from 1970.

Daughter of the Night, a superb Tim Greaves one-shot publication devoted to various cinematic adaptations of J. Sheridan Le Fanu's "Carmilla."

Volume 6 # 1 (July 1997) — Ingrid is featured in David Voigt's cover painting along with Raquel Welch and Veronica Carlson. The article "Hammer Heroines" is a 20-page tribute by Jessie Lilley and Ronald Dale Garmon to those heroines. Special features within the article include "Ingrid Pitt" and "Barbara Shelley" by Lilley; Christopher Lee recalling his favorite leading ladies, by Bill Kelley; "Video Revival" and "Hazel Court" by Bruce G. Hallenbeck; and "Caroline Munro" by Ted Newsom.

Volume 9 # 4/5 (September 1, 2000) — The July 1997 issue had been very good, but this one was downright spectacular. "Hammer Vamps" pulled out all the stops and devoted nearly 90 full-color pages to the 50 Sexiest Hammer beauties of all time, including two articles written by Ingrid, "Hammer Vamps" and a *Vampire Lovers* feature. Other contributors to this Amazonian effort included Fred Szebin ("Victoria Vetri," "Caroline Munro"), Tim Greaves ("Madeline Smith," "Yutte Stensgaard," "Valerie Leon"), Greaves and Bruce G. Hallenbeck ("Busty Babes and Sexy Sirens of Hammer Horror," "Hammer Films' Top 10 Sexiest Scenes," "Hammer's Erotic Horror Landmark"), Michael Reed ("Veronica Carlson," "Collinson Twins"), Steve Biodrowski ("Martine Beswicke"), Alan Jones ("Caroline Munro: *The Black Cat*"), and Ted Newsom ("Hazel Court"). This issue is basically the magazine forerunner of Marcus Hearn's equally spectacular coffee-table book *Hammer Glamour* (Titan Books, 2009). Ingrid wrote a regular column for the magazine.

Film Ex

V. 2 # 1, Summer 1992 — *Film Ex* was published by Kim Holston, co-author of *Science Fiction, Horror and Fantasy Film Sequels, Series and Remakes* (which features a foreword by Ingrid) et al. This issue features an article by Kim entitled "In Search of Ingrid Pitt: A Big Chapter in the History of Moviegoing" (memories of reactions from Army bases around the world, walking twenty blocks to see Ingrid in *The House That Dripped Blood*, and seeing her on stage in London in *Don't Bother to Dress*).

Filmfax

62 (August–September 1997) — Cover photo from *The House That Dripped Blood*, plus, "An Interview with Ingrid Pitt" by Al Taylor.

House of Hammer/Halls of Horror

28 (1984) — The legendary British monster magazine never featured Ingrid on any covers, but this issue boasts a "Close-Up on Ingrid Pitt" by Greg Turnbull, a generously illustrated five-page feature that includes a filmography.

The House That Hammer Built

#7 (February 1998) — Another superlative Hammer fanzine, this effort originated in the UK from Dr. Wayne Kinsey and built into a comprehensive guide to Hammer's fantasy films. This issue features coverage of *The Vampire Lovers* and *Lust for a Vampire* (and other Hammer classics from 1969–1970), and sports a very nicely done cover of Ingrid by Dr. Kinsey. Wayne is the author of three excellent books about the little company that could: *Hammer Films: The Bray Studio Years* (Reynolds & Hearn, 2002), *Hammer Films: The Elstree Studio Years* (Tomahawk Press, 2007), and *Hammer Films: A Life in Pictures* (Tomahawk Press, 2009).

Ingrid Pitt: Queen of Horror

(1996) — A one-shot fanzine published by One-Shot Publications (Tim Greaves) two years after the excellent *Daughter of the Night*. Ace production job, chock-full of stills and information ("Welcome to the Pitt of Horror"), and an interview with Ingrid by Kevin Collins, it's among the top single-subject fanzines ever produced.

Little Shoppe of Horrors

Not simply the best fanzine ever devoted to our beloved Hammer Films, but one of the best fanzines, ever, period. An incredible labor of love by publisher Richard Klemensen, each issue is a book unto itself and a true testament to quality and commitment.

#16 (August 2004) — Actually an upgrade and expanding of the eighth issue, this edition features a super new color cover by comic artist Bruce Timm, as well as a back cover reproduction of a Ralph Bates painting by Hammer heroine Veronica Carlson. In-depth research, interviews and behind-the-scenes information make it positively the last word on the Karnstein Trilogy. Kicking the issue off is the fourth part of the continuing "Ladies of Hammer" series, containing interviews with Hazel Court (Bruce G. Hallenbeck) and Yvonne Monlaur (Richard Klemensen), followed by "The Making of *The Vampire Lovers*" by Hallenbeck, which also contained interviews with Harry Fine (Klemensen), Tudor Gates (Hallenbeck), Harry Robinson (various), Roy Ward Baker (John and David Stoker), Scott MacGregor (Sue and Colin Cowie), Ingrid (Greg Turnbull), Maddy Smith (Hallenbeck), Kate O'Mara (Turnbull), Pippa Steele (Hallenbeck), John Forbes Robertson (Wayne Kinsey), Douglas Wilmer (Uwe Sommerlad), Elandra "Kirsten Betts" Meredith (Oscar Martinez), and Ferdy Mayne (Ted Newsom). Hallenbeck also contributes "Making of" articles for *Lust for a Vampire* and *Twins of Evil*, along with quite a few more interviews with the principals of those films. The issue is rounded off with a memoir of Mike Raven by Dennis Meikle.

#20 (June 2008) — This issue features an unparalleled, uncensored history of Amicus

Everything you always wanted to know about Amicus, but didn't know who to ask; look no further than the definitive history in *Little Shoppe of Horrors* #20 (courtesy Richard Klemensen and Mark Maddox).

Productions, "Scream and Scream Again" by Philip Nutman. Everything you always wanted to know about Amicus, but didn't know who to ask, all wrapped up in gorgeous color covers by Mark Maddox (a collage of Amicus's most famous monsters) and Bruce Timm (a spot-on EC–Jack Davis tribute), both of which feature Ingrid. Each film gets its fair share of space, and *The House That Dripped Blood* receives its due in an article entitled "The Anthology Reaches Its Zenith."

Monsterscene

8 (Summer, 1996)—The eighth issue of this short-lived spiritual descendant of *Famous Monsters* featured a cover painting of Ingrid by legendary *FM* alumnus Basil Gogos, plus extensive coverage of the Karnstein Trilogy by publisher-editor Stephen Smith. Unfortunately, the magazine would only last for three more issues after this one; the tenth and eleventh featured a column by Ingrid, "Pitt of Horror," which was also the name of the fanzine she produced at this time (see below), as well as the header for her articles for *Shivers* (that's down there, too) and the name of her website (that's back a bit).

Pitt of Horror 1/2

The ultimate Ingrid Pitt fanzine, produced by Ingrid herself, this "Special Limited Collector's Preview Edition" was, unfortunately, the only issue produced. Physically and graphically, it's quite an attractive publication, with full-color covers, a color centerfold of Hammer lobby cards, and lots of photos of Ingrid. But it's more than just a pretty face; it's a lot of fun. There's an article by Marcus Hearn on *The Vampire Lovers*, British horror writer Stephen Laws' interview with Ingrid, a short piece on autograph collecting by Peter Robbins, a short story by Ingrid entitled "Palfrey's Bane," a crossword puzzle, and even Ingrid's recipe for borscht! Ingrid also contributed a recipe to *It Came from the Kitchen* by Geoff Isaac Gordon Reid (BearManor Media, 2007).

Scream Queens Illustrated Poster Book

5 (1998)—Published by Market Square Productions in PITTsburgh, Pennsylvania, the fifth issue featured full-color photos and opens up to a 21" × 33" nude poster of Ingrid. Market Square also published the "Slice Girls" poster book, featuring Steffanie Pitt, and produced the Slice Girls' maxi-single "Wanna Haunt Me."

Pitt of Horror #1/2 — If you want something done right, then do it yourself, which Ingrid certainly did with the only issue of this digest.

Shivers

32 — The cover features another famous photo of Ingrid, the charming shot of her with fangs and a cup of tea (from *The House That Dripped Blood*); she's also featured in a nicely done color centerfold, a collage of her most famous roles, plus a four-page interview by Howard Maxford, "Revelations and Revolutions: Ingrid Pitt."

39 — The cover features an inset photo and a blurb touting her article inside, "The Pitt of Horror." The article combines news and Ingrid's always sharp wit on a variety of subjects, as well as new photos of her and her cars: "You're wondering 'Why the photos of the old banger,' aren't you? (And you'd *better* mean the car...)" Ingrid contributed columns to all of the issues after that; the magazine ended publication in 2008.

"In Her Own Write": Ingrid Pitt's Books

Since 1980 and the publication of her first novel *Cuckoo Run*, Ingrid Pitt has been in demand as much as a writer as an actress. In addition to the books in this chapter and articles or columns listed in the previous chapter, she writes regular columns for *TV & Film Memorabilia* and *Motoring & Leisure*, *Micro Mart* (a weekly British computer-trading magazine), the Glasgow-based *Bite Me*, *It's Alive*, and *The Cricketer*, her own website, and the British website Den of Geek, as well as the new *Monster-Mania* magazine. "Some of my columns have been running for ten years or more. Never missed a deadline and proud of it!" she told me in an e-mail.

Cuckoo Run
(London: Troubador Books, 1980)

Review: Ingrid's first book is the slam-bang pulp-fiction tale of a woman, Nina Dalton, who, like Roger O. Thornhill in *North by Northwest*, is drawn into a web of intrigue through a case of mistaken identity. She becomes, in her own words, "a cross between James Bond and Mata Hari," with a dash of Modesty Blaise thrown in, and the results are quite enjoyable. The book brims with the excitement and enthusiasm of every first work, and Ingrid is already showing she has as much of a way with words as she does with acting; for instance, describing a bald man as having a "Kojak hair style," and works in all sorts of neat little cultural references, like when somebody mentions the great train robber Ronnie Biggs. All of Ingrid's fictional works contain strong autobiographical elements: Ingrid loves motor-racing (husband Tony Rudlin was a racing driver and Lotus Team Manager), flying and karate, so Nina spends lots of time in cars, planes, and hand-to-hand combat. Ingrid loves South America; so does Nina. It shows that her acting experience and innate storytelling ability had equipped her to write a very cinematic book; this would have made a very entertaining vehicle had it been filmed. "I took it to Cubby Broccoli. It was about a woman named Nina Dalton who is pursued across South America in the mistaken belief that she is a spy. Cubby said she was a female Bond. He was being very kind."

Ingrid's first book, the long out-of-print *Cuckoo Run*.

Bertie the Bus
(London: Spastics Soc, 1981)

Review: A charming 32-page children's book featuring the popular supporting character from *Thomas the Tank Engine and Friends.*

The Peróns (with Tony Rudlin)
(London: Methuen, 1982)

Eva's Spell (paperback title)
(London: Methuen, 1985)

Promo shot for Ingrid's children's book *Bertie the Bus* (courtesy Ingrid Pitt).

Review: The Perons' supporters (and there are still many) cite their efforts to eliminate poverty, dignify workers, and promote women's suffrage, while their critics call them demagogues and dictators. Ingrid and Tony's epic novel of the Perons' rise and fall can best be called "faction" — a work of fiction with a strong basis in fact. Ingrid and Tony's admiration for and relationship with the Perons is well-documented, as is their love for Argentina, but they don't shy away from portraying the Perons as opportunistic and worse. The notable thing about the novel is the way in which it puts a human face, whether it is a good face or bad one, on these historical figures. The pace never lags despite the epic sweep and some unexpected pleasures come in the smallest of details: "Peron breathed in a grateful lungful of smoke and let it trickle out through his nose." As might be expected, the intrigue is thick enough to be cut by machetes; there's power and sex and money and murder and even a Black Mass. And for those who think this may have been slipped in to capitalize on one of the author's associations with the horror genre, the subject of this scene, Jose Lopez Rega, really *was* a practitioner, and was known as "The Warlock." Ingrid returned to Argentina for a visit in 2006 for the BBC 4 Radio program *Sentimental Journey*, hosted by Arthur Smith; it aired on August 5, 2006. Barbro Ryan says, "Ingrid was asked by a producer at the BBC where she would like to go, somewhere where she had had a good time. She suggested Buenos Aires. There was a few seconds' silence and then the producer said he would be back to her. He rang her later and said she could go — two weeks in Buenos Aires."

"I guess they expected me to say somewhere like Bath or Madame Tussaud's," says Ingrid.

A book describing the power and passions of the Peróns, as told by friends Ingrid and Tony.

Katarina
(London: Methuen, 1986)

Review: Another work based on history: The majority of the novel takes place in the Treblinka death camp, where on August 2, 1943, the prisoners staged a revolt. Although there were some Nazi casualties, the toll on the prisoners was much higher. Of some 1,500 prisoners, only about 600 managed to escape into the forest, and only 40 or 50 are known to have survived until the end of the war. Obviously Ingrid's most personal work, the novel is gripping and horrifying, and what surely must have been incredibly painful memories are described in vivid detail: "In the wash house, Katarina witnessed the last sad tragedy in the young girl's life. She had been trying to lift one of the bulky bundles of repossessed clothing up onto the edge of the boiler. In her weakened state, the load was too great. To encourage her to greater efforts a guard smashed the metal edge of his rifle butt into the small of her back. The blow to her spine was the end. With a little sigh she sank to her knees and jerked forward, her head thudding into the pool of slime that had collected under the wash tank." The book is dedicated to her mother and to John Hough, who directed Ingrid on *The Zoo Gang*, as well as *Twins of Evil*, for Hammer.

Ingrid's harrowing tale of a brave woman in a concentration camp, told with firsthand knowledge.

Life's a Scream: The Autobiography of Ingrid Pitt
(London: William Heinemann, 1999)

Review: As the headline for Ingrid's biography in the *Where Eagles Dare* pressbook exclaims: "Ingrid Pitt's Real-Life Saga Would Make a Movie Thriller in Itself!" And this was thirty years before she put the amazing account of her life and career to paper. Also one of the rare cases where the hyperbole was, if anything, understated. The years between that publicity piece and the words straight from the source brought even more adventure and experience; some good, some great, some terrible, some even beyond comprehension, but all faced by a woman for whom the term "survivor" would seem somewhat inadequate. In the end, the woman, like the book, is considerably more than just the sum of the parts: "Surviving doesn't make one special — but it does make one extraordinarily lucky. Although I have appeared on the stage, on television and in films, and have had several books published, I believe my most important achievement was to bring into this world an extraordinary human being who will carry on what my mother taught us about love and inner strength — about the destruction that hate breeds; about happiness, contentment, and not blaming others when things don't work out. She taught us not to lead a useless life, to strive to become a better person, to live with love in one's heart ... to be happy." Ingrid was nominated for a Talkies Award for her reading of the audio book version; she has also read other books on tape, such as *Delta of Venus* by Anaïs Nin and *Travels with Diana Hunter* by Regine Sands.

Darkness Before Dawn
(Baltimore: Luminary Press, 2004)

Review: An expanded and revised paperback version of *Life's a Scream*, published by Luminary Press, a division of the legendary fanzine *Midnight Marquee* (Susan Svehla does the cover design and revised layout design). And it's a new, nifty full-color cover, too — a nicely done collage of Ingrid's most famous roles. There are twice as many photos as the original, and a new chapter that covers Ingrid's life between 1999 and 2004.

The Ingrid Pitt Bedside Companion for Vampire Lovers
(London: B. T. Batsford, 1998)

Review: The first of Ingrid's popular *Bedside Companion* series had something for every vampire fan: histories of the origins of the vampire, real and reputed vampires, writers who created and continue the traditions, and movies that did the same. It's breezy yet knowledgeable, insightful and incisive, hilariously funny and delightfully naughty, and sure to cause controversy in certain quarters with some of its opinions. This applies

Flyer for a book signing by Ingrid for *Life's a Scream* (courtesy Ingrid Pitt).

Books: *The Ingrid Pitt Bedside Companion for Vampire Lovers* (1998)

Whether you're a vampire lover or just love vampires, it's a must-read.

A room with a view: a shot from Ingrid's room at Castle Dracula, overlooking the famed Borgo Pass.

to both social ("[T]he resurrection is as important to the Christian religion as it is to Vampirism. The qualification is death. In many ways, the church works like a giant corporate vampire. Regardless of the wishes of those it targets, it moves in and imposes its will and emaciates the body it acquires.") and pop-cultural ("Tod Browning's idea of taking the stage version of Dracula as a template came with built-in flaws. These flaws have been exaggerated by time, and make the film so slow and talky that it is almost a life-sentence to sit through it. I know that sort of remark could get me burned at the stake but what can I do? I must call it as I see it."). And, boy, she just does not like Liz Taylor, not no way, not no how. The cover features Ingrid in the classic shot from *The House That Dripped Blood*; inside, the book is well-laid-out and lavishly illustrated with photos from an international selection of vampire movies. That year, Ingrid appeared on the Sci-Fi Channel in a promotional interview segment for the book. She discussed the changing role of women in horror films; of herself, she said, "You don't become the 'Queen of Horror' if you're not the predator." She also appeared at the 2000 World Dracula Conference in the real land of the Borgo Pass to promote and sign the book. As reported by *The Guardian* on Tuesday, May 30, 2000, "Ingrid Pitt, the first lady of Hammer Horror films, emerges pale-faced from the toilets of the *Favorit* Night Club, a seedy dive in the Romanian town of Poiana Brasov. 'They're bloody disgusting and the paper is scratchy as hell,' she says. 'Sorry,' says a bouncer, 'the cleaner doesn't come on Sundays.'" Later, after two attendees engage in a knife fight to determine who the better vampire is, they reported, "Ingrid Pitt, signing copies of her *Bedside Companion for Vampire Lovers* in the *Favorit* lobby, thinks she would win that one.... 'Dracula is my raison d'être,' says Pitt, who played Countess Dracula in the Hammer films. 'When I go in for the kill in a movie, I go into it with venom and viciousness. It's a bloody recommendable way of venting your anger.'" Barbro Ryan told me, "Ingrid was asked if she would like to do a Dracula Tour of Romania by the Tourist Board. She enjoyed ... the country, but as she spent most of the day on the coach, all she saw was the scenery passing by."

The Ingrid Pitt Bedside Companion for Ghost Hunters (London: B. T. Batsford, 1999)

Review: Ingrid provides a look at the world of ghosts in her second *Bedside Companion*, a fascinating read for those who "*Do* believe in spooks." Or, as Uri Geller says in his foreword, "These pages are full of foolhardy mortals who thought the power of their reason was stronger than the supernatural. I am not that stupid." She movingly recounts her own experience among the Native Americans, and takes thorough, objective looks at many other spook tales. The scope is wide, and it practically screams to be read; who can resist chapters titled "Ghostly Gazumping" or "Possession and Danny Kaye" or especially "James Dean — The Little Bastard" (cleverly, not what the title implies)? As with the previous *Companion*, there's also a guide to the best ghost movies.

The Ingrid Pitt Book of Murder, Torture and Depravity
(London: B. T. Batsford, 2000)

Review: How and why we kill each other has always fascinated us, and Ingrid gives an overview of some of the more spectacular examples of humanity's inhumanity to itself. Of course, the model for *Countess Dracula*, Countess Erzebet (or Elizabeth) Bathory, is included, and, again, the accounts of her real-life atrocities make the Hammer film seem quite tame indeed. Stabbing a gypsy in the neck with a hairpin? Kid stuff compared to hanging them nude in a see-through Iron Maiden and then bathing in their blood as it flowed down on her. Some of the other usual suspects are included; Ed Gein, Josef Mengele, Ivan the Terrible, and Caligula. But Ingrid, as always, takes pains to point out the inconsistencies of the accepted social order as we know it: "When the Inquisition was in full swing in the Middle Ages, was torture and burning any less horrific because it was done in the name of the Holy Cross by men of the cloth? Exactly what is the difference between [the hangman] and the run-of-the-mill serial killer who can only get his pleasure from killing?" Like her *Companion* books, this one is lavishly illustrated, mostly with photographs, but also with some enthusiastically gory drawings.

The Mammoth Book of Vampire Stories by Women
Stephen Jones, editor (New York: Carroll & Graf, 2001)

Review: This is part of the Mammoth series of omnibus editions that range in subject matter from Arthurian legends to gay erotica to sex, drugs and rock 'n' roll to the world's greatest chess games ... everything, apparently, except actual mammoths. As Ingrid says in the introduction, "Fashions change, and the urbane vampire created by Byron and cemented in place by Stoker has had to move on. There are now new age vampires aplenty, waiting in the shadows, just out of sight, ready to slither forth and seek new victims. Are you, like me, ready for the new dusk...?" True to her words, there are very few pre–Anne Rice authors represented; "Luella," "The Haunted House" and "Good Lady Ducayne" are the only turn-of-the-century examples of the form, while all of the others are contemporary. Rice is included, as are other heavyweights like Chelsea Quinn Yarbro and Tanith Lee, but there are equally stellar contributions from underrated talents like Christa Faust (*Hoodtown*). Ingrid contributes "Hisako San," a wild, pulpy tale of a Japanese karate-woman vampire who is a result of the Atom Bomb dropped on Nagasaki, and whose victims rot alive. She's after the now–Senator who was part of the team that dropped the bomb, and the action builds to a furious climax that recalls the end of *House of Dracula*. Favorite line: "It was 9:45 P.M. and Brasher was beginning to think they had overreacted, seen too many Arnie Schwarzenegger films."

The Macros (Doctor Who: The Lost Stories)
Big Finish Productions Audiobook;
Ingrid Pitt & Tony Rudlin, 2010

In 1984, Ingrid and husband Tony were commissioned to write a Doctor Who adventure after her appearance in the "Warriors of the Deep" episodes. "The Macro Men," one of a number of ideas submitted, focused on the real-life story of the Philadelphia Experiment, which was attempted in World War II by the United States (they tried to make a naval destroyer invisible to radar). In Ingrid and Tony's version, the Doctor travels to 1943, boards the ship and becomes involved in a battle with microscopic creatures native to Earth but previously unknown to humans. Although accepted, the script only got to first draft episode stage, and was never made; it will finally see the light of day in 2010 in this audio series.

Bibliography

Books

Buckley, David. *The Thrill of It All.* London: Carlton Publishing Group, 2004.

Everson, William. *More Classics of the Horror Film.* Secaucus, NJ: Citadel Press, 1986.

Frank, Alan. *Horror Movies.* London: Octopus Books, 1976.

Hearn, Marcus. *Hammer Glamour.* London: Titan Books, 2009.

Holston, Kim, and Tom Winchester. *Science Fiction, Fantasy and Horror Film Sequels, Series and Remakes: An Illustrated Filmography.* Jefferson, NC: McFarland, 1990.

Hunter, Jack. *House of Horror: The Complete Hammer Films Story.* London: Creation Books, 1994.

Johnson, Tom, and Deborah Del Vecchio. *Hammer Films: An Exhaustive Filmography.* Jefferson, NC: McFarland, 1995.

Jones, Steven, editor. *The Mammoth Book of Vampire Stories by Women.* New York: Carroll & Graf, 2001.

Keeyes, Jon, with Linnea Quigley, Debbie Rochon, and Brinke Stevens. *Attack of the B Queens.* Baltimore, MD: Luminary Press, 2003.

Kinsey, Wayne. *Hammer Films: The Bray Studios Years.* Richmond, England: Reynolds & Hearn, 2002.

_____. *Hammer Films: The Elstree Studios Years.* Sheffield, England: Tomahawk Press, 2007.

Le Fanu, J. Sheridan. "Carmilla" from *The Vampire Lovers and Other Stories.* London: Fontana Books, 1970.

Marrero, Robert G. *Vampires: Hammer Style.* Key West, FL: RGM Publications, 1983.

McKay, Sinclair. *A Thing of Unspeakable Horror: The History of Hammer Films.* London: Aurum Press, 2007.

Meikle, Dennis. *A History of Horrors: The Rise and Fall of the House of Hammer.* Lanham, MD: Scarecrow Press, 2009.

Pitt, Ingrid. *Darkness Before Dawn.* Baltimore, MD: Luminary Press, 2004.

_____. *The Ingrid Pitt Bedside Companion for Vampire Lovers.* London: B.T. Batsford, 1998.

_____. *Life's a Scream: The Autobiography of Ingrid Pitt.* London: William Heinemann, 1999.

Stump, Paul. *Unknown Pleasures: A Cultural Biography of Roxy Music.* New York: Thunder's Mouth Press, 1999.

Winder, Simon. *The Man Who Saved Britain: A Personal Journey into the Disturbing World of James Bond.* New York: Farrar, Straus & Giroux, 2006.

Periodicals

Daughter of the Night. London: One-Shot Publications, 1994.

Famous Monsters of Filmland #86, 90, 122. New York: Warren Publishing, 1971, 1972, 1976.

Fangoria #22. New York, NY: Starlog Publications, 1981.

Film Ex EX V2#1. Wilmington, Delaware: Holston Publications.

Guide to Current and Coming Movies. US Army Publications, May 1971.

Halls of Horror #28. London: Quality Communications, 1984.

The House That Hammer Built #7. London, England: Wayne Kinsey, 1998.

Ingrid Pitt: Queen of Horror. London, England: One-Shot Publications, 1996.
Little Shoppe of Horrors #16, 20. Des Moines Iowa: Richard Klemensen, 2004, 2008.
Midnight Marquee #47. Baltimore, Md.: Midnight Marquee Press, 1994.
Monsterscene #8, 10, 11. Lombard, Illinois: GoGo Publications, 1996, 1997, 1998.
New York Magazine V4#7. New York: New York Media LLC, Feb. 1971.
Philadelphia Bulletin. Philadelphia: The Charter Company, 1969)
Philadelphia Daily News. Philadelphia: Philadelphia Media Holdings LLC, 3/30/73.
Photoplay 1972 Film Annual (UK). London: Argus Press, 1972.
Pitt of Horror. Richmond, England: Pitt of Horror, 1997.
Variety. Hollywood: Variety Incorporated, 3/3/71.

Websites

Den of Geek (www.denofgeek.com)
Internet Movie Database (www.imdb.com)
New York Times (www.nytimes.com)
Pitt of Horror (www.pittofhorror.com)
Turner Classic Movies (www.tcm.com)

Index

Numbers in ***bold italics*** indicate pages with photographs.

ABC Film Review 192
The Adventurer 154–155
Amicus 63, 105, 159, 169, 178, 196, 200, 202
Artemis '81 159–162
The Asylum 100, ***101***, 102–103
Aurelia ***16***, 18

Baker, Roy Ward 139
Bates, Ralph 144
Bathory, Erzebet 55, 57, 108, 215
BBC2 Playhouse 158
Bertie the Bus ***207***
Un Beso en el Puerto 35, ***36***, 37
Beyond the Rave 114–118
Bond, James Bond 40, 51, 77, 82–83, 90, 155, 205
Bones see *Parker*
Bride of Monster Mania 179–180
British Film Forever 188–189
Bulman ***172***–173
Burnt Offering: The Cult of the Wicker Man 182
Burton, Richard ***46***, ***47***, ***49***, 51–52, 91

Campanadas a Medianoche 25–29, ***26***
Carmilla 149
"Carmilla" 128, 134, 137, 144, 148–150, 198
Cast & Crew 188
Castle of Frankenstein 192
Charley's Aunt ***14***, ***15***, 18
Chimes at Midnight see *Campanadas a Medianoche*
Cinema Mil 191
Clemens, Brian 156–157
Click 71, ***72***
Collinson, Madeline 148
Collinson, Mary 148
The Comedy of Errors 164, ***165***, 166–167
Continental 196
Countess Dracula 44, 52, ***53***–***56***, 57
Crumpet! A Very British Sex Symbol 184–185
Cuckoo Run 205, ***206***
Cushing, Peter ***132***, 137, ***138***, 139, 177–179, 181, 196

Darkness Before Dawn 103, 105, 109, 210
Daughter of the Night 196, ***198***
Dial "M" for Murder ***8***, 9
Doctor Who 167, ***168***–***170***, 171
Doctor Zhivago 29, ***30***, 31–35
Dominator 105–106, ***107***, 108–109
Don't Bother to Dress 9, ***10***–***11***
Los Duendes de Andalucía 19–***20***
Dundee and the Culhane 151, ***152***
Duty Free 9

The Eamonn Andrews Show 185
Eastwood, Clint ***46***, ***48***, 51–52
Eva's Spell see *The Perons*
Ex-S 179

Falstaff see *Campanadas a Medianoche*
Famous Monsters of Filmland 196
Femme Fatales 196
Film Ex 199
Filmfax 199
The Final Option see *Who Dares Wins*
Flesh and Blood: The Hammer Heritage of Horror 178–179
A Funny Thing Happened on the Way to the Forum 37, ***38***, 39–41

Green Fingers 103–105

Hammer Films 4, 35, 40, 55, 57, 63, 105, 128, 131, 144, 156, 169, 177–179, 184, 189, 190, 191, 196, 199, 200
Hammer: The Studio That Dripped Blood 177–178
Hanna's War 95–96, ***97***, 98–100
The House ***171***–172
House of Hammer/Halls of Horror 199
The House That Dripped Blood 40, 57–58, ***59***–***62***, 63, ***64***
The House That Hammer Built 200

In Praise of Love 18
The Ingrid Pitt Bedside Companion for Ghost Hunters 214

The Ingrid Pitt Bedside Companion for Vampire Lovers 210, ***212***–213
The Ingrid Pitt Book of Murder, Torture and Depravity 215
Ingrid Pitt: Queen of Horror 200
Ironside 152–153

Jason King ***153***–154
Joe D'Amato at Eurofest 185

Katarina 209
A Kiss in the Harbour see *Un Beso en el Puerto*

The Last of the Gentleman Producers 183
Lee, Christopher 63, ***68***, 71, 178, 179, 181, 182, 186, 188, 199
Le Fanu, J. Sheridan 128, 134, 148–149
Life's a Scream 20, 29, 35, 37, 41, 52, 71, 77, 91, 100, 151, 156, 210, ***211***
Light Lunch 186–188
A Lion in Winter 18
Little Shoppe of Horrors ***140***, 200, ***201***
Lust for a Vampire 139, 141–142, ***143***–144, 149

The Mammoth Book of Vampire Stories by Women 215
The Man Most Likely to… ***17***–18
Martina Cole's Lady Killers 189
Mills, John 151, 158
The Mind of David Berglas 186
Minotaur 109–111, ***112***, 113–114
Mondo Rosso 186
Monsterscene 202
Mother Courage and Her Children 7
Movie Memories 185

New Faces 155–156
Nobody Ordered Love 64–***65***

Octopussy 77, ***78***, 79–83
O'Mara, Kate ***131***, 134–***135***
The Omegans 41, ***42***, 43–44

219

On Location: Where Eagles Dare 175–177
Once Upon a Time in Europe 180

Parker 83, **84**, 85–87
The Perfect Scary Movie 184
The Perons 207, **208**
Pertwee, Jon 40, **60**, **61**, 63–64, 168–169
Pitt, Ingrid: books 205–216; documentary appearances 175–185; films 19–135; magazines 192–204; stage career 7–18; television 151–174; website 192
Pitt, Steffanie (daughter) 103, 202
"The Pitt of Horror" (column) 200, 202
The Pitt of Horror (magazine) **203**
The Pitt Tapes **195**

The Return of Count Yorga 189–190

Rudlin, Tony (husband) **73**, 205, 207, 216

Sea of Dust 118, **119–120**, 121, **122**, 123, **124**, 125–126
Scream Queens Illustrated Poster Book 202
Sex at 24 Frames Per Second 182–183
Shivers 204
Smiley's People 162, **163**, 164
Smith, Madeline 24, **130**, **134**, **135**, 137
El Sonido de la Muerte **21–24**, 25
Sound of Horror see *El Sonido de la Muerte*
The Splendor of Andalucia see *Los Duendes de Andalucía*
Steele, Pippa **135**, 137
Stensgaard, Yutte 137, 143–144
A Streetcar Named Desire 7

The Tell-Tale Heart 126–127
Thriller 156–**157**
Transmutations see *Underworld*

Twins of Evil 144–145, **146**, 147–149

Underworld 91, **92**, 93–95
Urban Gothic 173–174

The Vampire Lovers 52, 57, 128–129, **130–132**, 133, **134–136**, 137, **138**–139, 144, 149, **197**

Welles, Orson **26**, 28–29
Where Eagles Dare 44, **45–46**, 47, **48–50**, 51–52, 175–177
Who Dares Wins 74, **75**, 76–77, 183
The Wicker Man 65, **66**, 67, **68–69**, 70–71, 175–177
The Wicker Man Enigma 180–182
Wild Geese II 87–88, **89**, 90–91, 183
Woman of Straw **12–14**, 18
Woodward, Edward 77, 184

The Zoo Gang 157–158